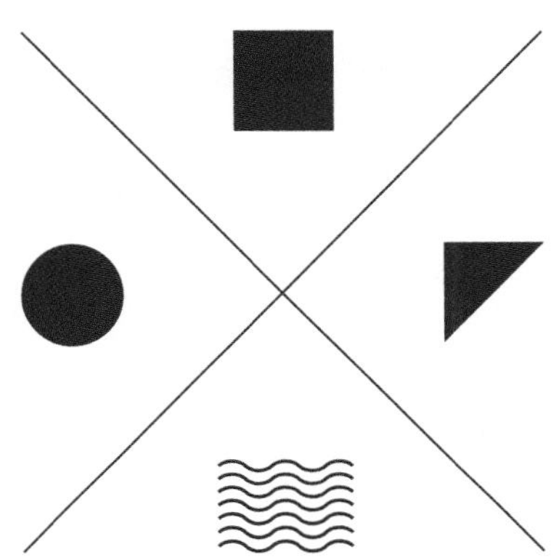

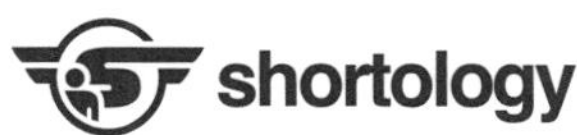 shortology

m a t t e o   c i v a s c h i

minimal film

/ / / / The cinematic world reimagined through graphic design.

SKIRA

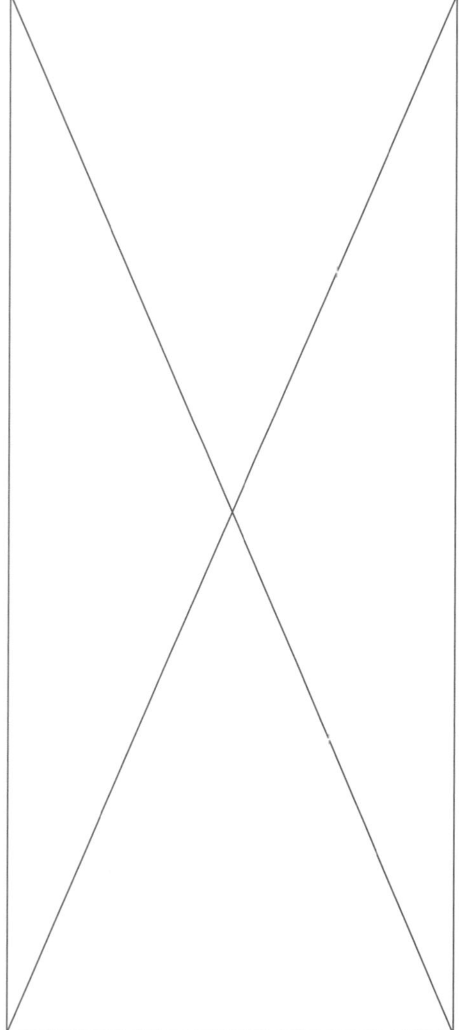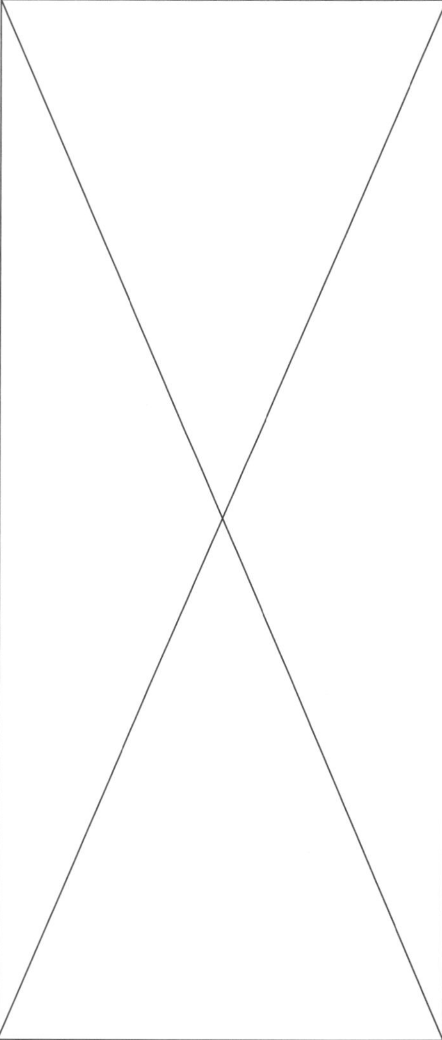

The first, rudimentary, form of language was born 32,000 years ago, in a cave in southern France. Some people also consider it the first art form, I see it more as the first graphical summary of history. Since then, those rock drawings and engravings have evolved in many ways, and one of these is infographics. This is a subject that I've been able to investigate thoroughly, due to it being a constant companion during my professional career as a designer. In recent years, I've concluded that not much has changed from the original cave pictograms to the most sophisticated and technological iPhone model. Signs and styles have evolved, dynamics were created, details and nuances have been added, but one thing has remained unchanged over time: synthesis. The use of infographics is extremely effective, because it is based on simplicity, essentiality, on the speed and ease of understanding of each defining element. In 2011, I started using infographics to portray the lives of

32,000 years ago

famous people and historical events (these days we call it "storytelling"). Starting from stick figure toilet signs (think back to the cave drawings… notice a certain resemblance?) and drawing heavily on that symbolic, simple, yet intuitive universe found in driver's ed manuals or on road signs, I created Shortology, an instant language able to narrate anything through pictograms. Endless days have been spent devising linear features and simple forms, strictly in black and white, which suddenly take shape and become thousands of stylized icons, to use as words in a uniquely communicative language.

From the first stories (Michael Jackson, Jesus, Napoleon, Marie Antoinette, Darth Vader) to now, around 20 publications have been generated, which were distributed almost all over the world. I don't presume that I've invented something new, I regard my work as an addition of new tales to the famous cave ones: a cynical and ruthless visual synthesis, just like 32,000 years ago, but with an added touch of irony.

Shortology has allowed me to look at films with different eyes, reinterpreting and pruning them to isolate the bare essence. The best example is *The Lord of the Rings*: hours and hours of adventures, a myriad of characters, battles, spells, ruthless enemies, flying dragons and epic journeys synthesized by a ring which, following a long arrow to indicate an action, ends up inside a volcano. Done.

Of course, in analyzing a film to synthesize and deciding to leave out incredible events or the detailed reconstructions that make up the plot, I feel an increasingly deep responsibility for "throwing it all away".
But the art of synthesis is just that: a loaded gun ready to fire at anything that isn't vital to the story. What remains then, trivially, is exactly what we would use if we were to briefly describe a movie to someone.

Then came the realization: to draw the bag containing methamphetamine crystals for TV's *Breaking Bad* series, I absolutely had to make use of color. And not only that – I had to invest a lot of time in understanding the form they had to take... regular? Irregular? Geometric? At one point, I used essential shapes only: triangles and squares, equidistant from each other, in essence creating a mathematical pattern. It was a graphic art that struck me immediately because it was something I'd never done before. Trying to enrich it with a background color, it hit me: I was facing something new and different, or better, I had pushed Shortology to an even more extreme visual synthesis. I took that file, saved it in a folder called "The Minimal Film Project" and whispered to myself, "See you soon, *Breaking Bad* bag!". In that moment, the idea of the book you're holding in your hands was born (for the record: I then kept the "bag with irregular shapes" for the project that I was finishing!).

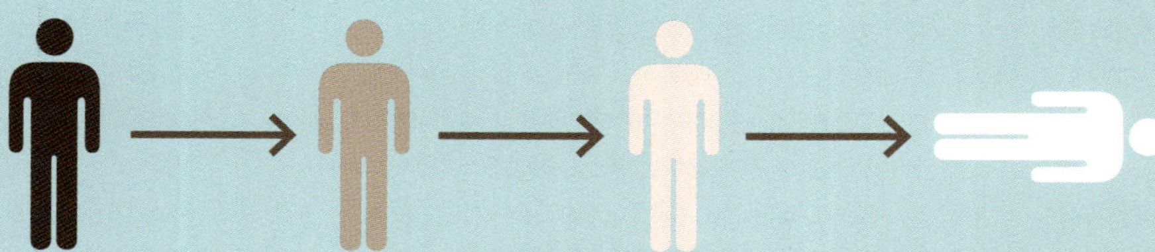

michael jackson

the lord of the rings

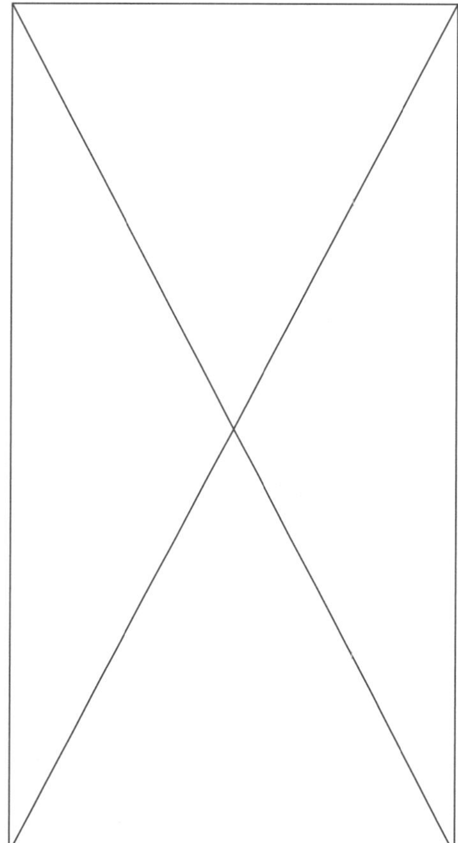 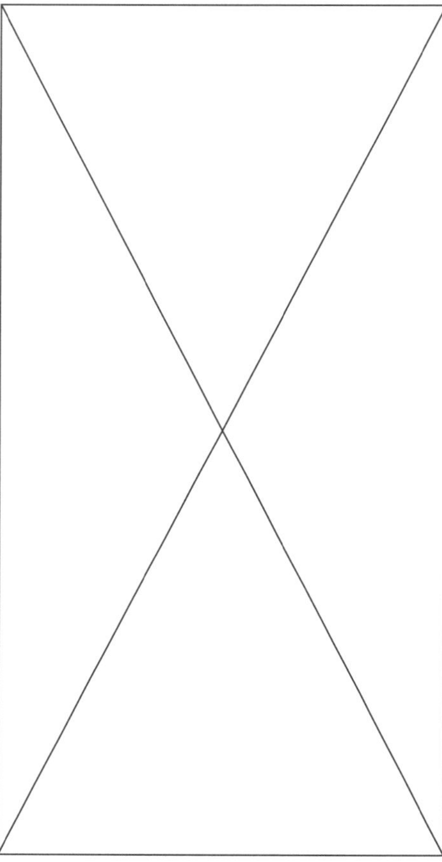

This is a book about cinema told through the visual magic of graphic design, or a graphic design book narrated through the evocative magic of cinema, you decide! It's a book about emotions, the indelible indentations that cinema has left on our imagination as viewers and as lovers of the seventh art. You will find most of the films that have made history: from the immortal *Star Wars* film saga to art house movies, passing through TV series, which have now become the diamonds in Hollywood productions' crowns, drastically changing the way in which we enjoy these magical products. *Game of Thrones* may be consumed as a long, single continuum lasting several weeks, or taken in small, individual doses – episode by episode (sometimes shocking, sometimes

the book

exciting). *Breaking Bad* has re-defined the approach to script-writing, character description, and the portrayal of incredible yet dramatically realistic situations. This has been done to the point that, for me, cinema (yes, you read right, cinema!) is divided into "before *Breaking Bad*" and "after *Breaking Bad*". And if TV can change the way films are made, then it deserves the same artistic consideration.

This book is a visual hug, something that you could do without, but will become indispensable if you love it. This is a book for anyone who is in constant search of aesthetic beauty or a different point of view. In the illustrations you will find, above all, shapes and colors, but also a small series of equally functional icons to explain the

film. The style and atmosphere are a tribute to the magical world of 1960s and 70s design with its greatest creatives, designers and architects (Joe Colombo, Max Huber, Gio Ponti and Armando Testa above all). I hope it will fill your eyes with joy.

Ah, paging through it you might ask yourself: "But what are those numbers in the top right-hand corner for? If I told you, I'd have to kill you. But I will give you a hint: after reading the book, go to page 248.

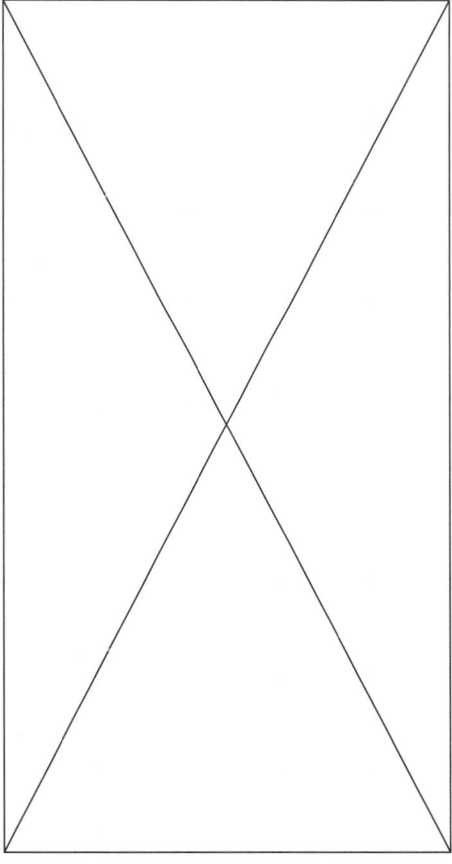

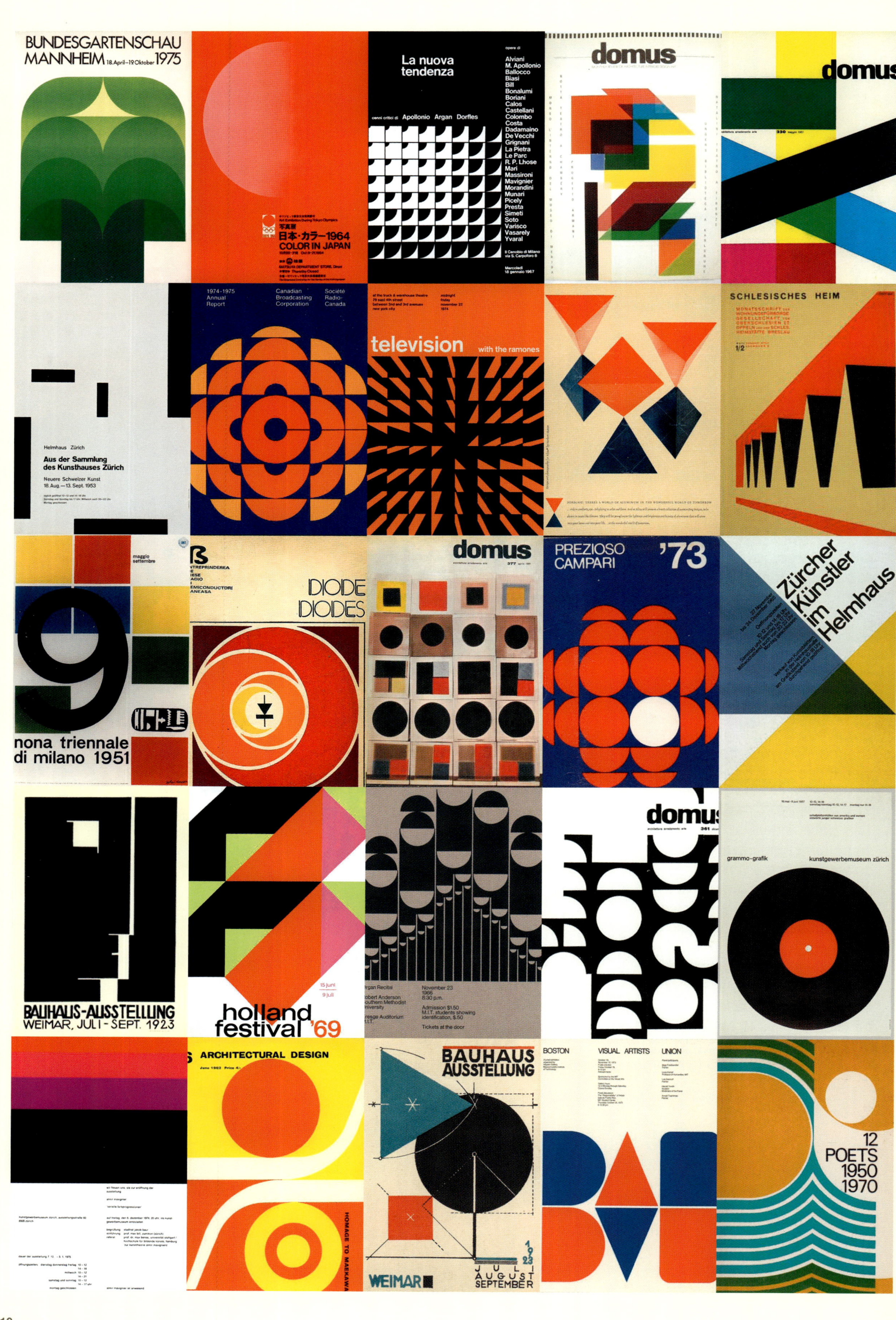

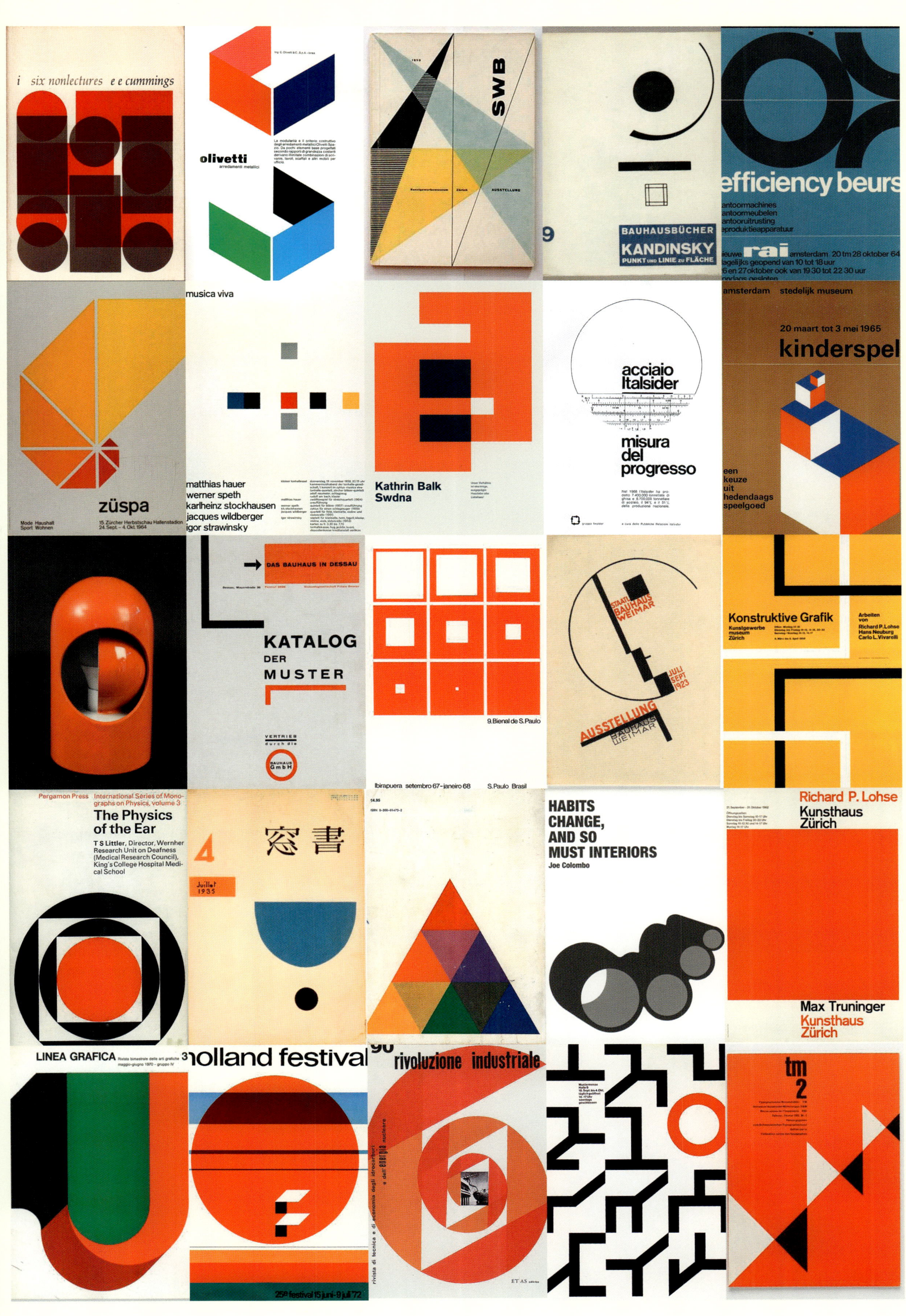

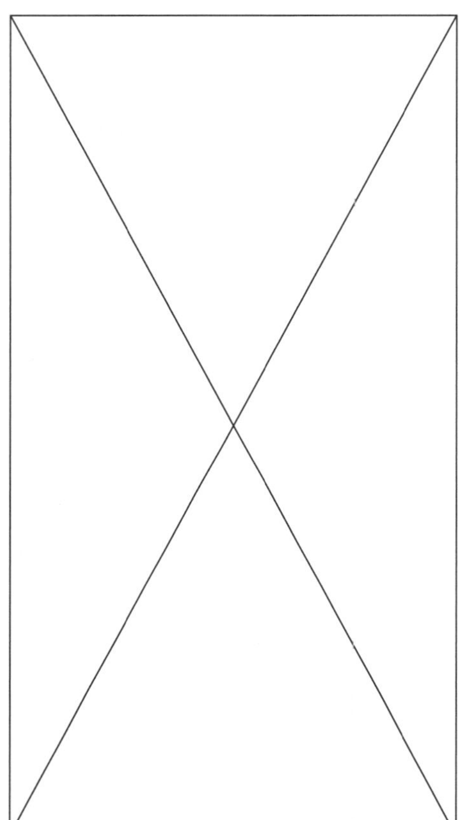 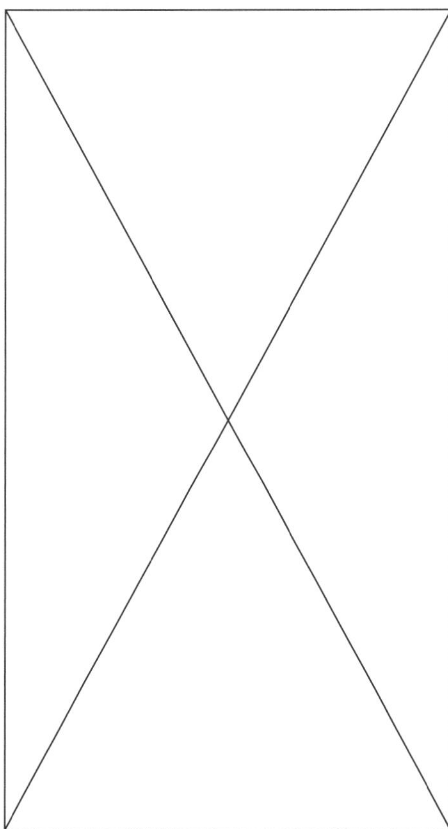

Everything around us is made up of matter, and each element can be assimilated into a specific form, whether spherical, trapezoidal, conical, square, rectangular or sinusoidal. Each element observed by our brain is subconsciously revised, deconstructed and reduced to the simplest geometric and essential forms, or stripped of unnecessary detail and trappings, to increase its memorability. Basically, our mind constantly creates a schematic synthesis to retain and pigeonhole the greatest amount of input possible.

This book, just like the Shortology philosophy, is based precisely on this concept: do away with the superfluous to concentrate on the essential.

shapes and colors

What is the core of a complex and elaborate form? What is the hallmark of an object? And again: what are the proportions and measures that make it unique compared to other, seemingly similar ones?

If we apply this deconstruction to the cinematic world, the results are astonishing. This is what The Minimal Film Project does: it represents the emotion of cinema through the extreme synthesis and simplicity of form. For example: a white circle resting on a blue expanse is enough to depict Wilson, the ball in *Cast Away*; two white triangles perfectly perpendicular to a red color are enough to evoke "Dracula"; a light blue cross on a white background (wavy in the upper part to symbolize the liquid state) becomes the "milk-plus" of the protagonists in *A Clockwork Orange*.

And then there is the color, or better, the color combinations that, in addition to making each illustration pack an effective visual punch, emphasize the general narrative suspense of the film: a blue triangle on a light blue background for *Jaws*; the black of the sphere and inclined slope, paired with a bright orange background, catapult us into the mysterious world of *Raiders of the Lost Ark* and make us imagine Harrison Ford being chased and about to be crushed by a huge ball.

A chromatic parallelism is to be found in the scene in which a group of men are digging with spades and pickaxes against the light of sunset. In other cases, the colors are matched to suggest a strong visual contrast, bringing back energy to the eyes of the beholder: it is not by coincidence that the background of *Alien* is green, or that the two shades of gray in *Titanic* (to symbolize both the fog and limited visibility) contrast with the dark blue and burgundy hull and a simple white triangle: the iceberg.

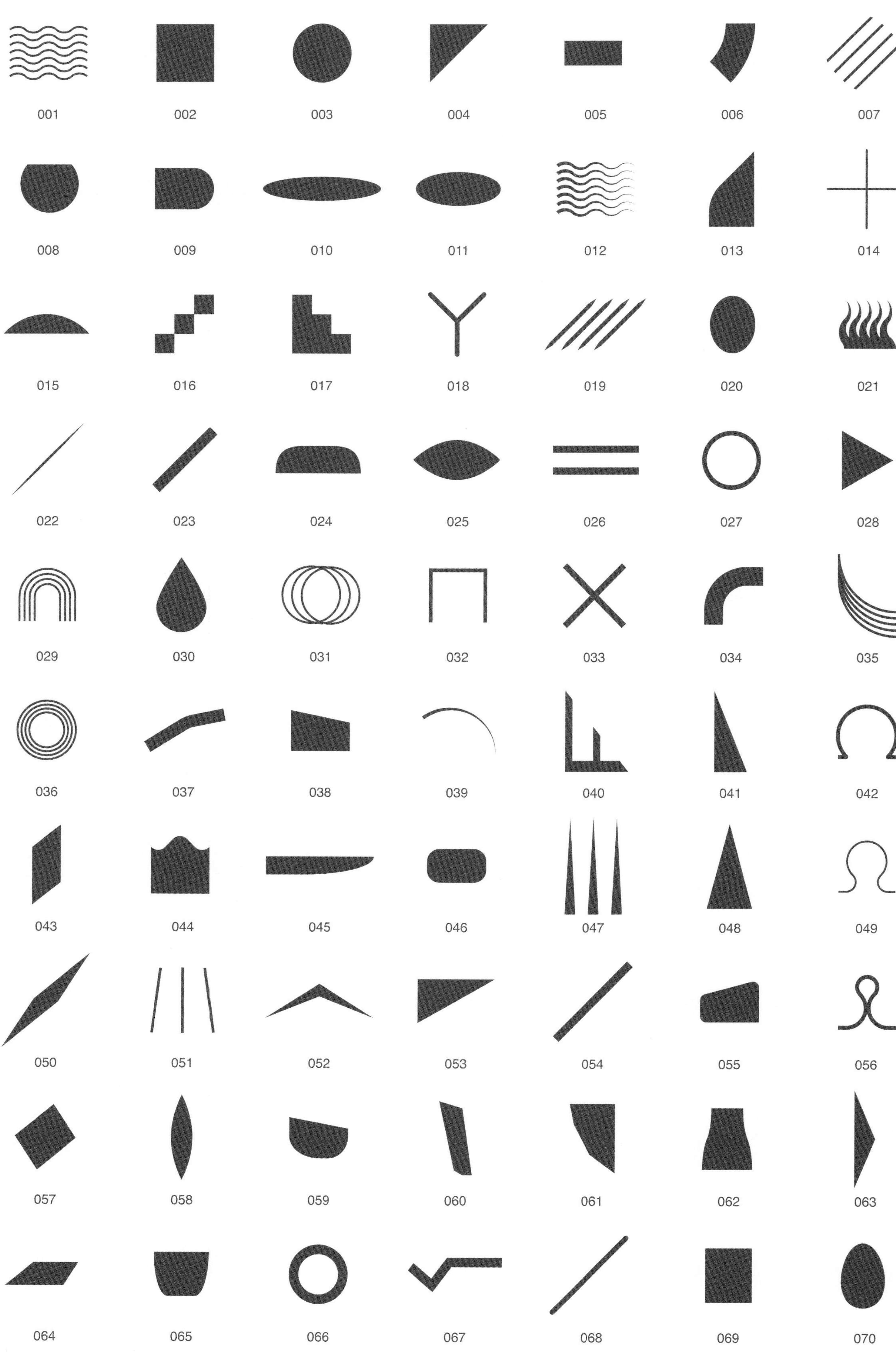

001
002
003
004
005
006
007
008
009
010
011
012
013
014
015
016
017
018
019
020
021
022
023
024
025
026
027
028
029
030
031
032
033
034
035
036
037
038
039
040
041
042
043
044
045
046
047
048
049
050
051
052
053
054
055
056
057
058
059
060
061
062
063
064
065
066
067
068
069
070

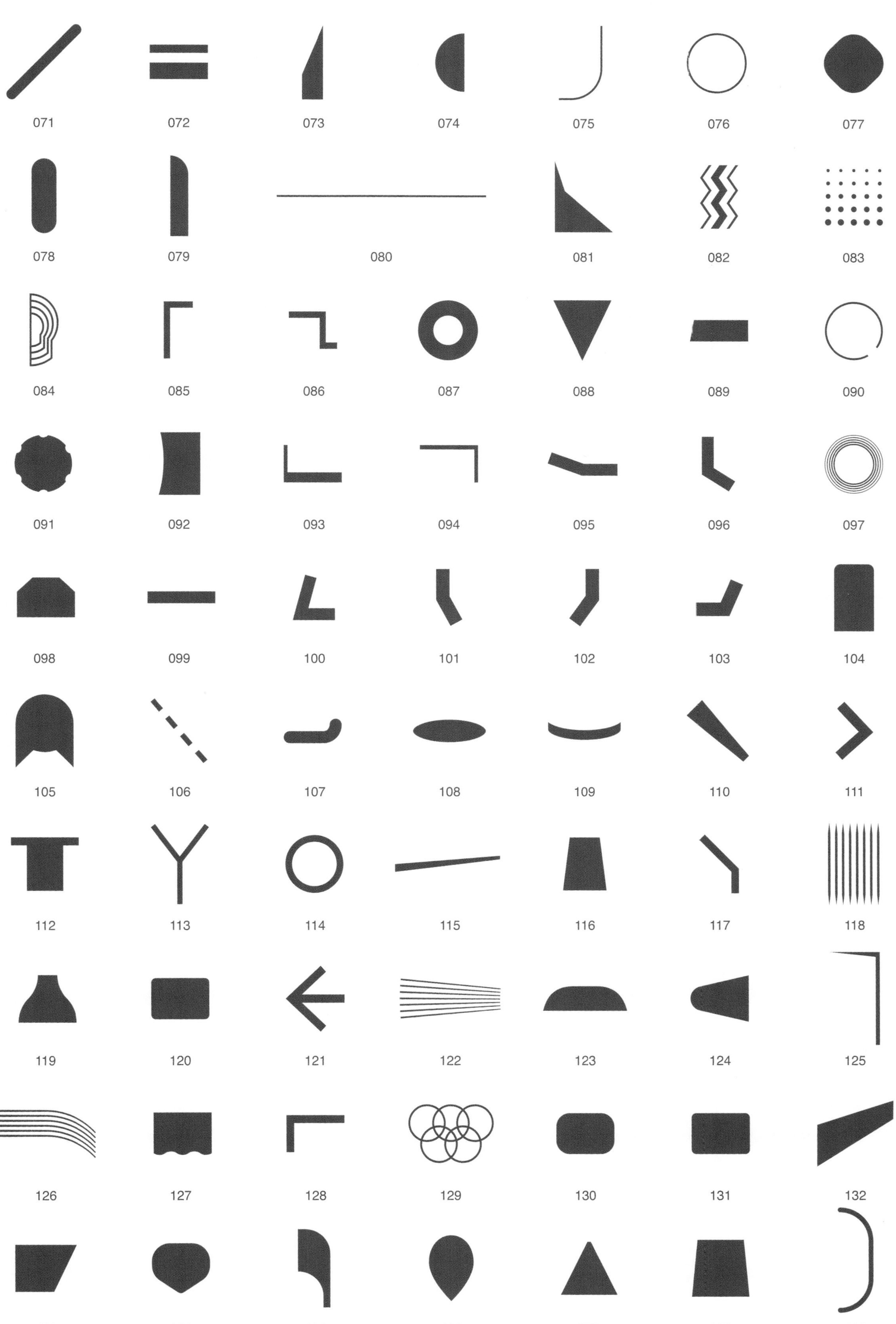

071
072
073
074
075
076
077
078
079
080
081
082
083
084
085
086
087
088
089
090
091
092
093
094
095
096
097
098
099
100
101
102
103
104
105
106
107
108
109
110
111
112
113
114
115
116
117
118
119
120
121
122
123
124
125
126
127
128
129
130
131
132
133
134
135
136
137
138
139

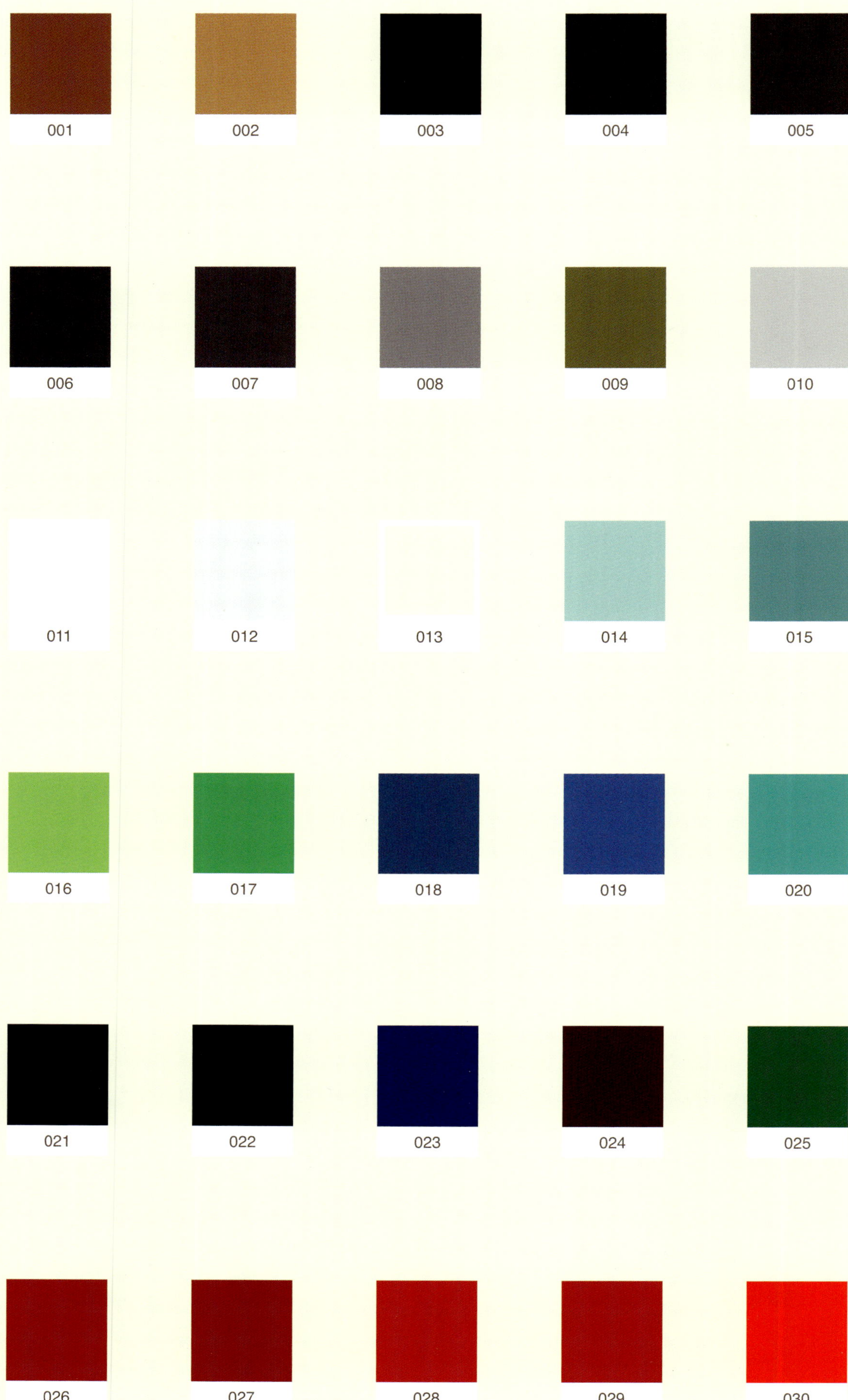

001
002
003
004
005
006
007
008
009
010
011
012
013
014
015
016
017
018
019
020
021
022
023
024
025
026
027
028
029
030

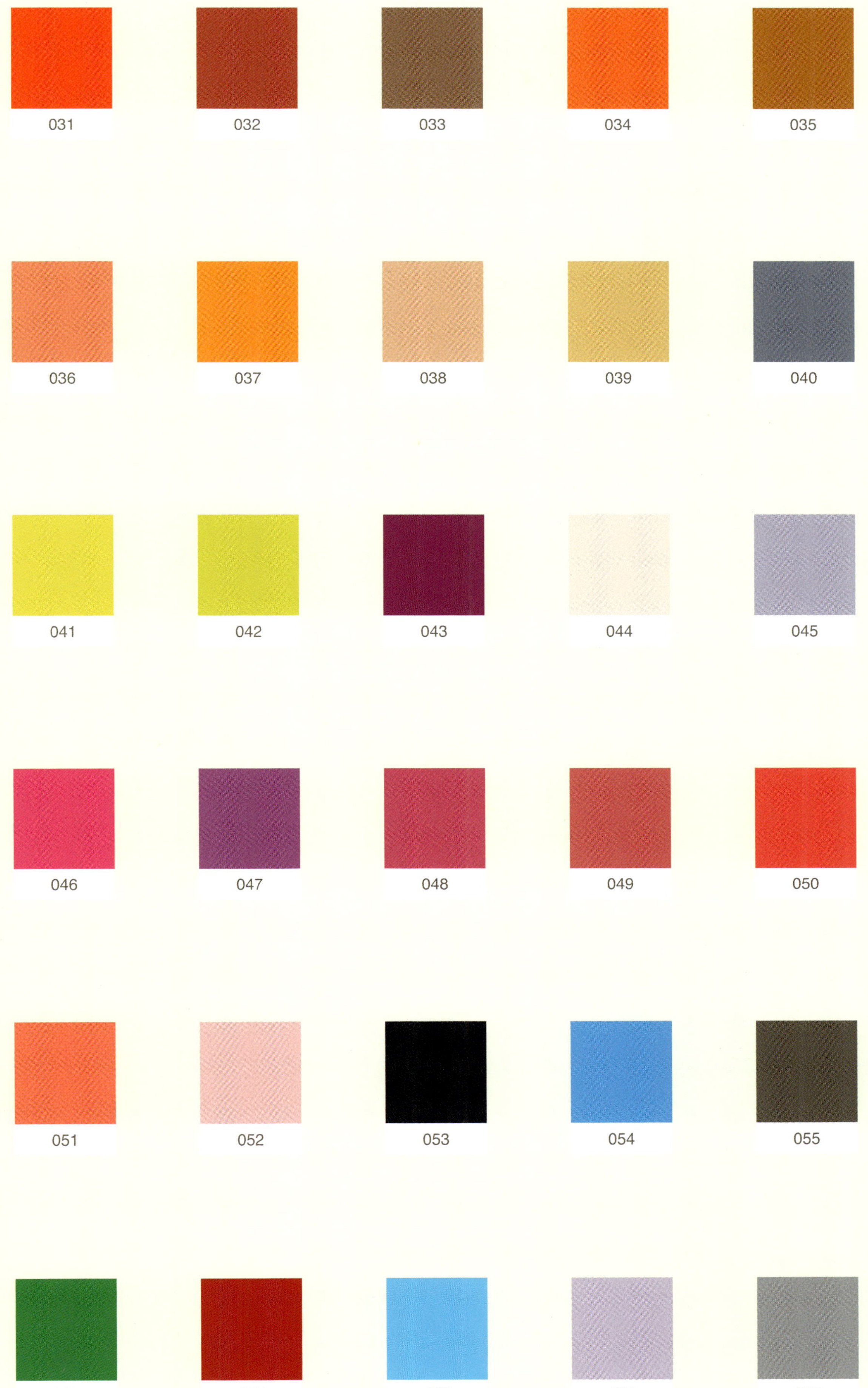

031
032
033
034
035
036
037
038
039
040
041
042
043
044
045
046
047
048
049
050
051
052
053
054
055
056
057
058
059
060

shapes   **colors**

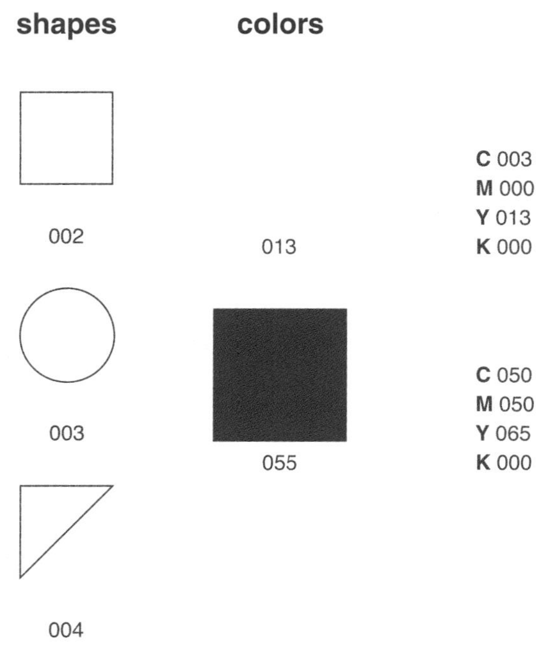

002   013

003   055

C 003
M 000
Y 013
K 000

C 050
M 050
Y 065
K 000

Key to the colors
used in the
composition of the
movie poster design
board.
The percentages
of the four-color
process are
indicated next to
each color.

004

Key to the shapes
used in the
composition of the
movie poster design
board.

movie title / / /
movie tag-line

movie title

movie tag-line

In cinematography this is the slogan or catchphrase with which a film is presented.
On advertising posters, it's usually placed near the title and conveys the sense in a concise way.

design boards

poster   image

Shortology icons

Shortology icons are used to tell a bit more about the film, such as the plot, or even a single scene.

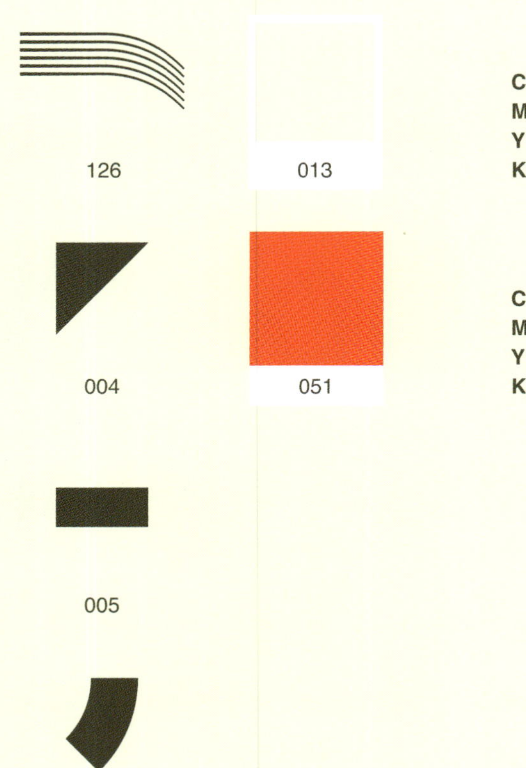

126

013

C 003
M 000
Y 013
K 000

004

051

C 001
M 073
Y 057
K 000

005

006

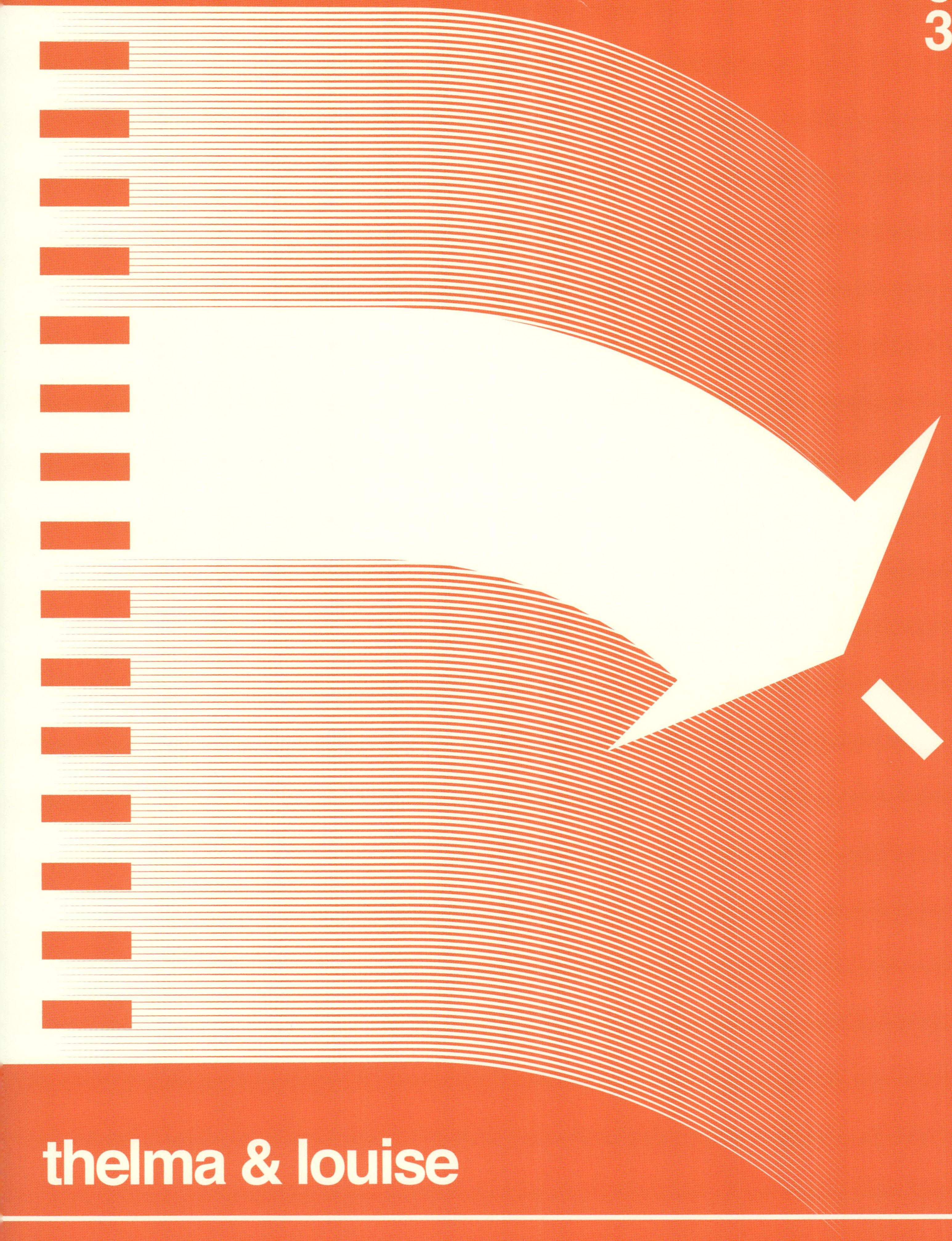

thelma & louise

somebody said get a life... so they did.

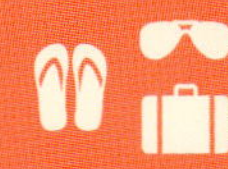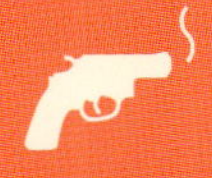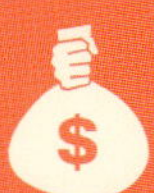

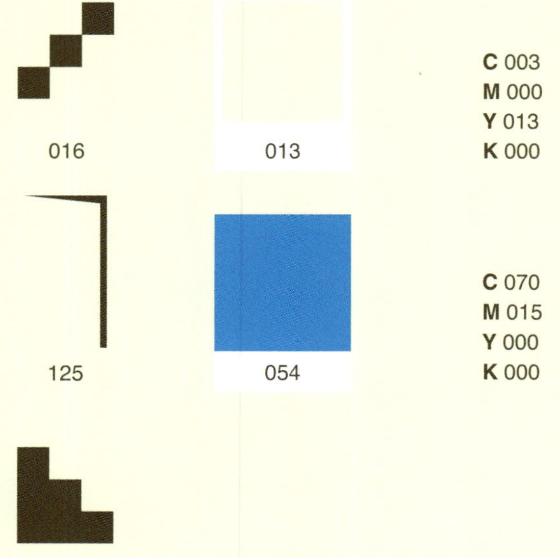

016

013

C 003
M 000
Y 013
K 000

125

054

C 070
M 015
Y 000
K 000

017

the truman show

all the world's a stage...

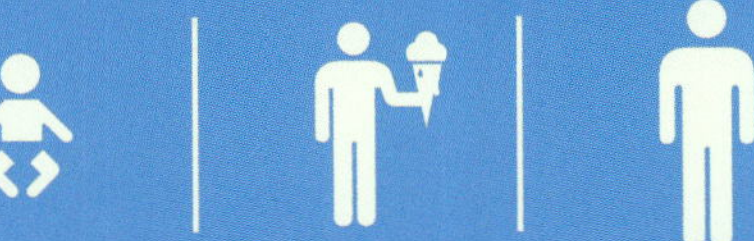

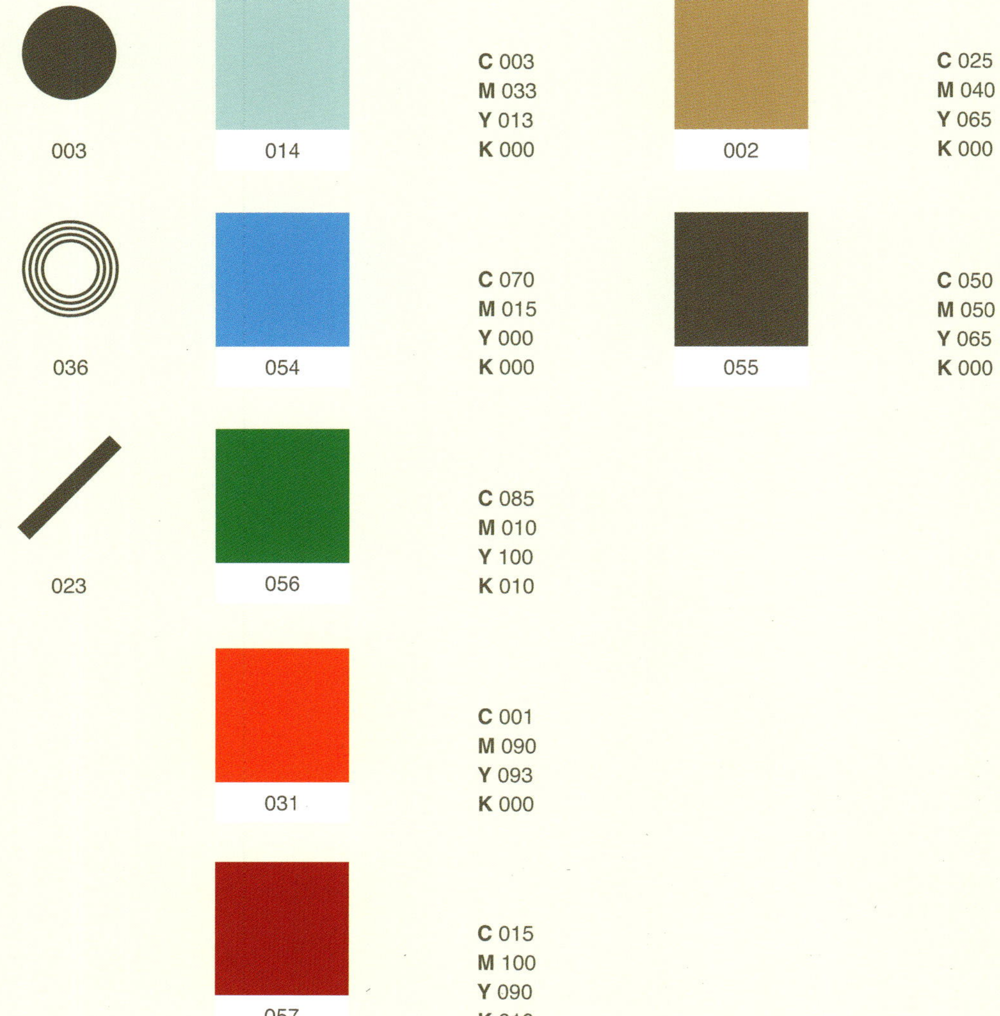

003
036
023
014
C 003
M 033
Y 013
K 000
054
C 070
M 015
Y 000
K 000
056
C 085
M 010
Y 100
K 010
031
C 001
M 090
Y 093
K 000
057
C 015
M 100
Y 090
K 010
002
C 025
M 040
Y 065
K 000
055
C 050
M 050
Y 065
K 000

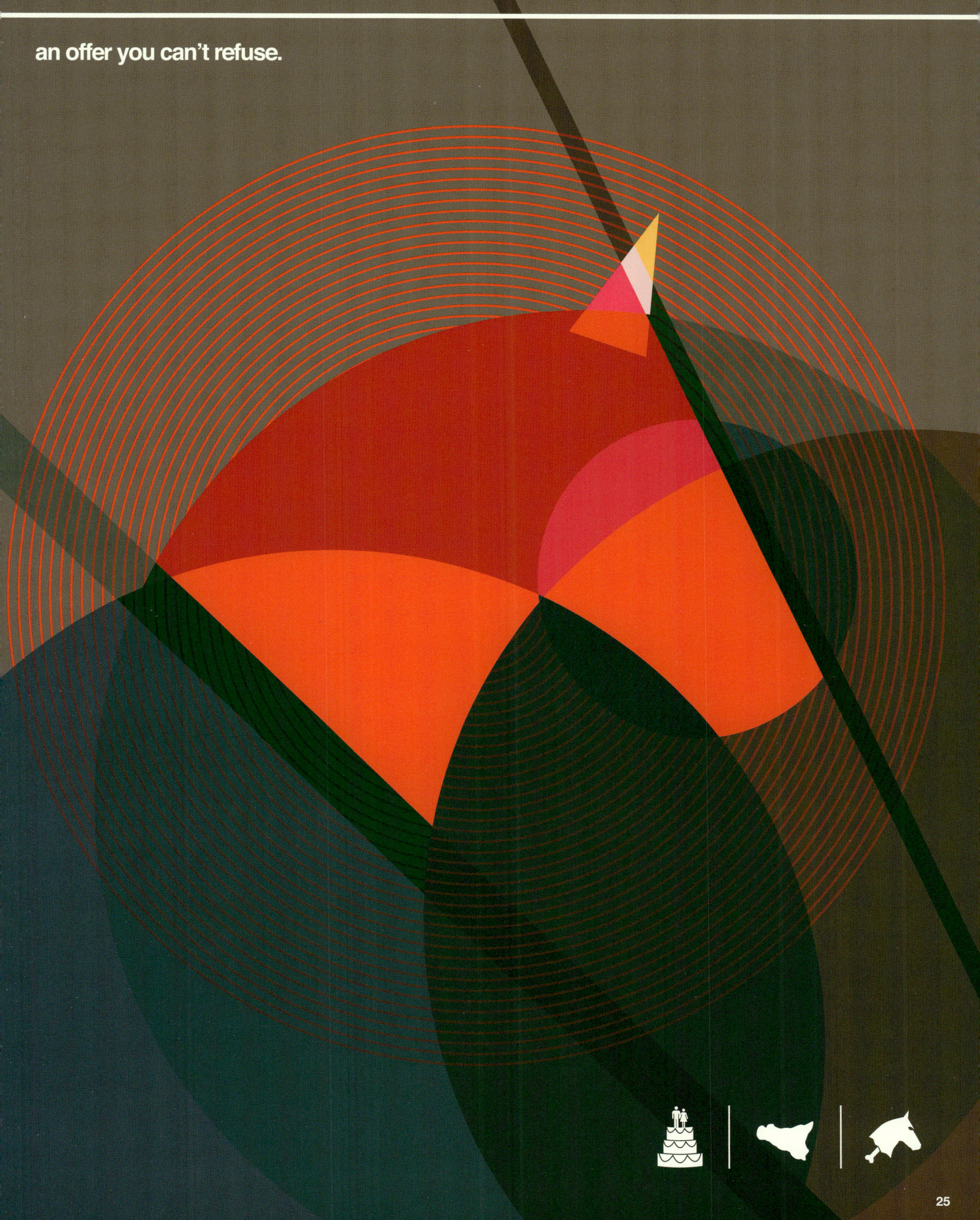
19
55
the godfather
an offer you can't refuse.

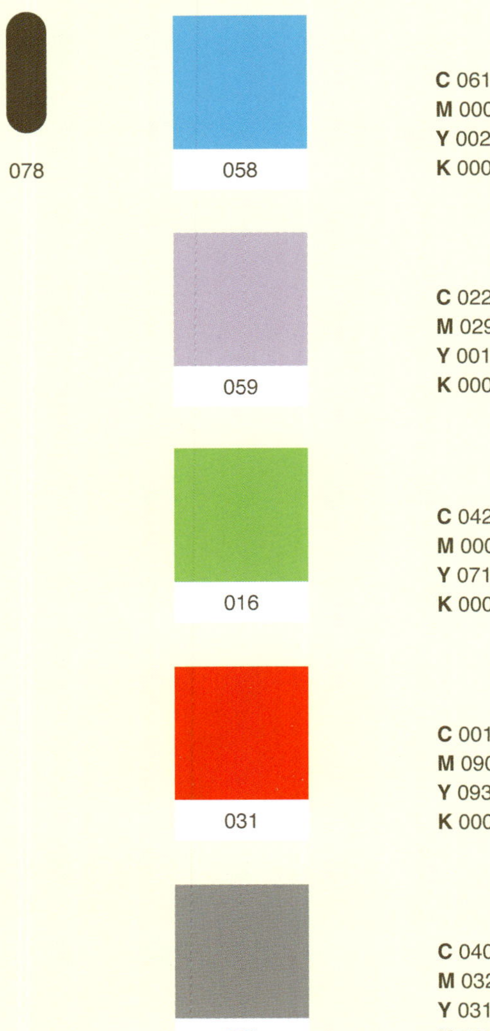

078

058

C 061
M 000
Y 002
K 000

059

C 022
M 029
Y 001
K 000

016

C 042
M 000
Y 071
K 000

031

C 001
M 090
Y 093
K 000

060

C 040
M 032
Y 031
K 000

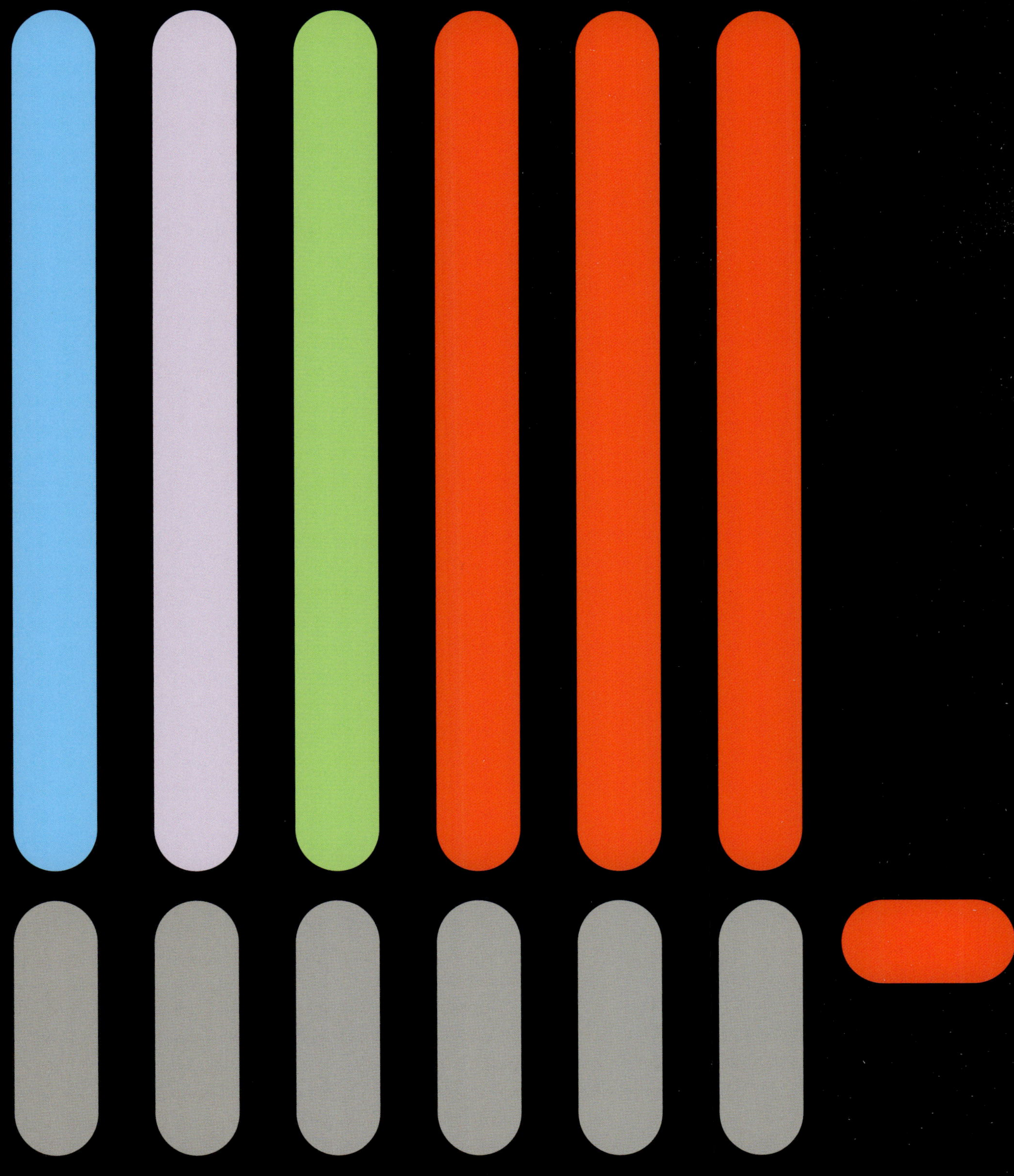
11
38
star wars
a long time ago in a galaxy far, far away...

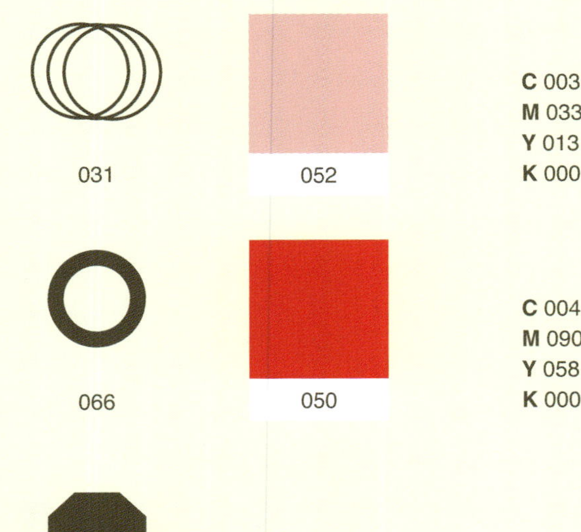

031

052

066

050

098

C 003
M 033
Y 013
K 000

C 004
M 090
Y 058
K 000

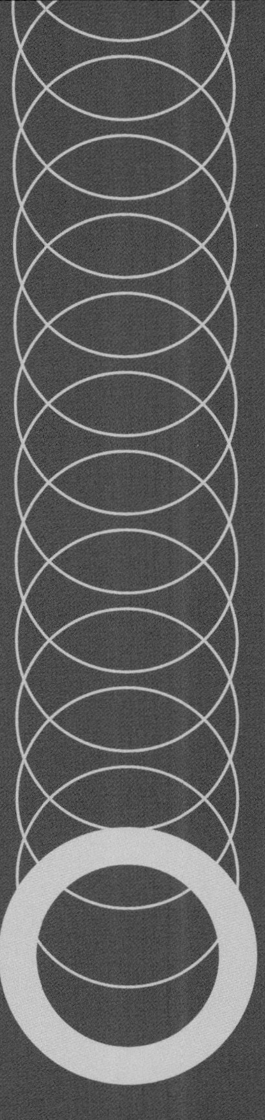

the lord of the rings

one ring to rule them all.

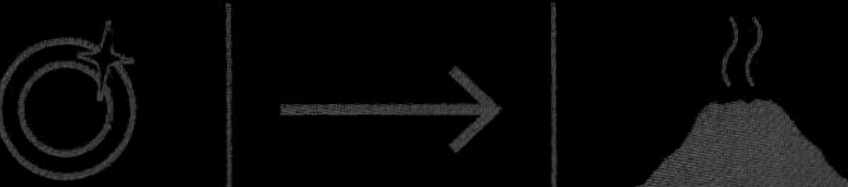

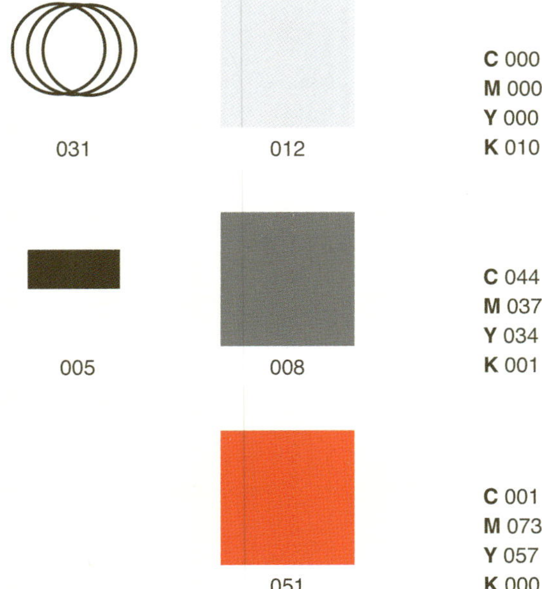

031

012

C 000
M 000
Y 000
K 010

005

008

C 044
M 037
Y 034
K 001

051

C 001
M 073
Y 057
K 000

schindler's list

whoever saves one life, saves the world entire.

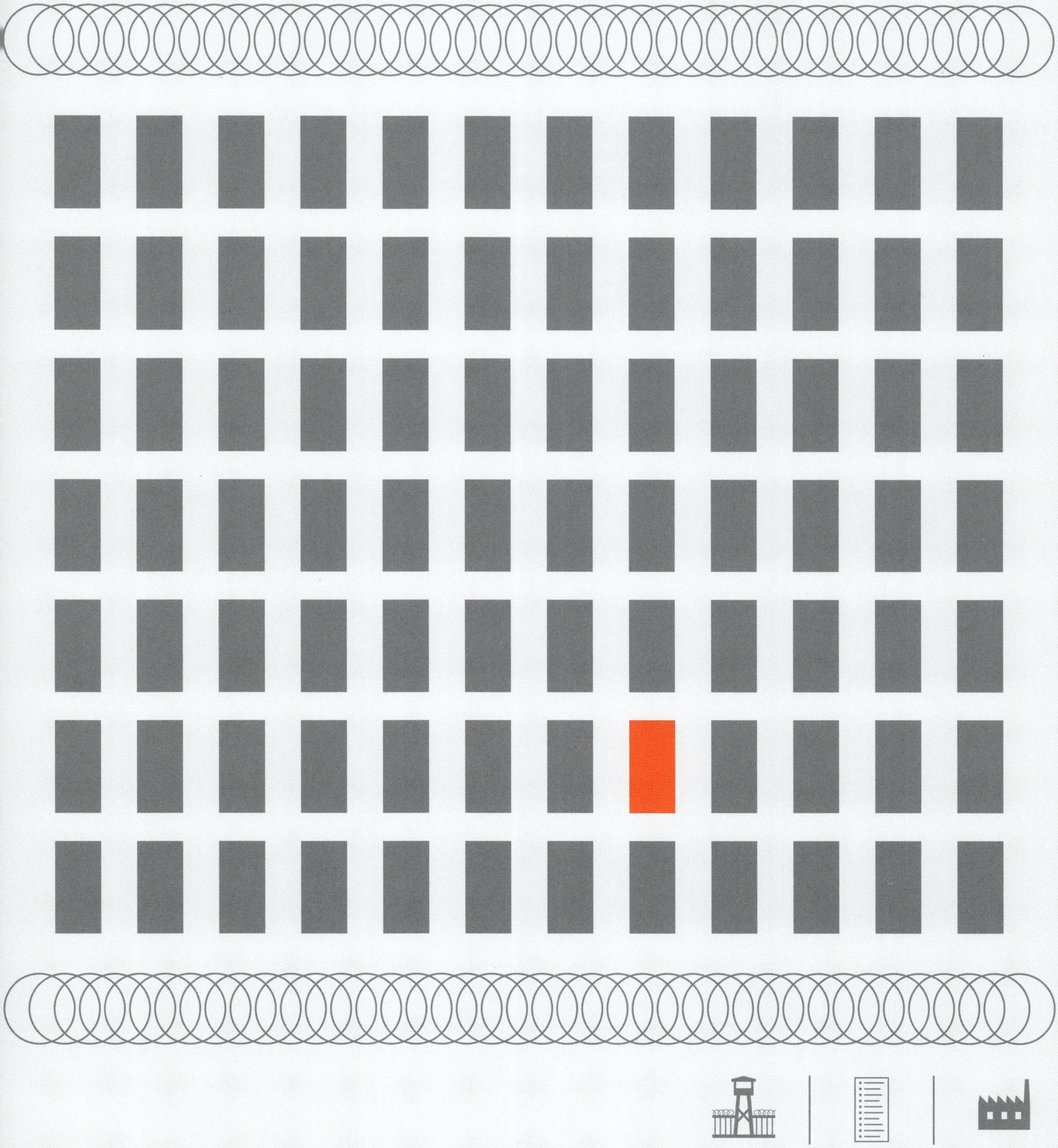

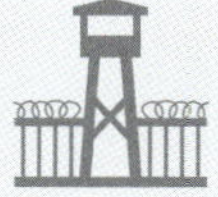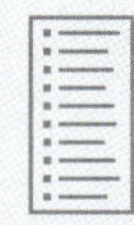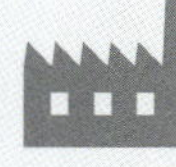

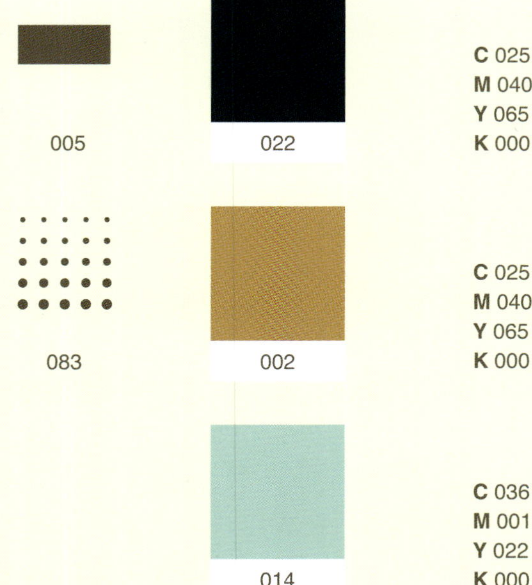

005

022

C 025
M 040
Y 065
K 000

083

002

C 025
M 040
Y 065
K 000

014

C 036
M 001
Y 022
K 000

pulp fiction

pulp (pulp) n. 1. a soft, wet shapeless mass of matter.
2. a book dealing with lurid or sensational subjects,
often printed on low-quality paper manufactured from wood pulp.

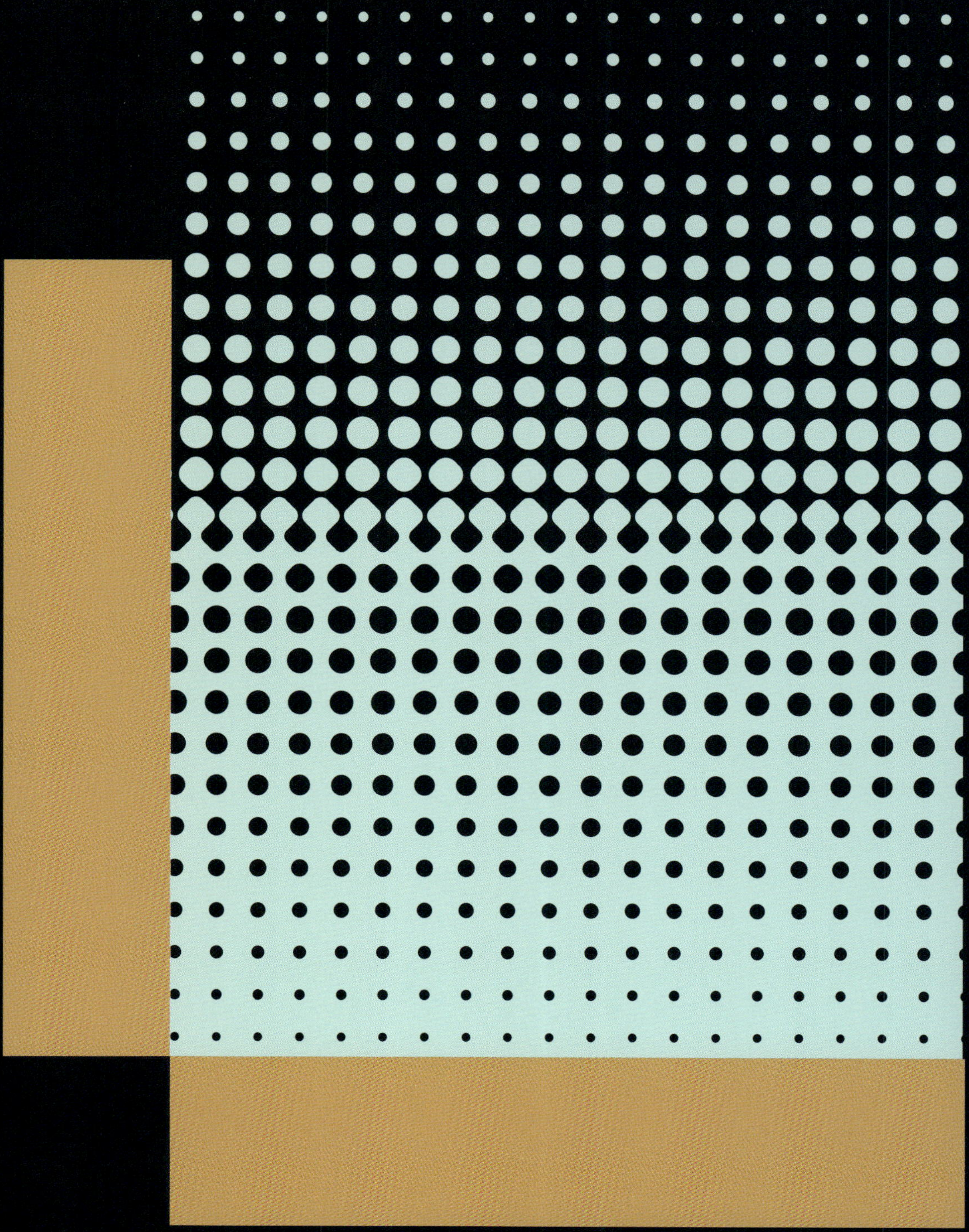

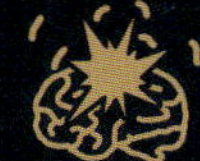
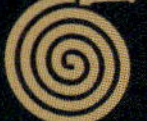

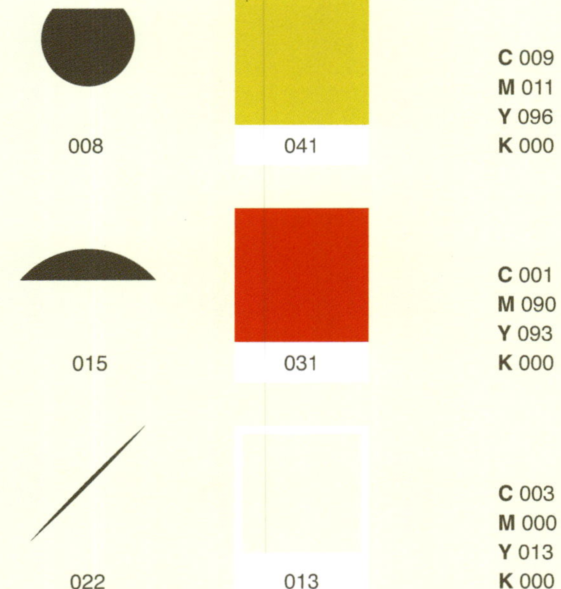

008 041 **C** 009 **M** 011 **Y** 096 **K** 000

015 031 **C** 001 **M** 090 **Y** 093 **K** 000

022 013 **C** 003 **M** 000 **Y** 013 **K** 000

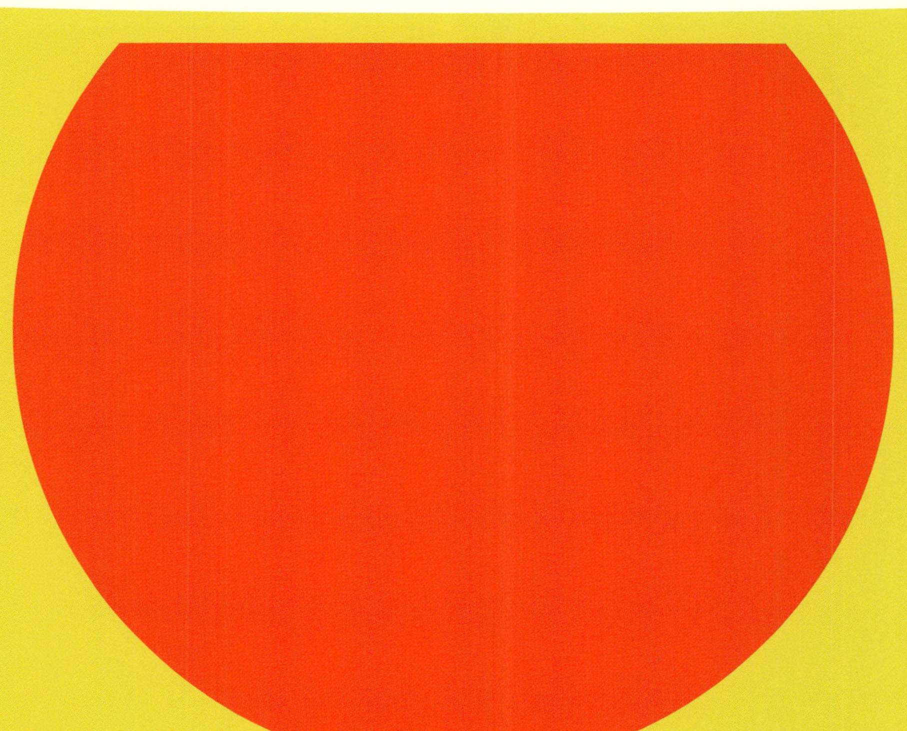

01
01
kill bill
a roaring rampage of revenge.
35

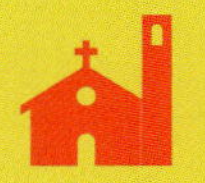
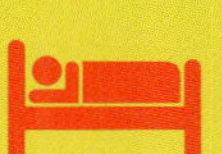
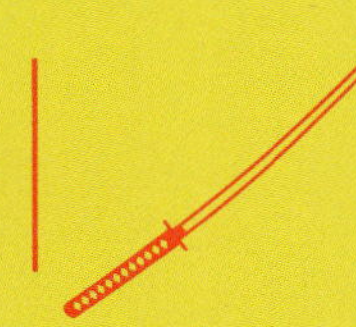

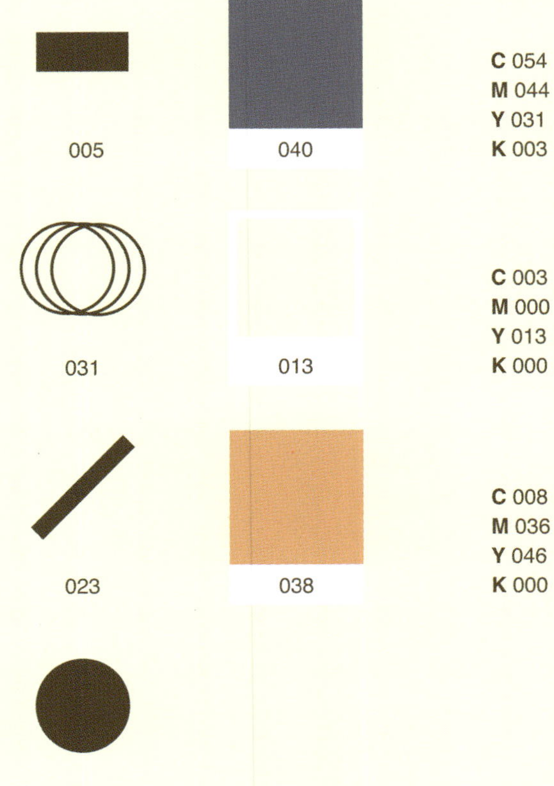

005

040

C 054
M 044
Y 031
K 003

031

013

C 003
M 000
Y 013
K 000

023

038

C 008
M 036
Y 046
K 000

003

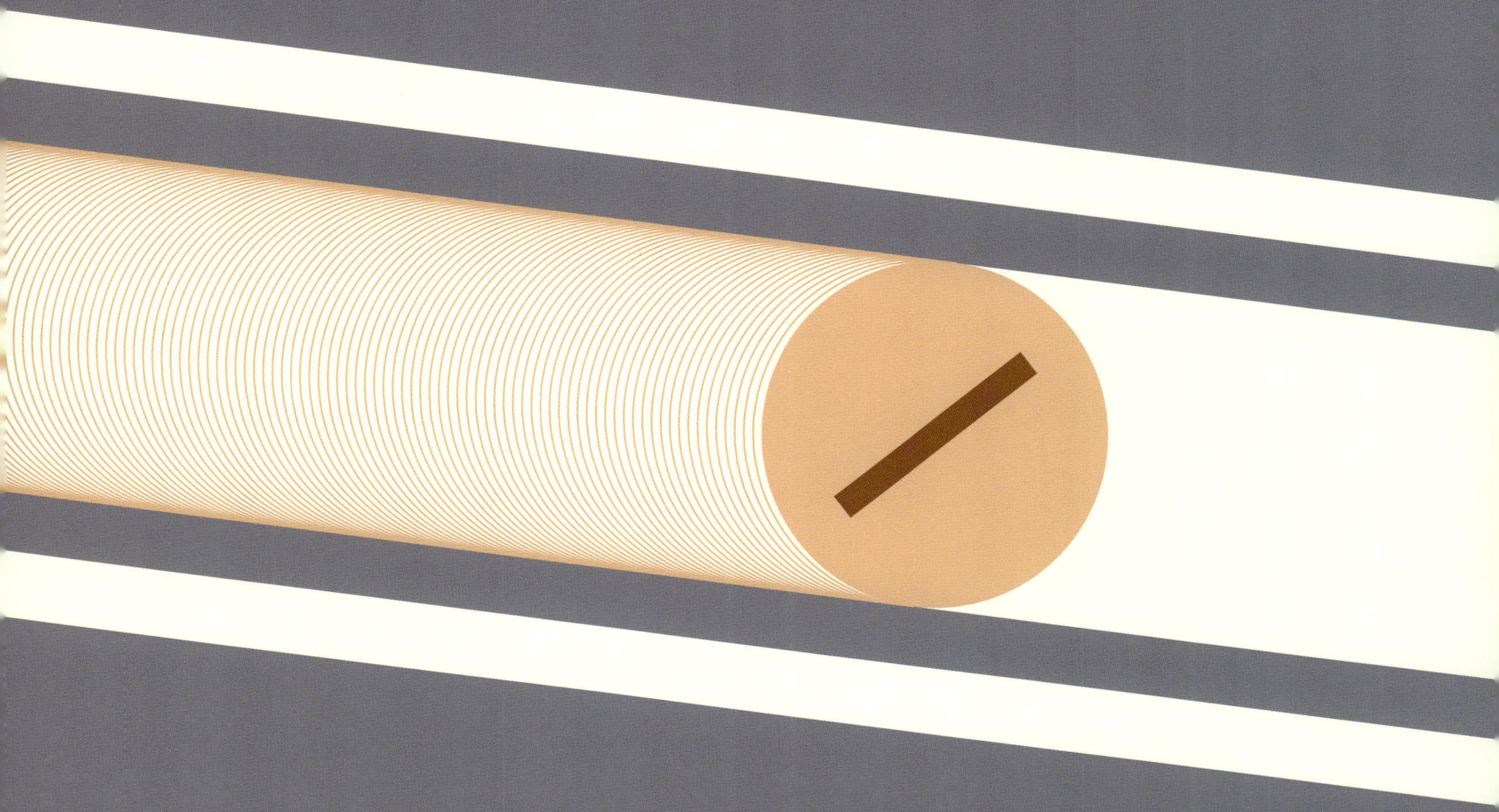

minority report

everybody runs.

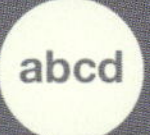
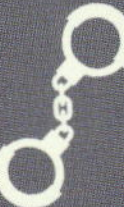

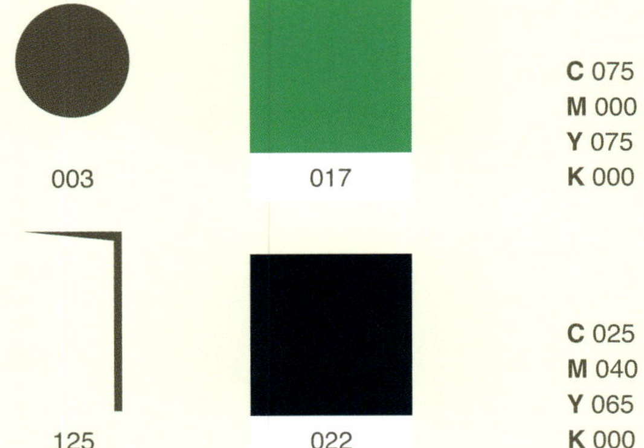

003   017   **C** 075
                      M 000
                      Y 075
                      K 000

125   022   **C** 025
                      M 040
                      Y 065
                      K 000

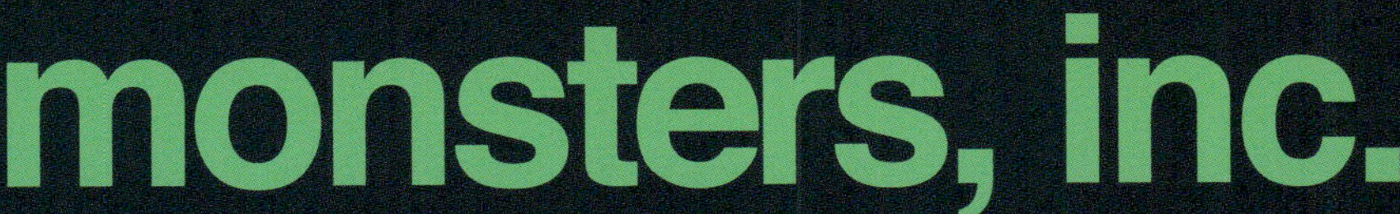

monsters, inc.

we scare because we care.

 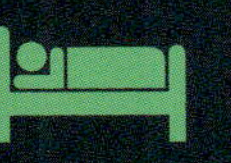 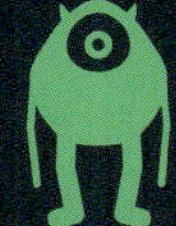

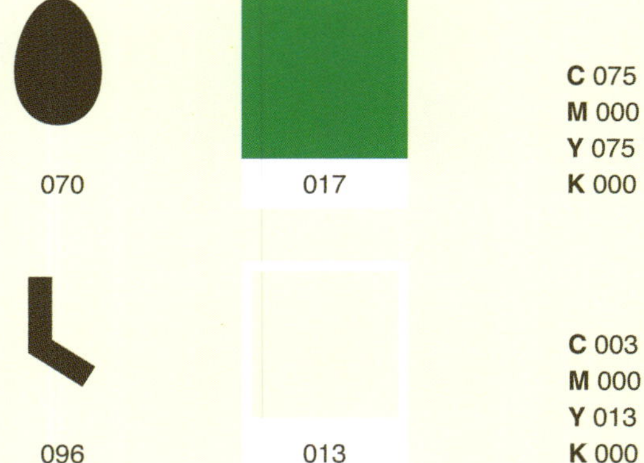

070   017

C 075
M 000
Y 075
K 000

096   013

C 003
M 000
Y 013
K 000

alien

in space, no one can hear you scream.

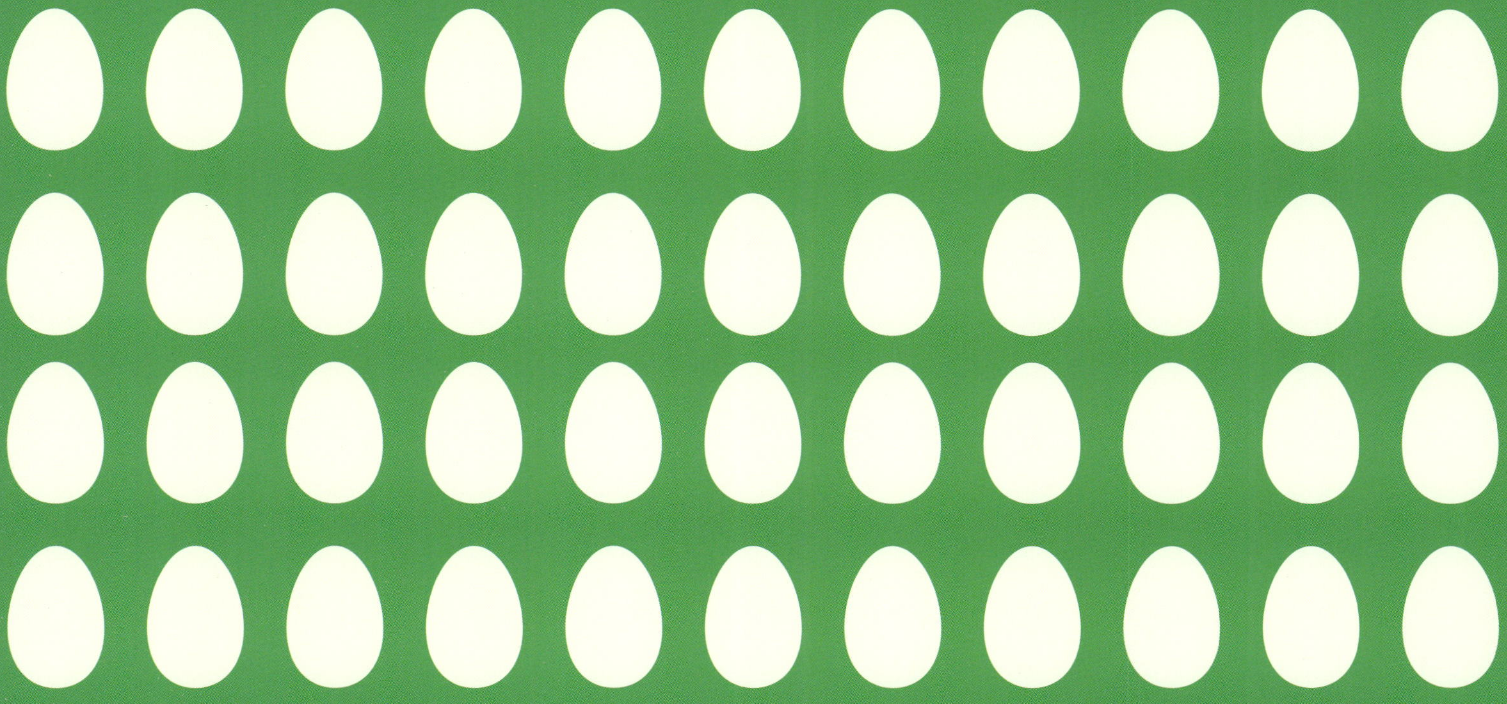

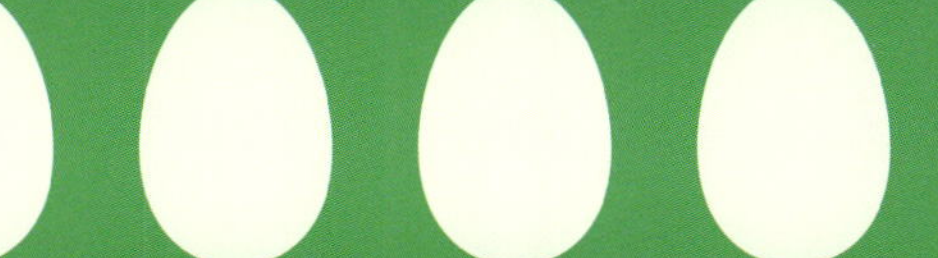

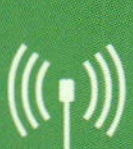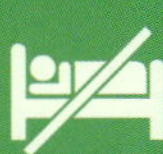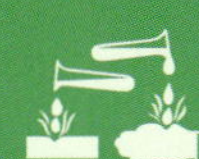

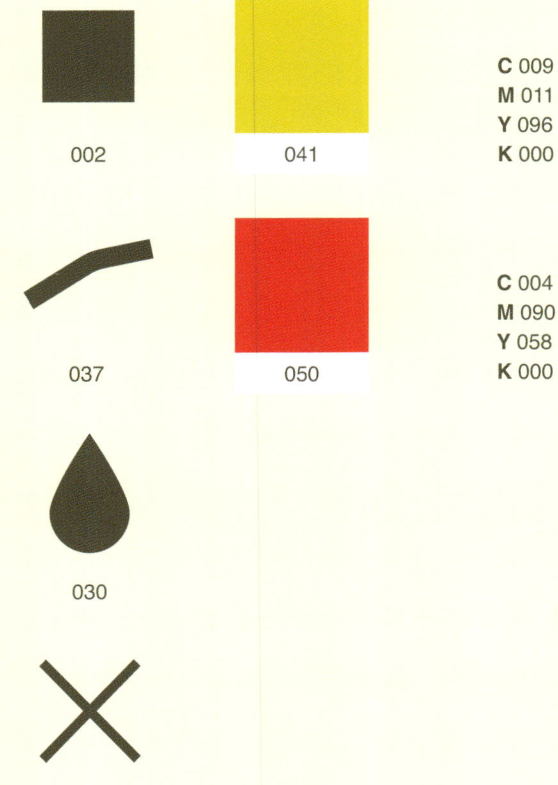

002   041   **C** 009
                      M 011
                      Y 096
                      K 000

037   050   **C** 004
                      M 090
                      Y 058
                      K 000

030

033

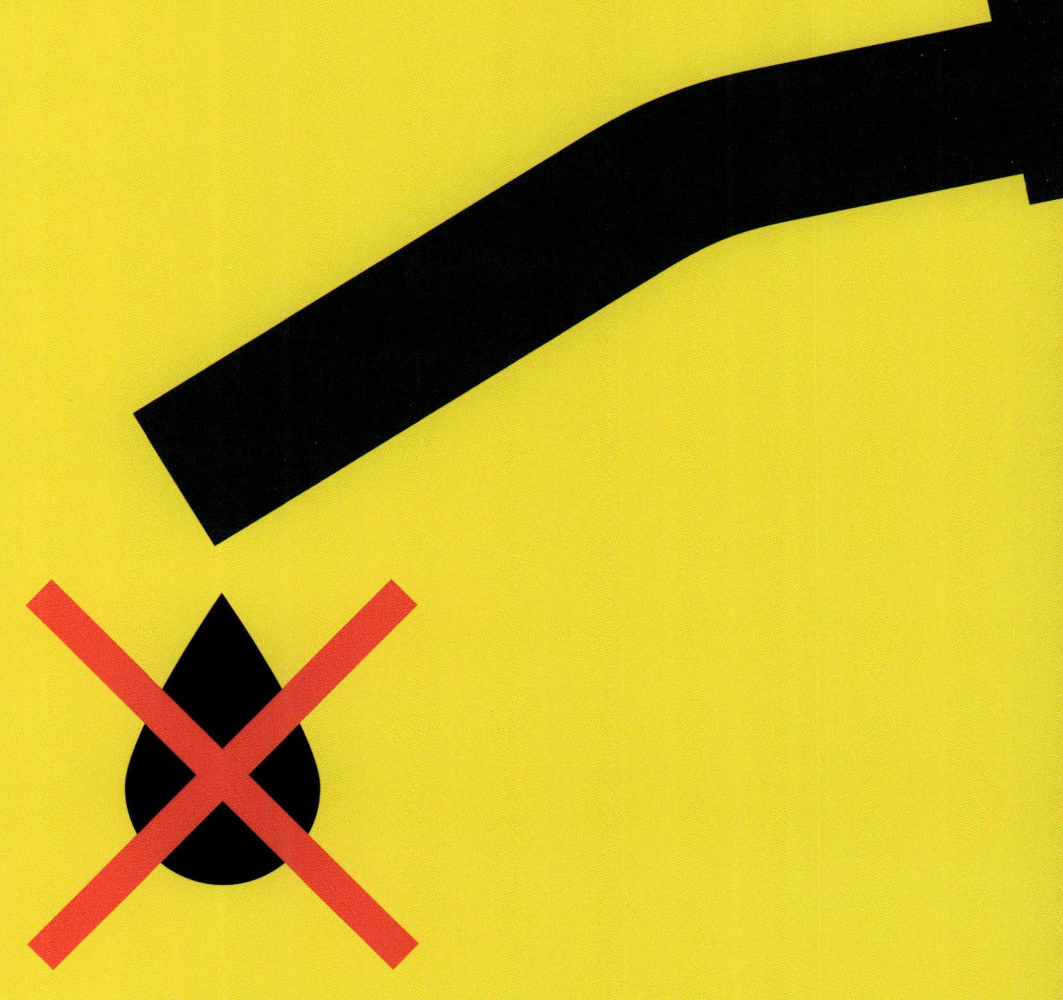

19
73
mad max
the maximum force of the future.

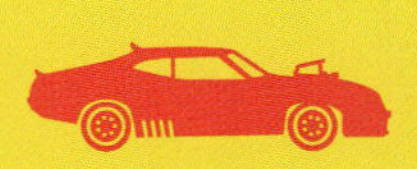

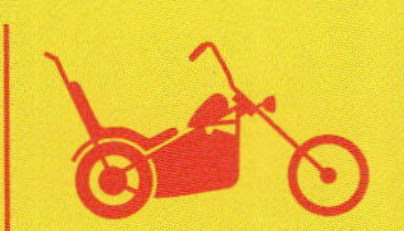

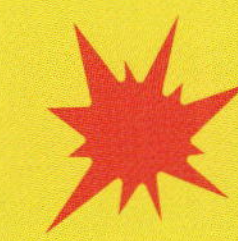

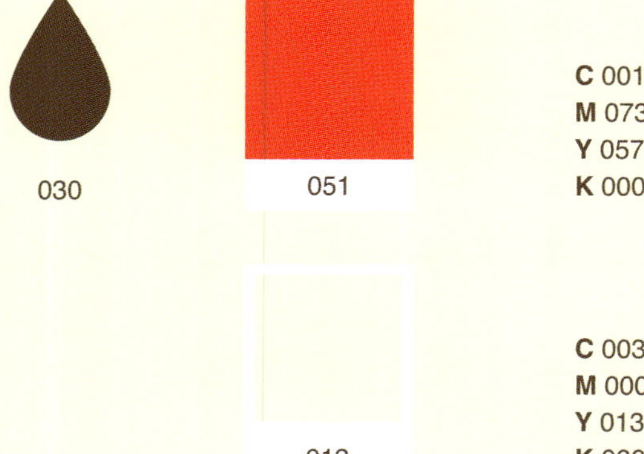

030

051

C 001
M 073
Y 057
K 000

013

C 003
M 000
Y 013
K 000

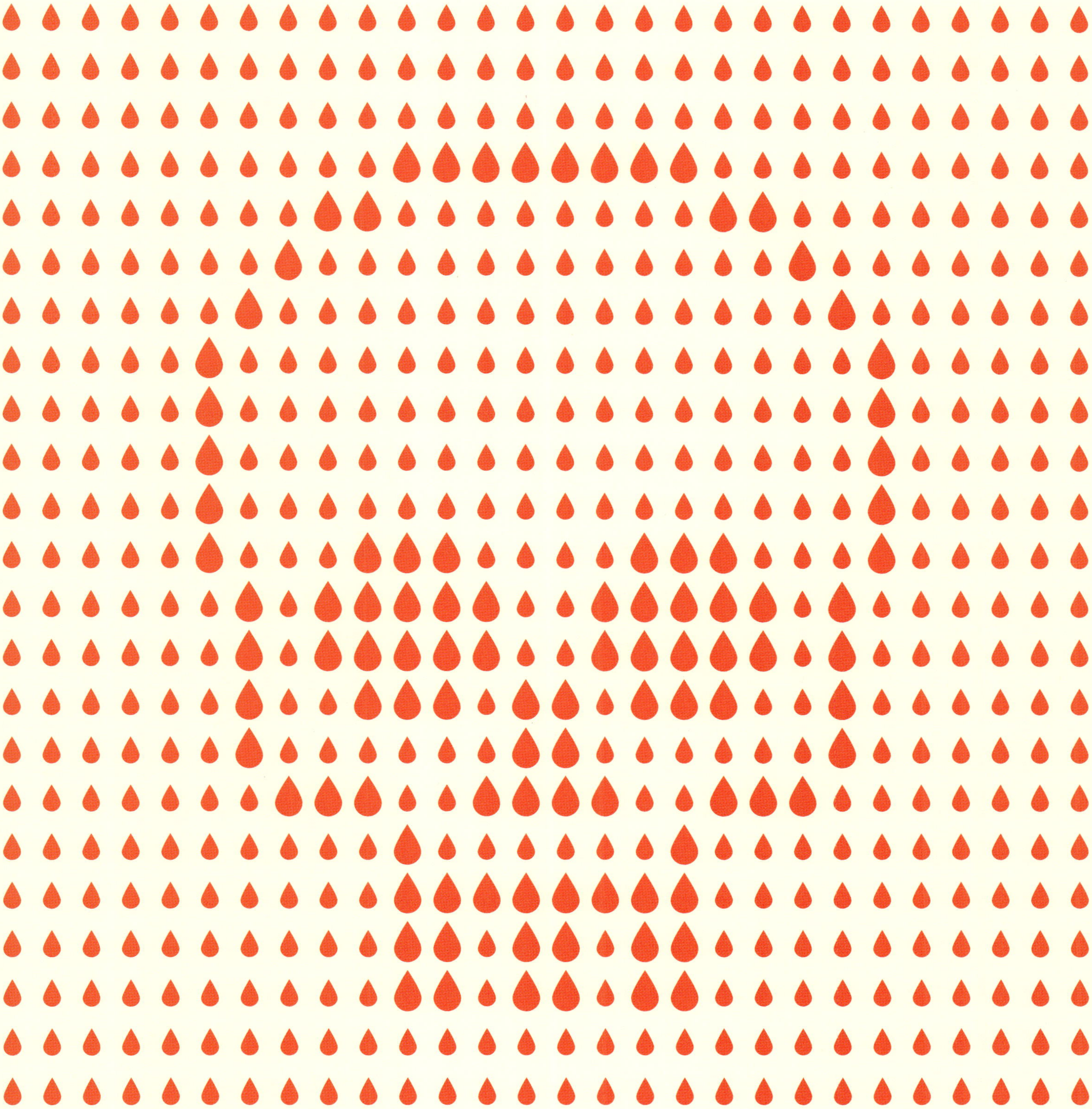

game of thrones

all men must die.

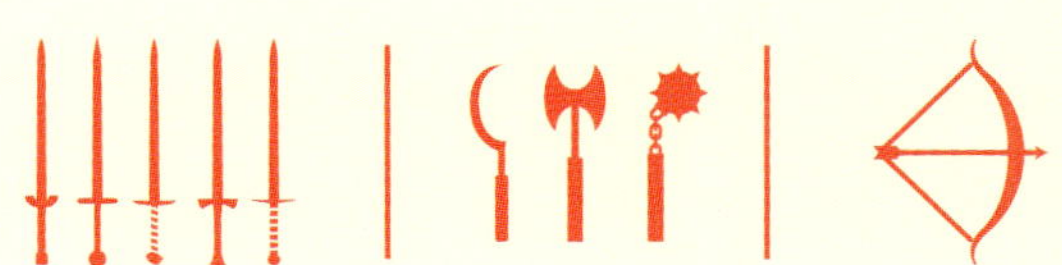

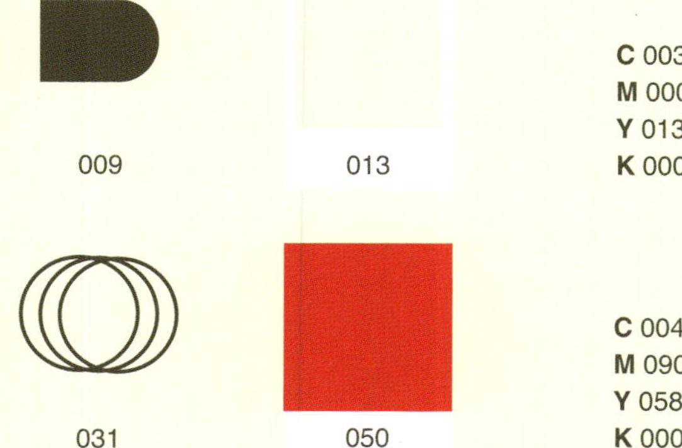

009

013

C 003
M 000
Y 013
K 000

031

050

C 004
M 090
Y 058
K 000

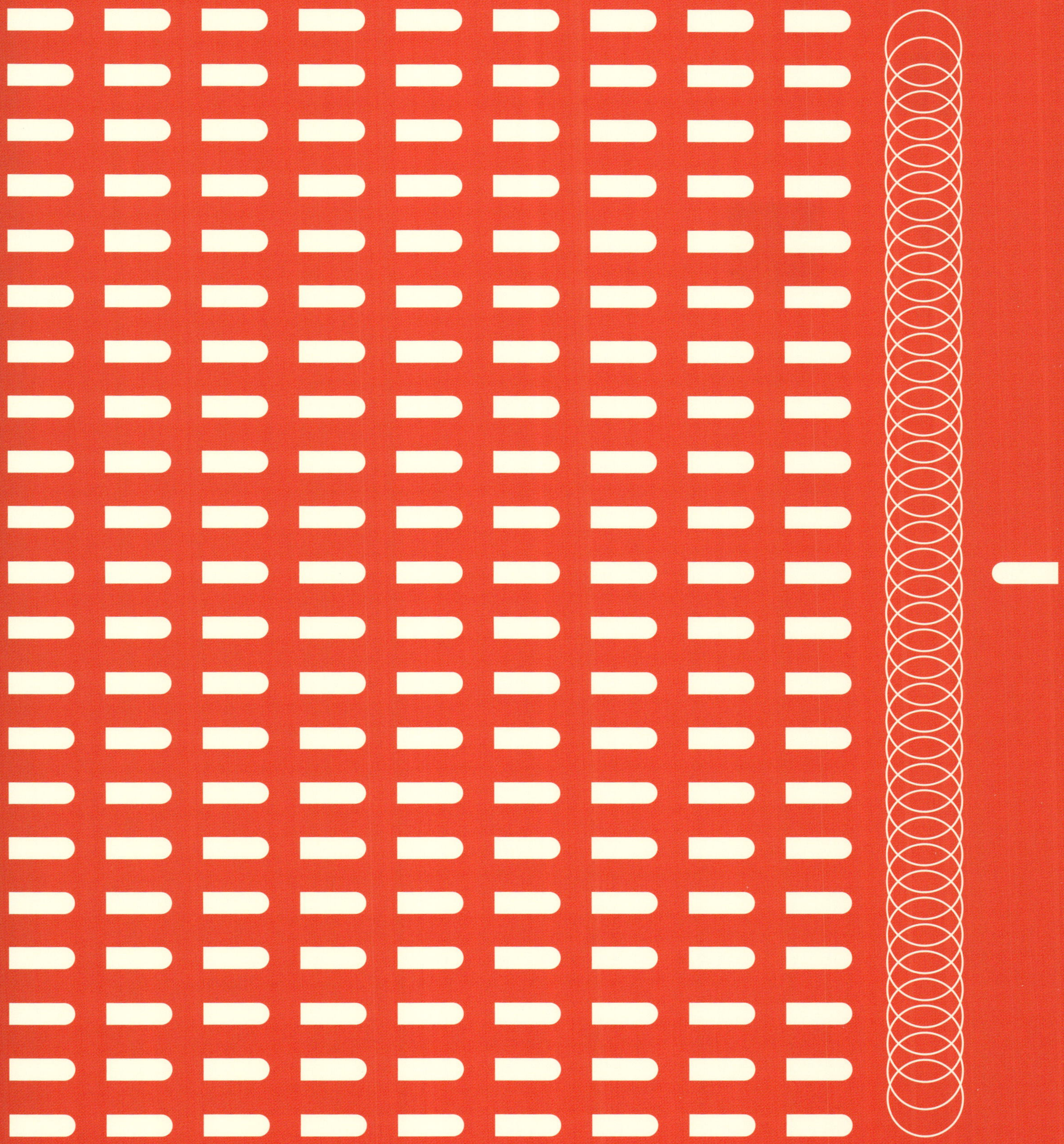

full metal jacket

in vietnam the wind doesn't blow. it sucks.

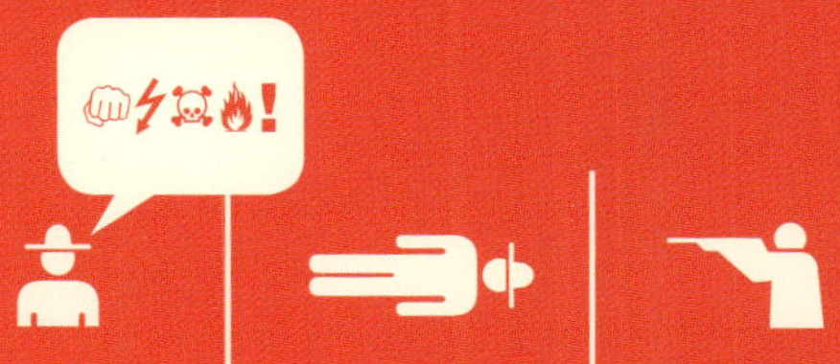

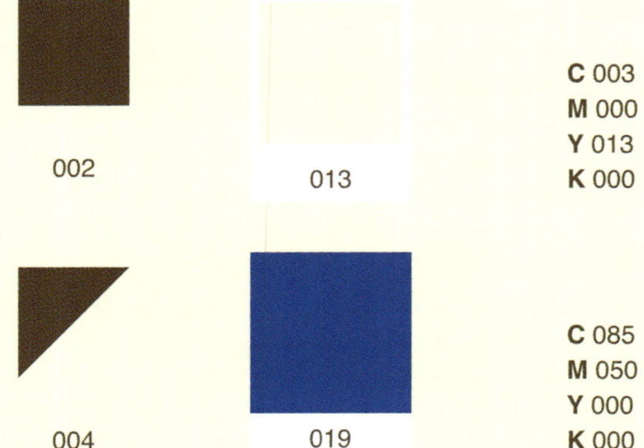

002

004

013

019

C 003
M 000
Y 013
K 000

C 085
M 050
Y 000
K 000

breaking bad

all becomes crystal clear.

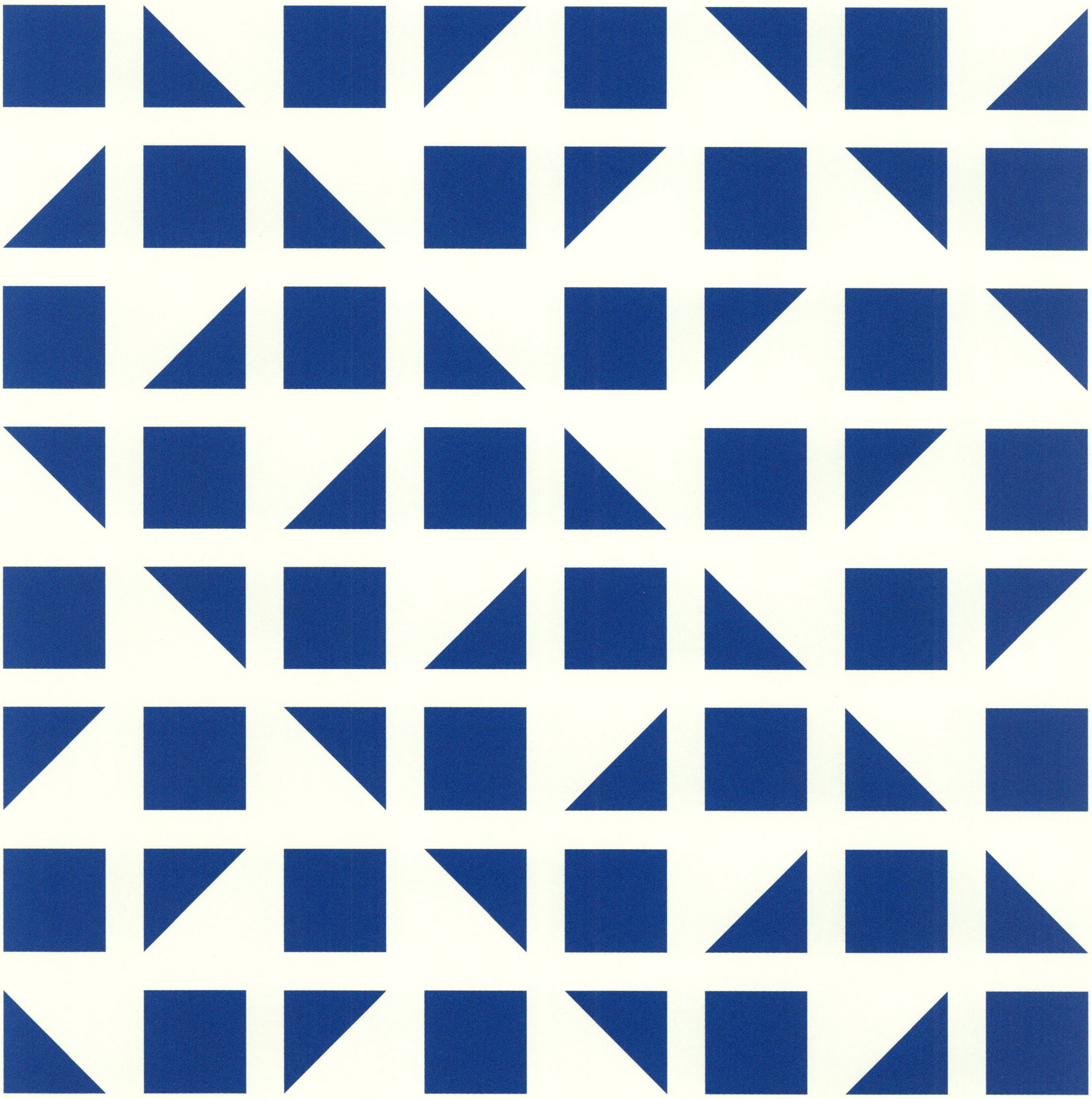

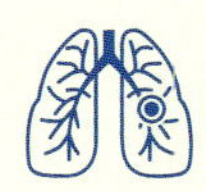 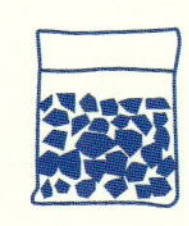 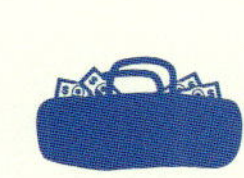

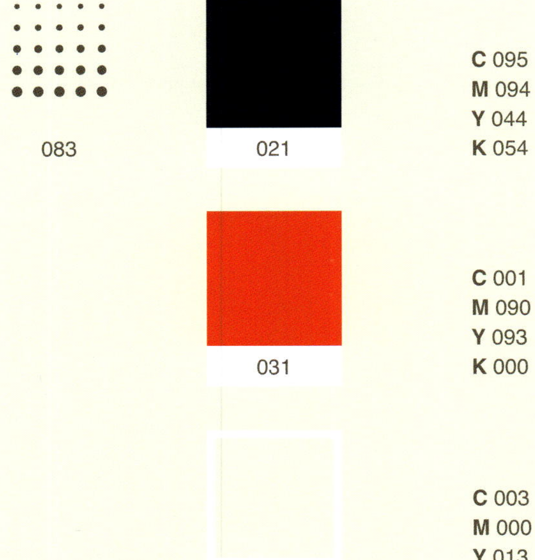

083

021

C 095
M 094
Y 044
K 054

031

C 001
M 090
Y 093
K 000

013

C 003
M 000
Y 013
K 000

blade runner 2049

sometimes to love someone, you gotta be a stranger.

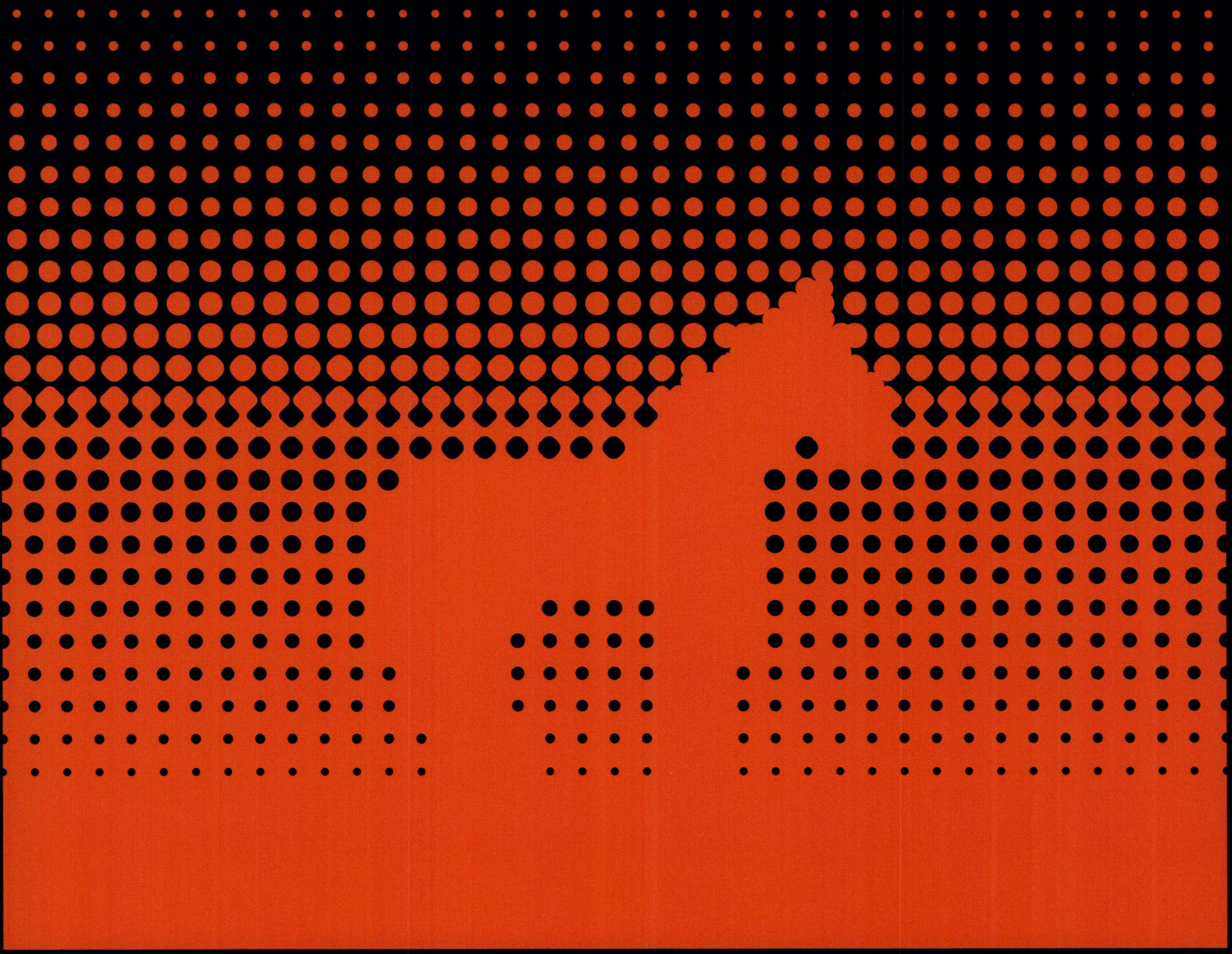

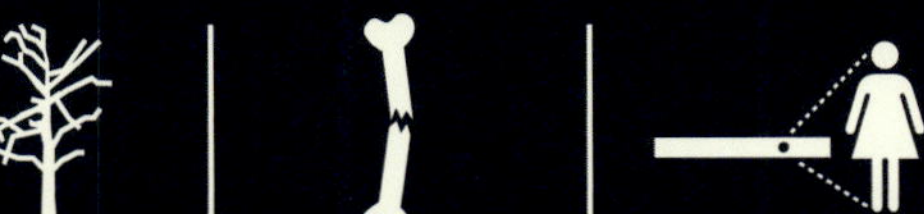

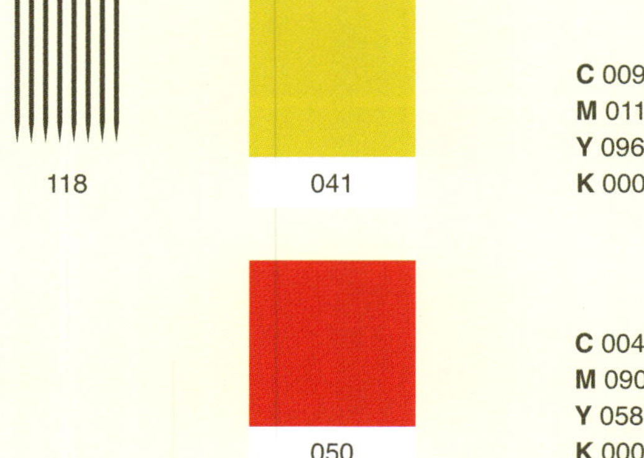

118

041

C 009
M 011
Y 096
K 000

050

C 004
M 090
Y 058
K 000

rain man

a journey through understanding and fellowship.

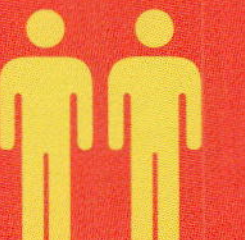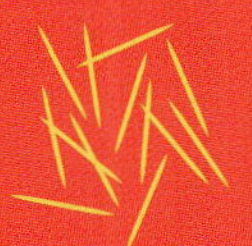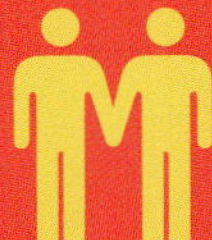

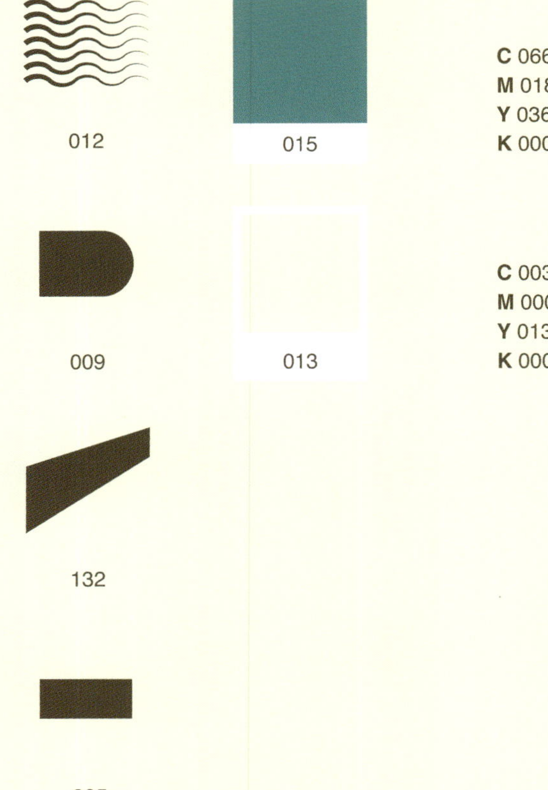

012

015

C 066
M 018
Y 036
K 000

009

013

C 003
M 000
Y 013
K 000

132

005

wild tales / / /
we can all lose control.

relatos salvajes

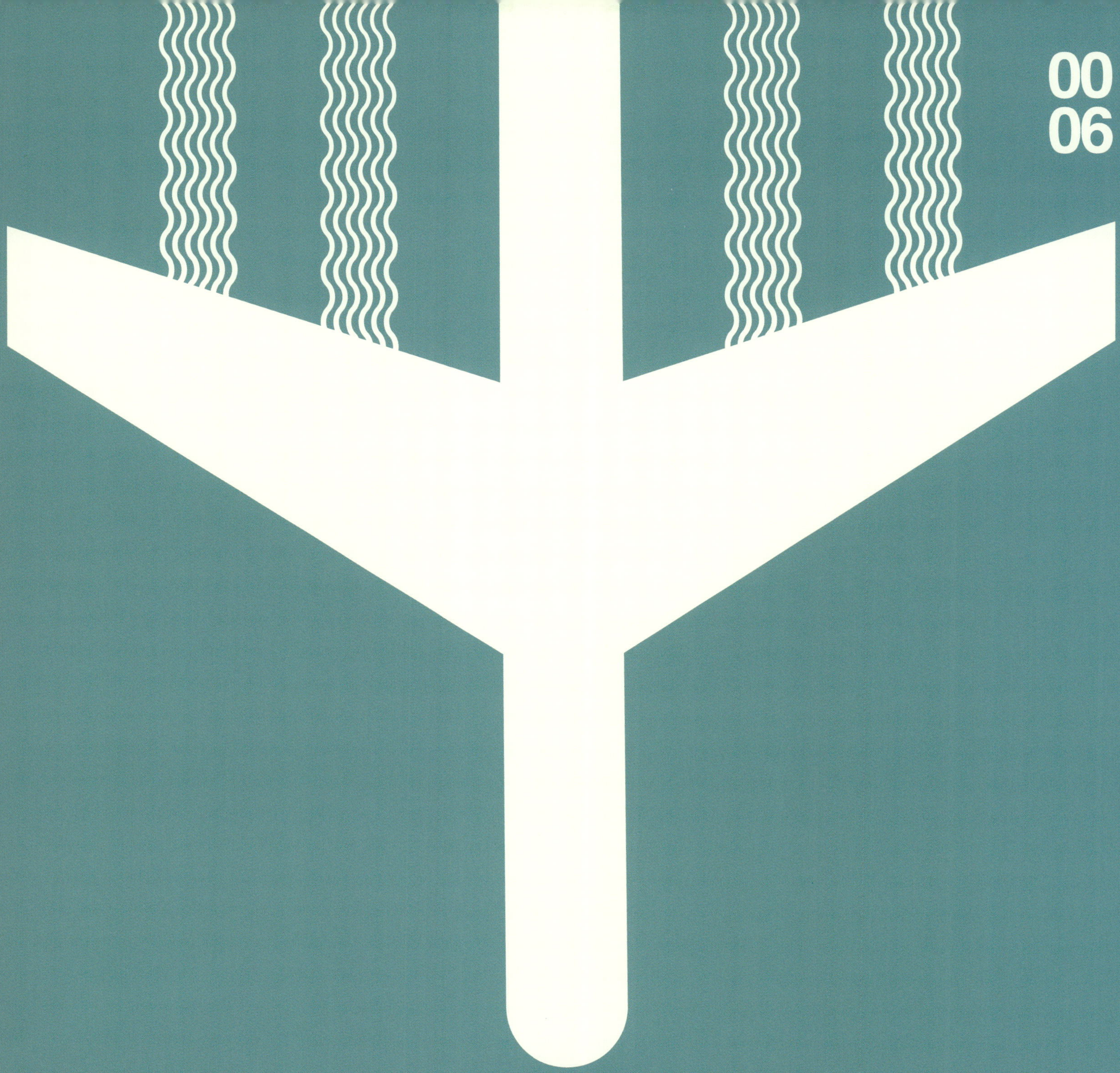

todos podemos perder el control.

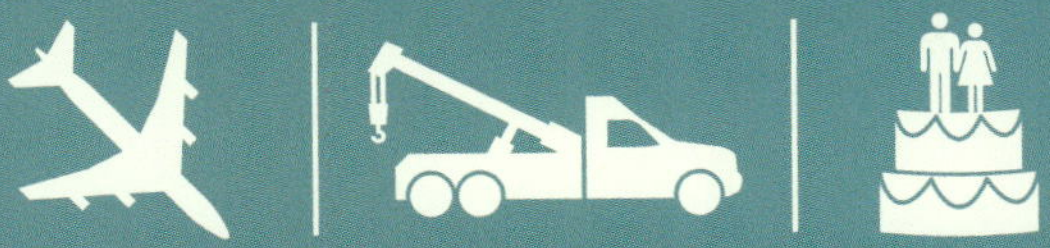

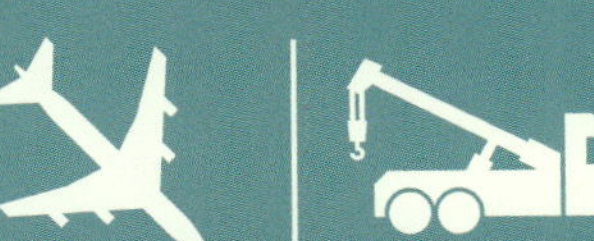

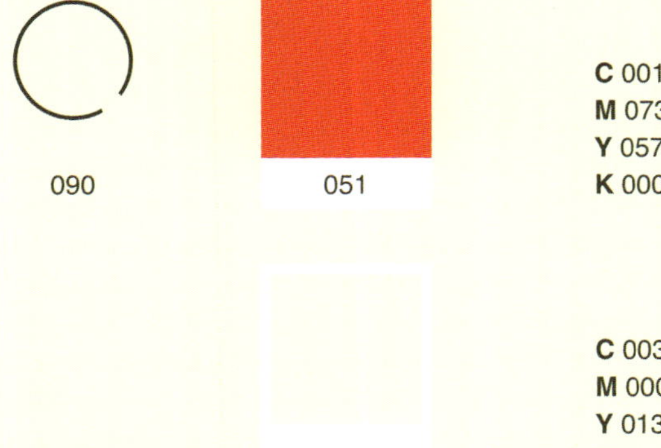

090

051

C 001
M 073
Y 057
K 000

013

C 003
M 000
Y 013
K 000

arrival

why are they here?

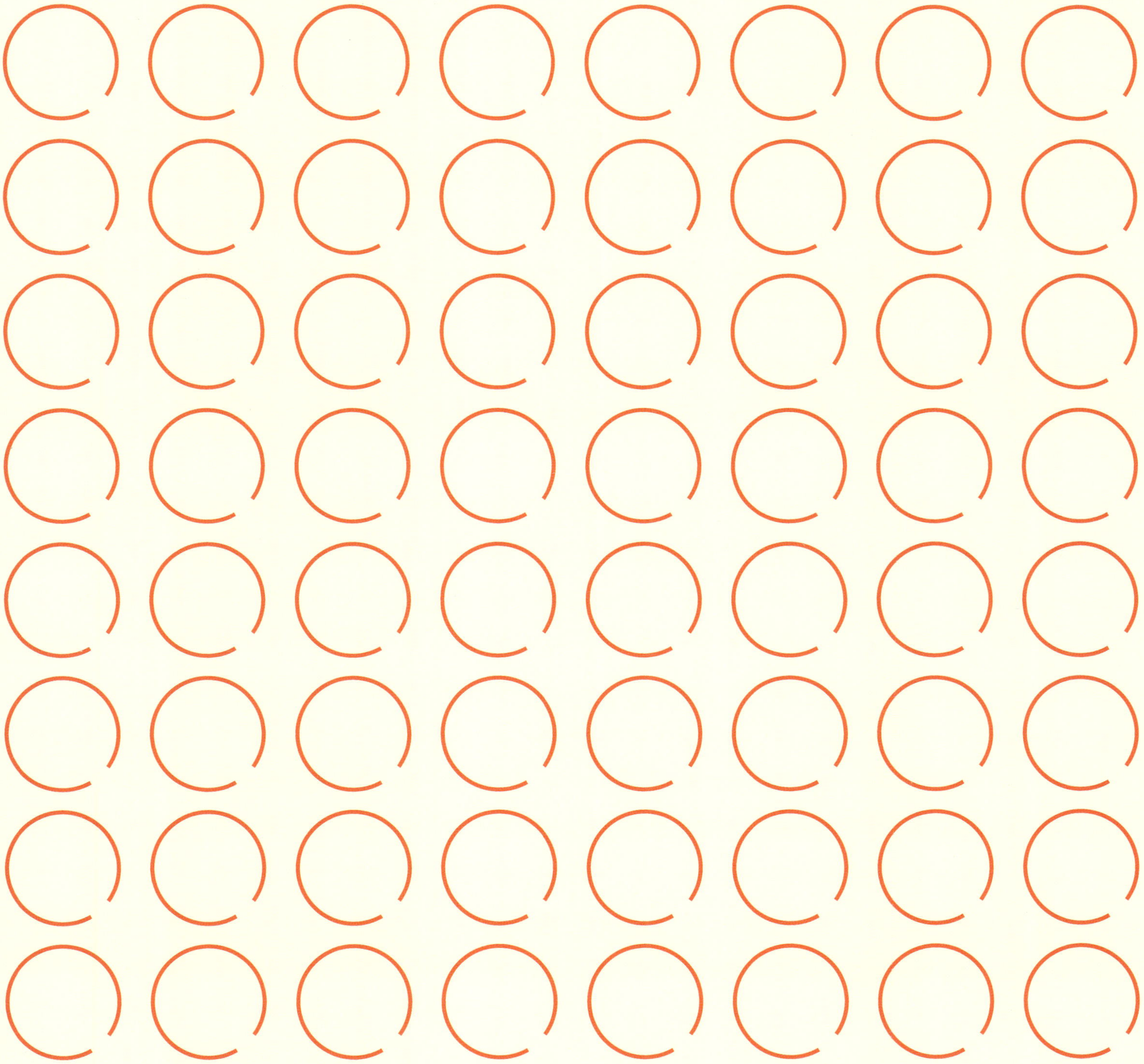

abcd... | 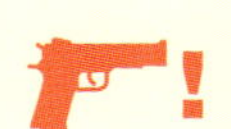

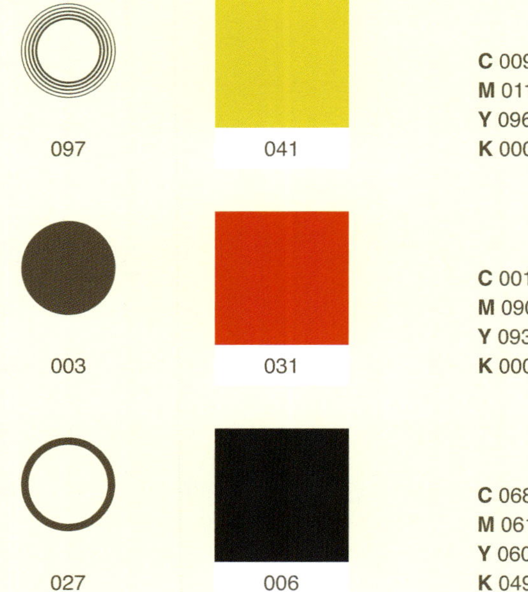

097

041

C 009
M 011
Y 096
K 000

003

031

C 001
M 090
Y 093
K 000

027

006

C 068
M 061
Y 060
K 049

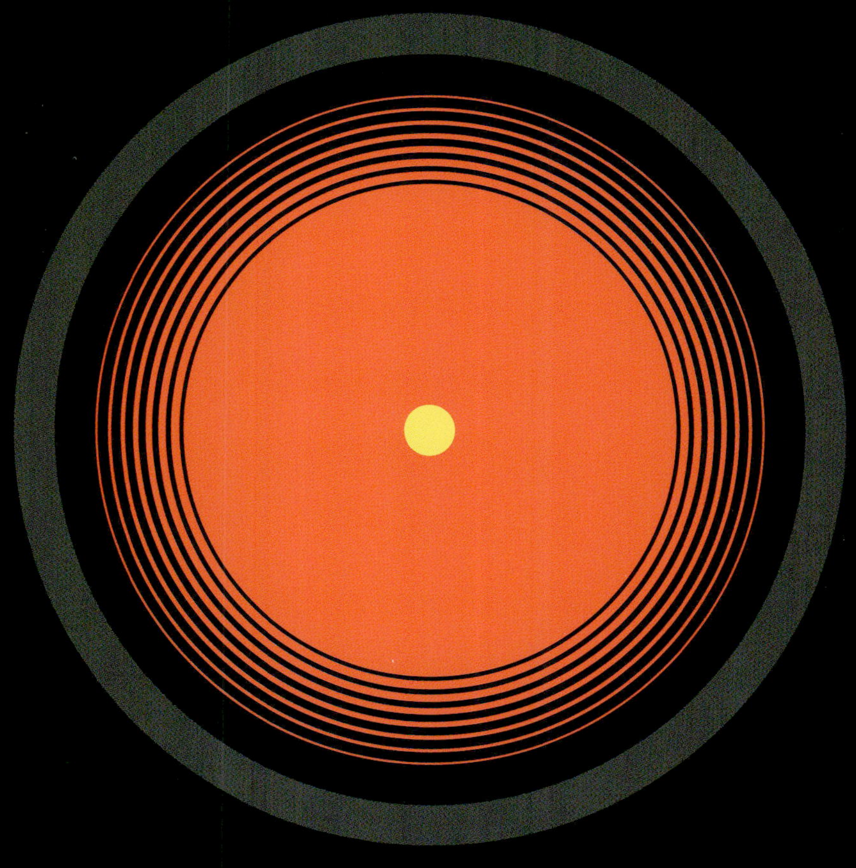

2001: a space odyssey

an epic drama of adventure and exploration.

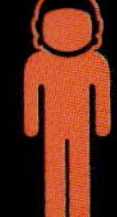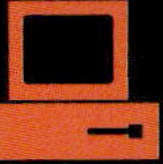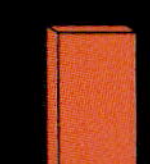

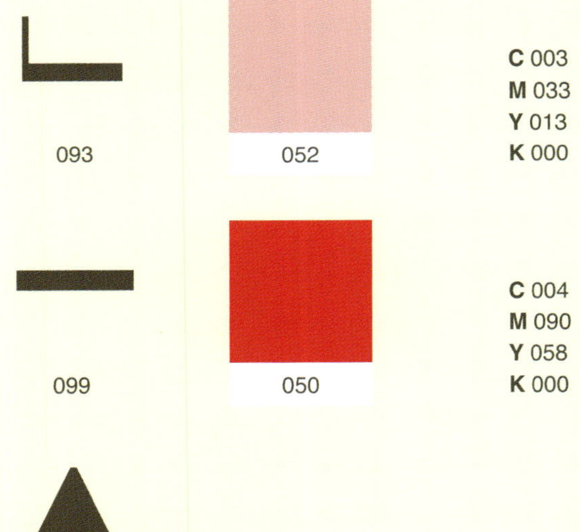

093

099

137

052

C 003
M 033
Y 013
K 000

050

C 004
M 090
Y 058
K 000

rogue one

a rebellion built on hope.

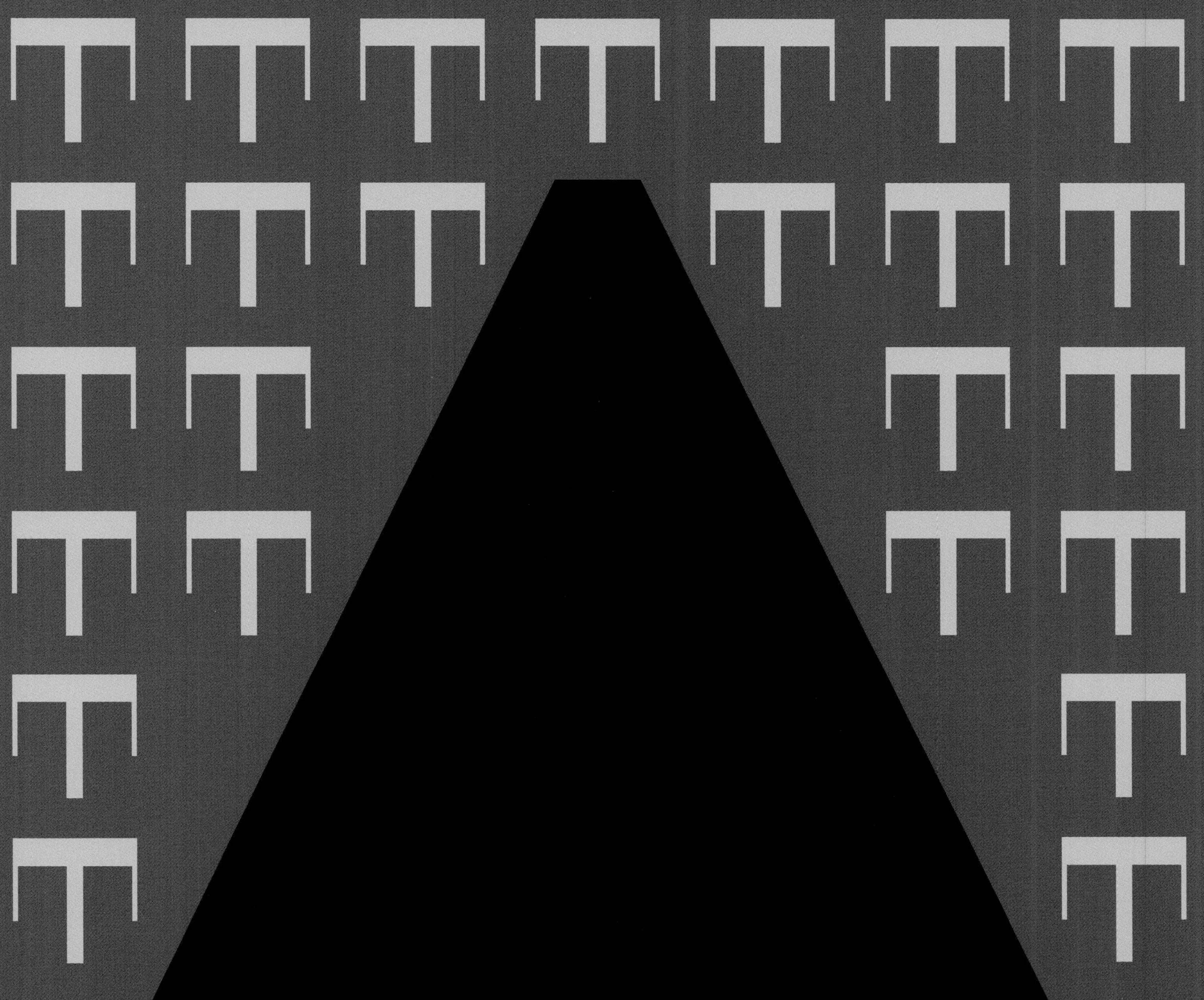

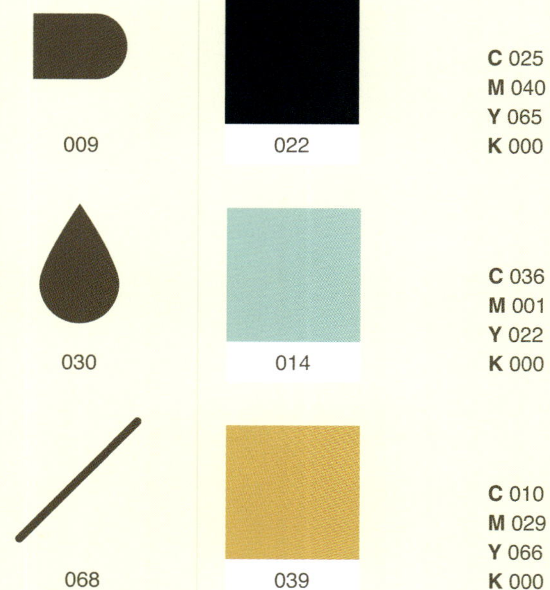

009

022

C 025
M 040
Y 065
K 000

030

014

C 036
M 001
Y 022
K 000

068

039

C 010
M 029
Y 066
K 000

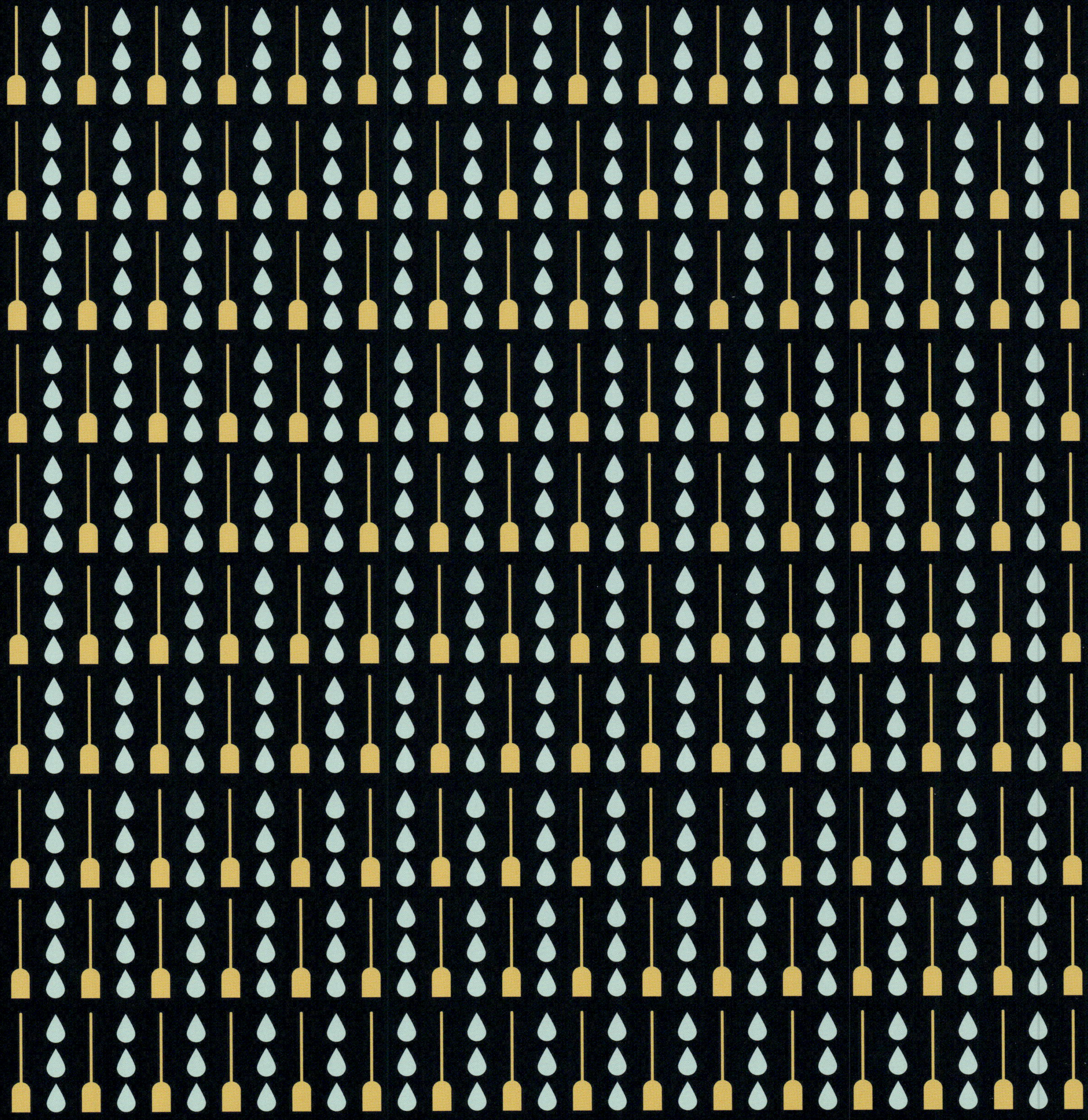

fantasia

where every sound creates a picture.

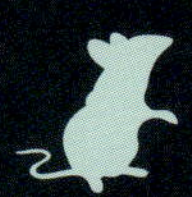 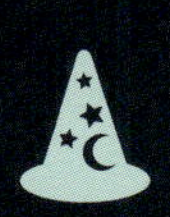 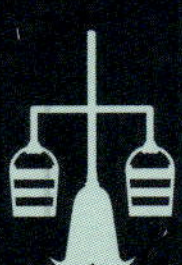

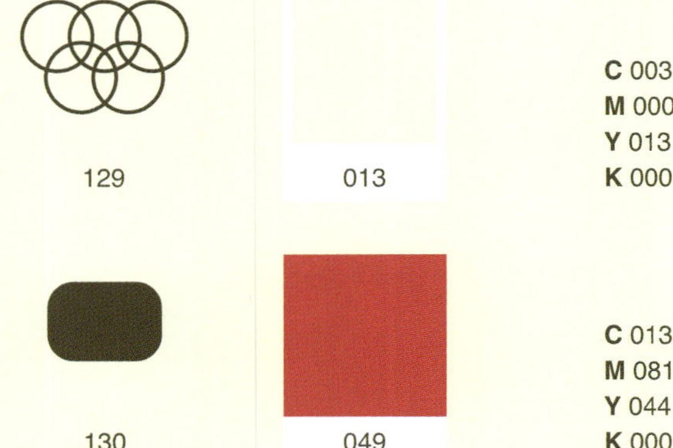

129

013

C 003
M 000
Y 013
K 000

130

049

C 013
M 081
Y 044
K 000

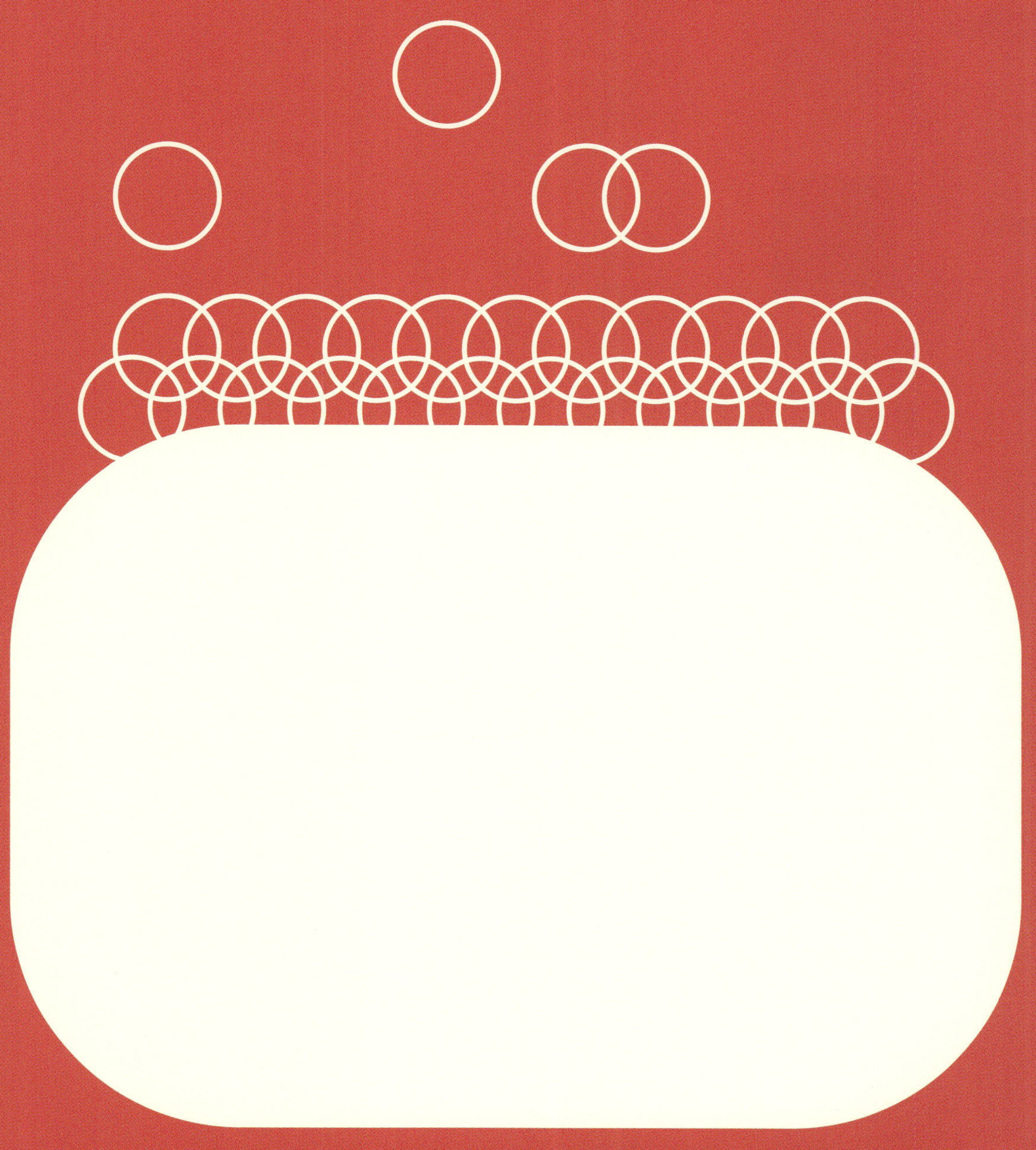

fight club

how much can you know about yourself if you've never been in a fight?

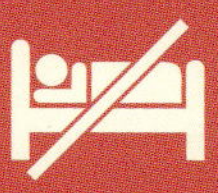 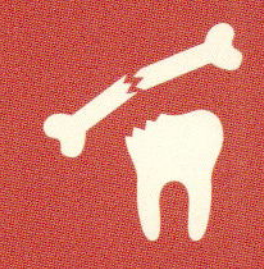 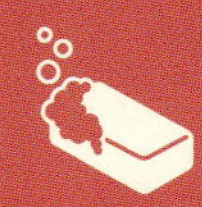

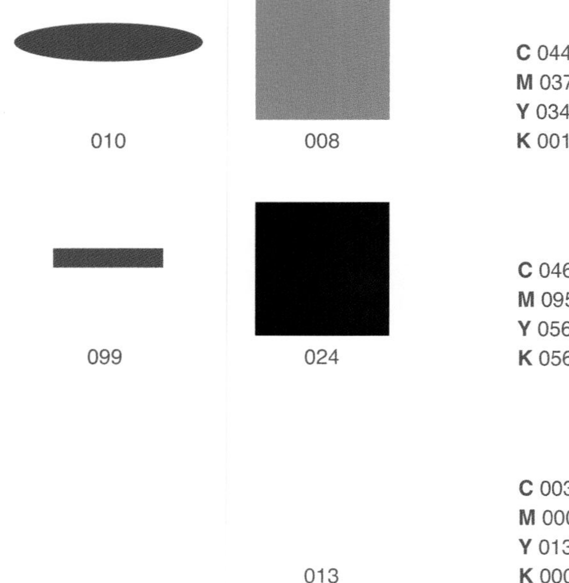

010

008

C 044
M 037
Y 034
K 001

099

024

C 046
M 095
Y 056
K 056

013

C 003
M 000
Y 013
K 000

star trek

welcome aboard the united space ship enterprise. where it goes, no program has ever gone before.

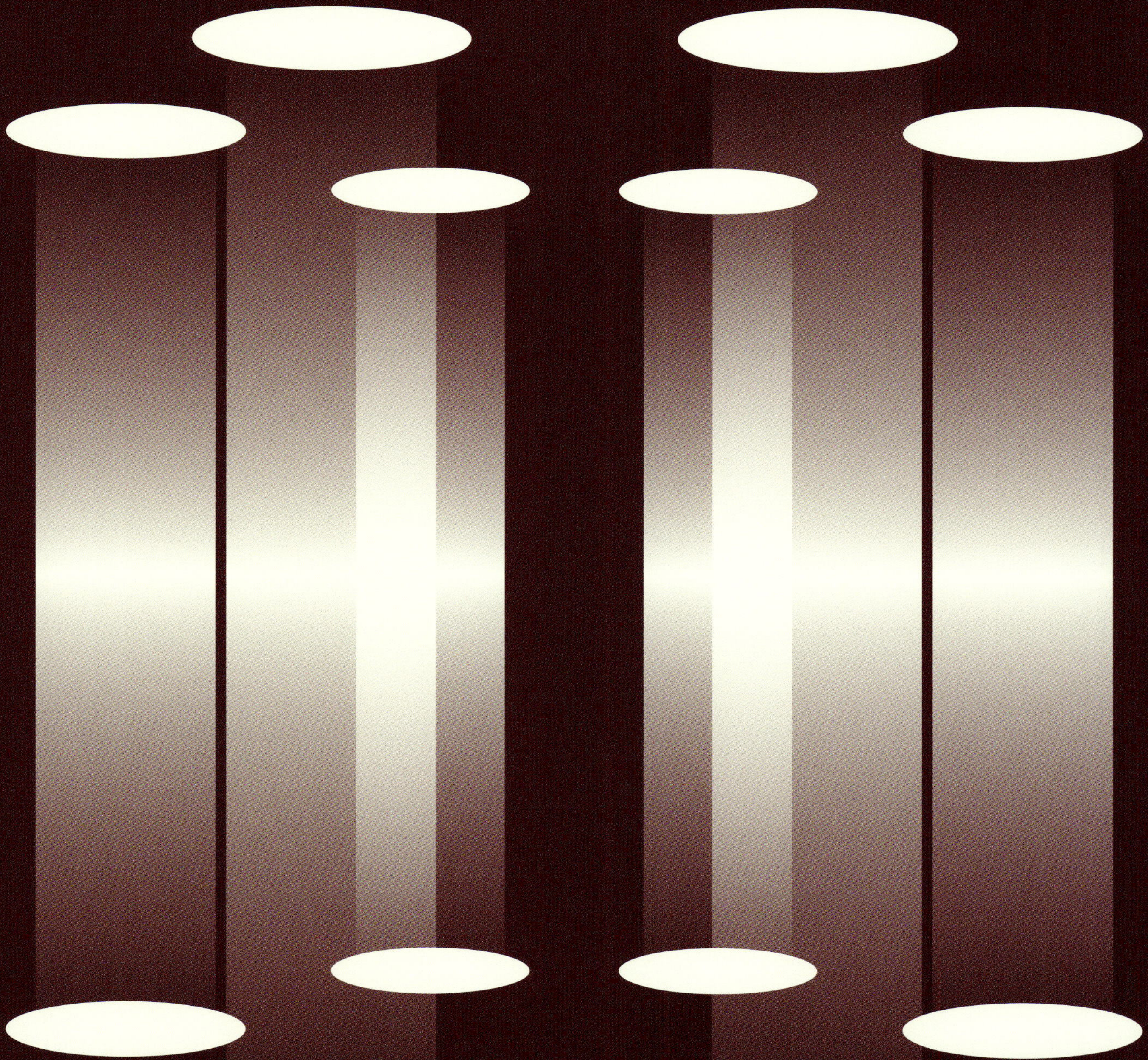

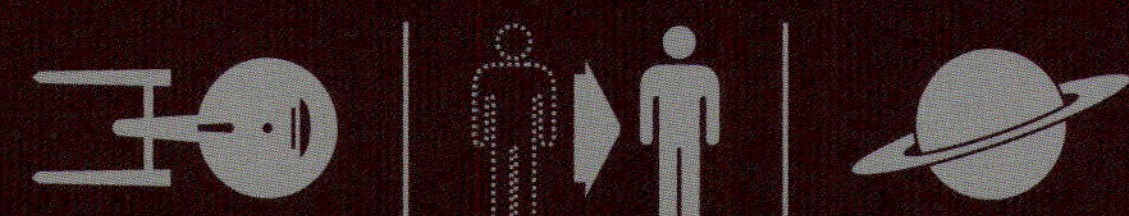

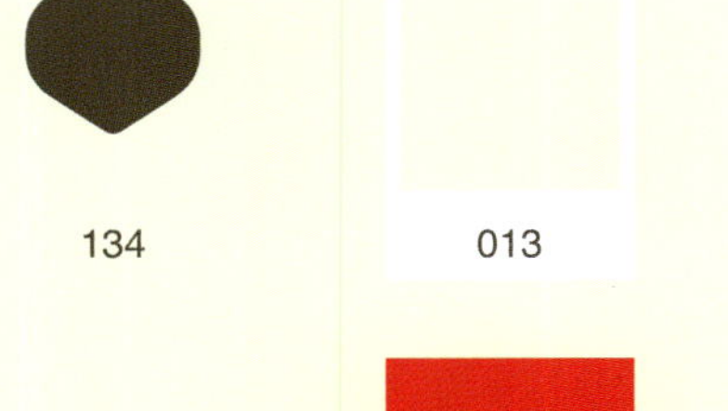

134

013

C 003
M 000
Y 013
K 000

050

C 004
M 090
Y 058
K 000

american beauty

… look closer.

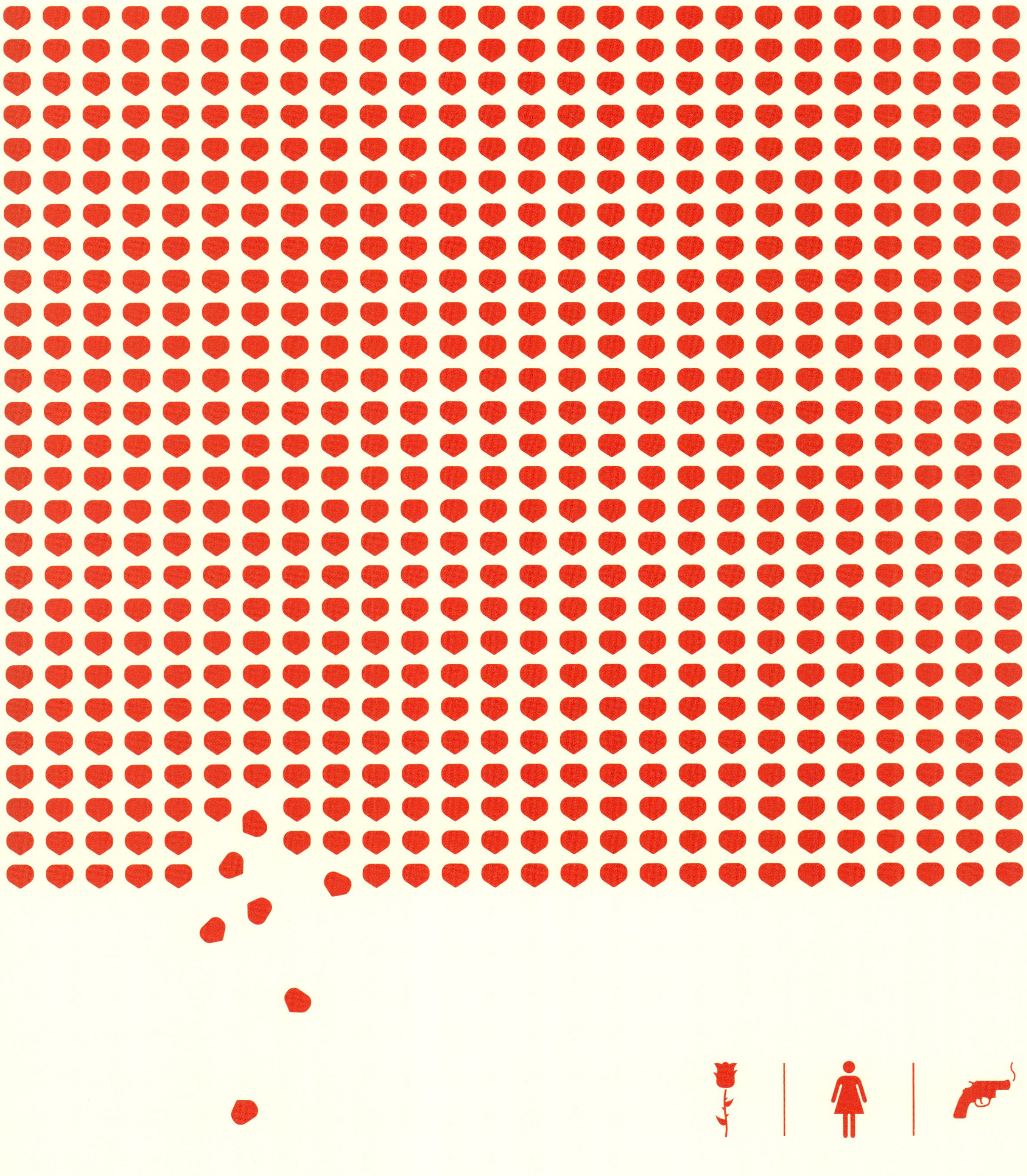

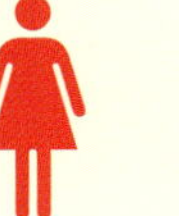 | 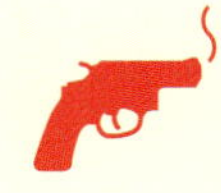

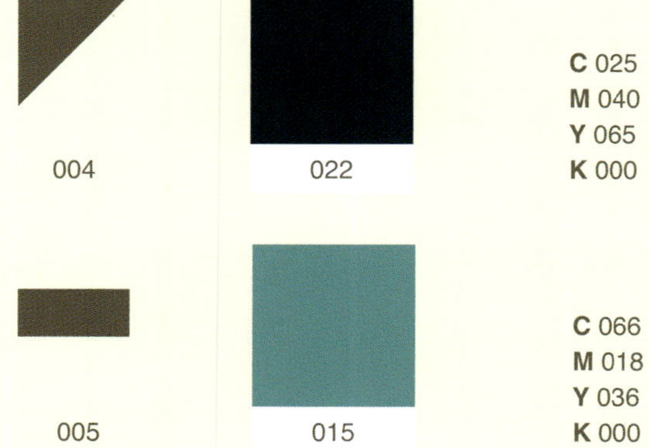

004

005

022

015

C 025
M 040
Y 065
K 000

C 066
M 018
Y 036
K 000

jaws

on the fourth of july, fishing season will open... on you.

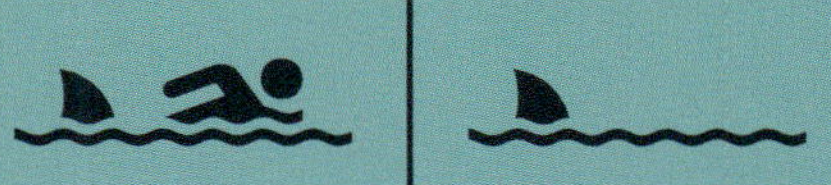

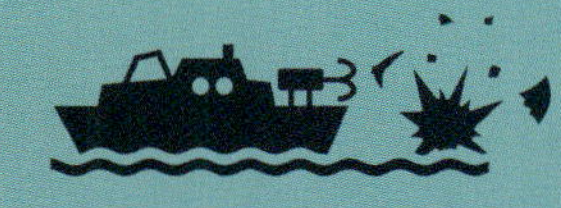

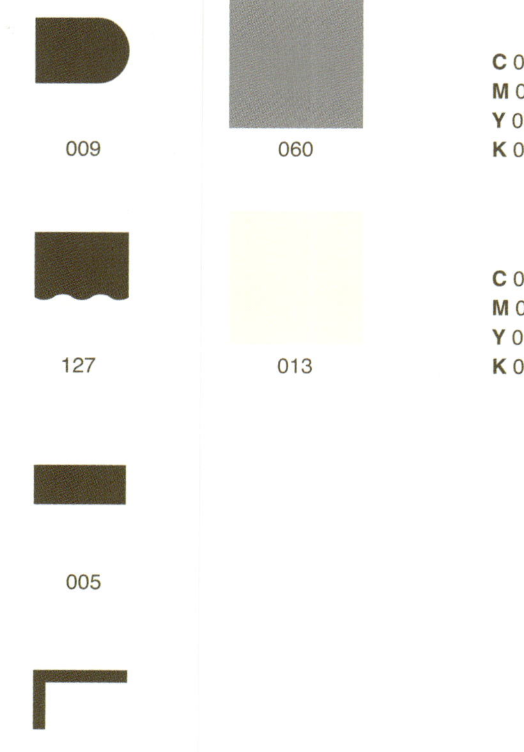

009

060

C 040
M 032
Y 031
K 000

127

013

C 003
M 000
Y 013
K 000

005

128

60
00 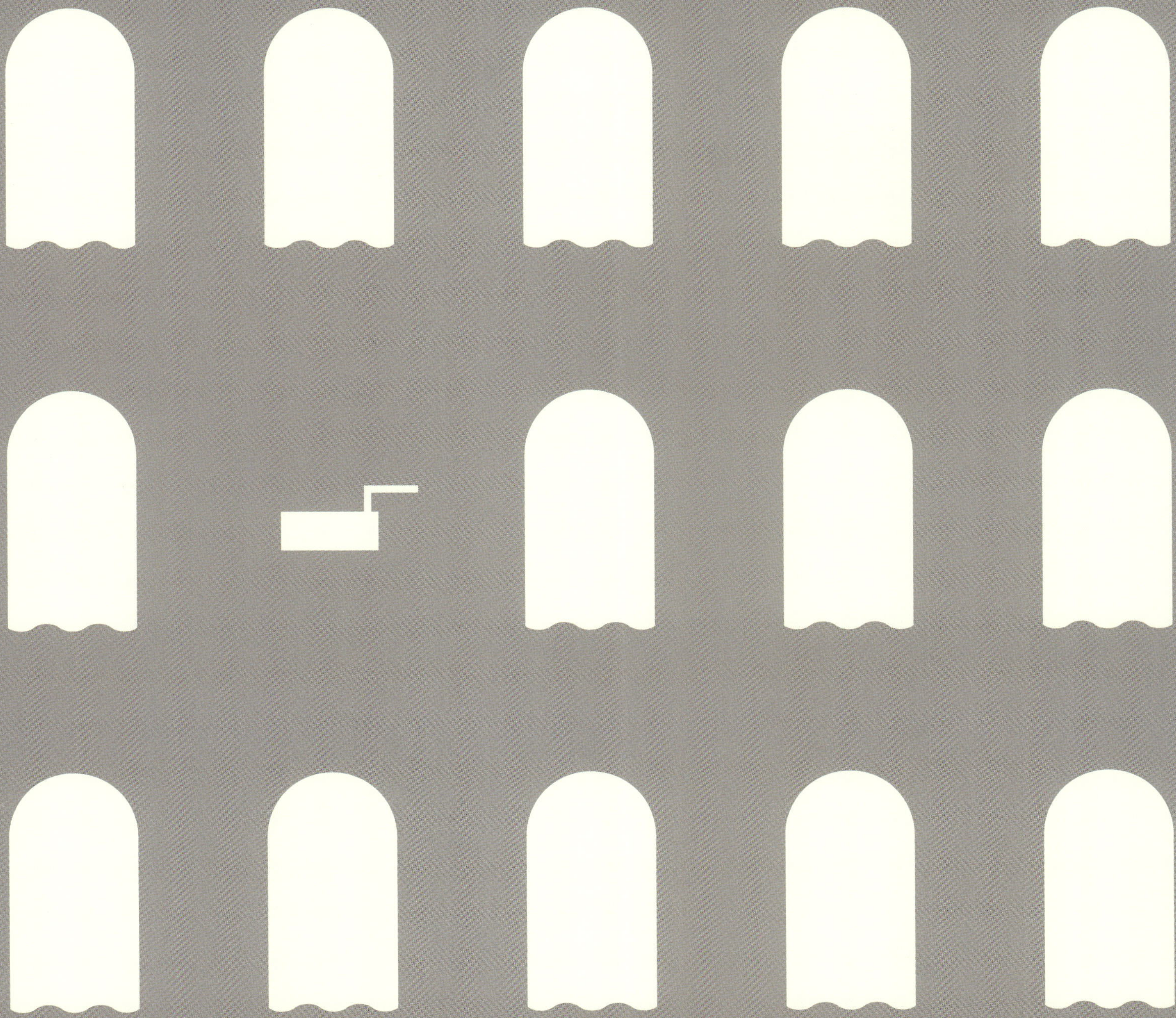
73
ghostbusters
they're here to save the world.

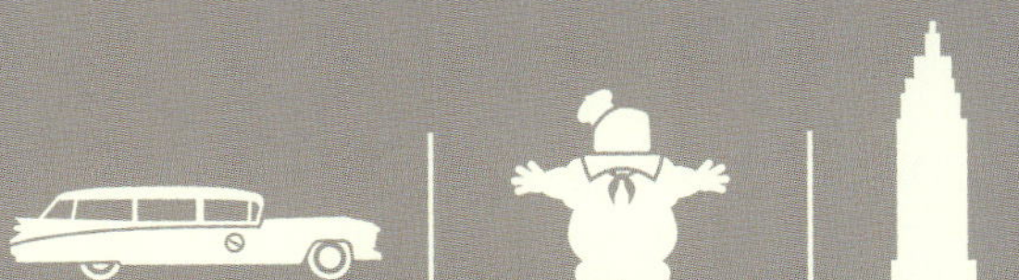

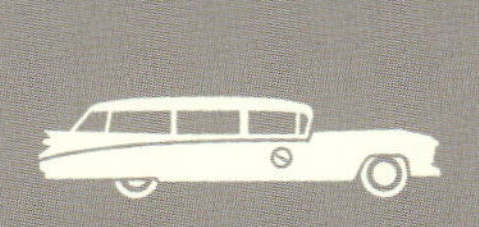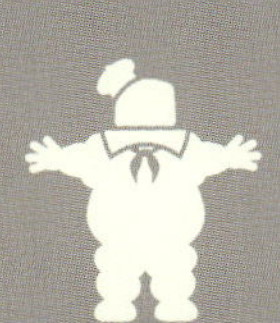

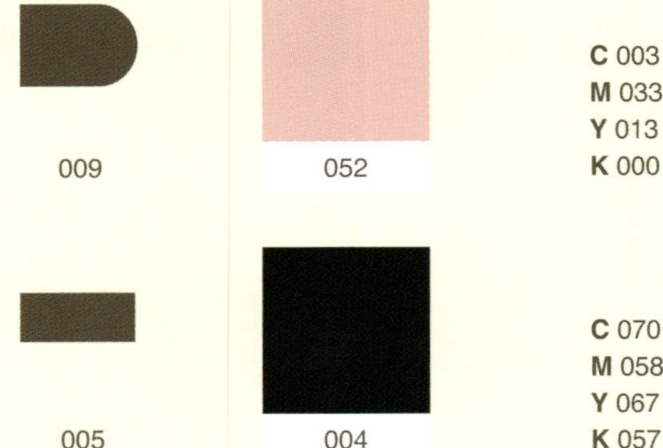

009

005

052

004

C 003
M 033
Y 013
K 000

C 070
M 058
Y 067
K 057

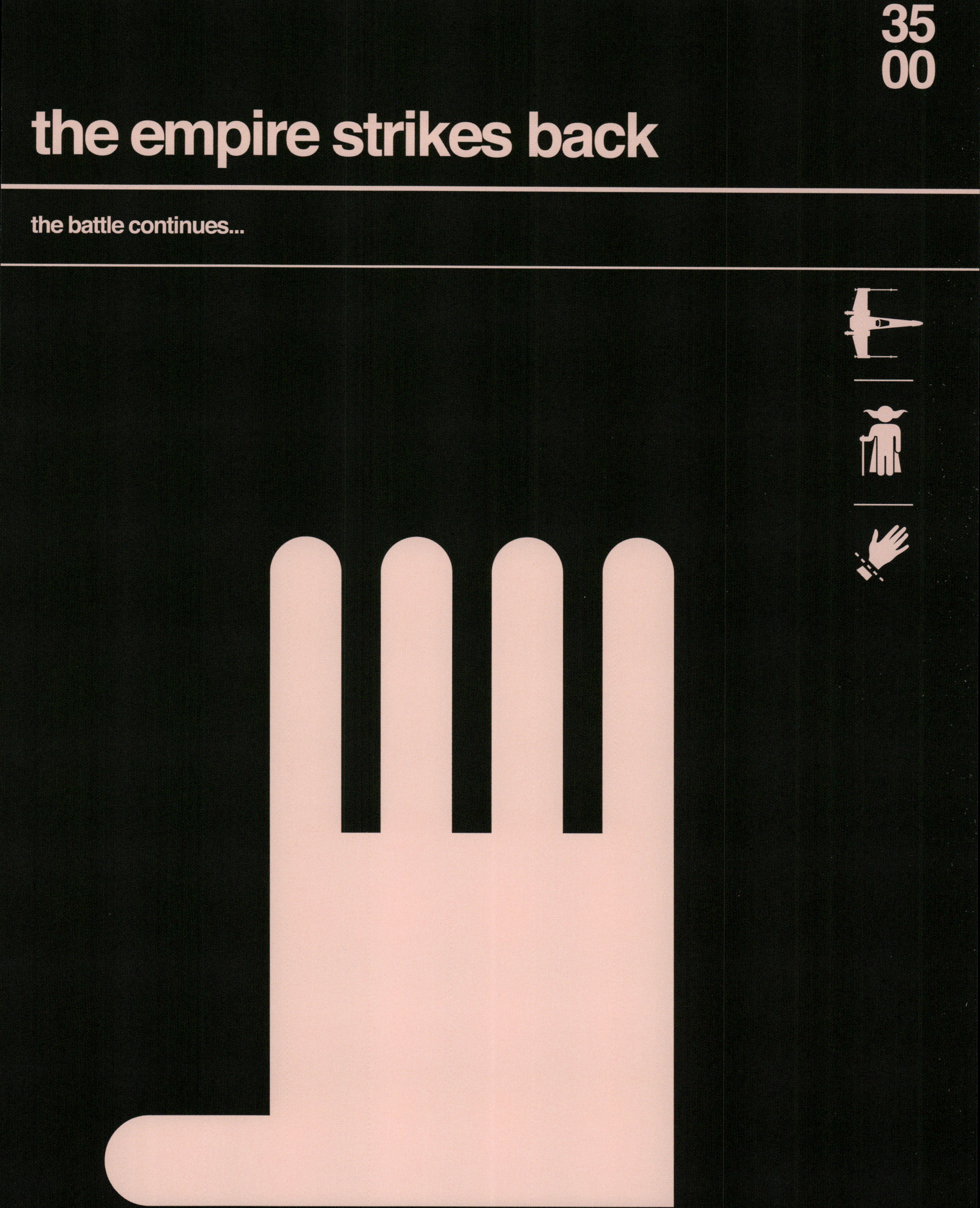

the empire strikes back

the battle continues...

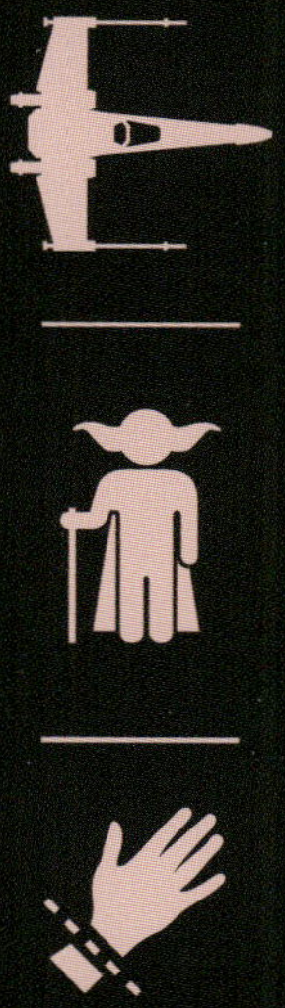

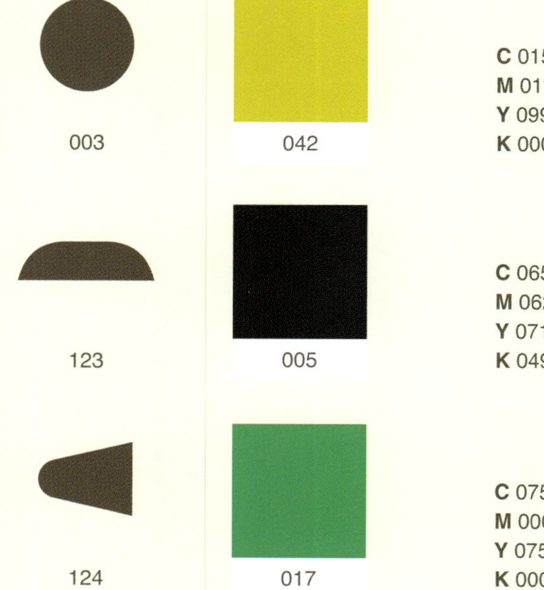

003   042

C 015
M 011
Y 099
K 000

123   005

C 065
M 062
Y 071
K 049

124   017

C 075
M 000
Y 075
K 000

the exorcist

the devil inside.

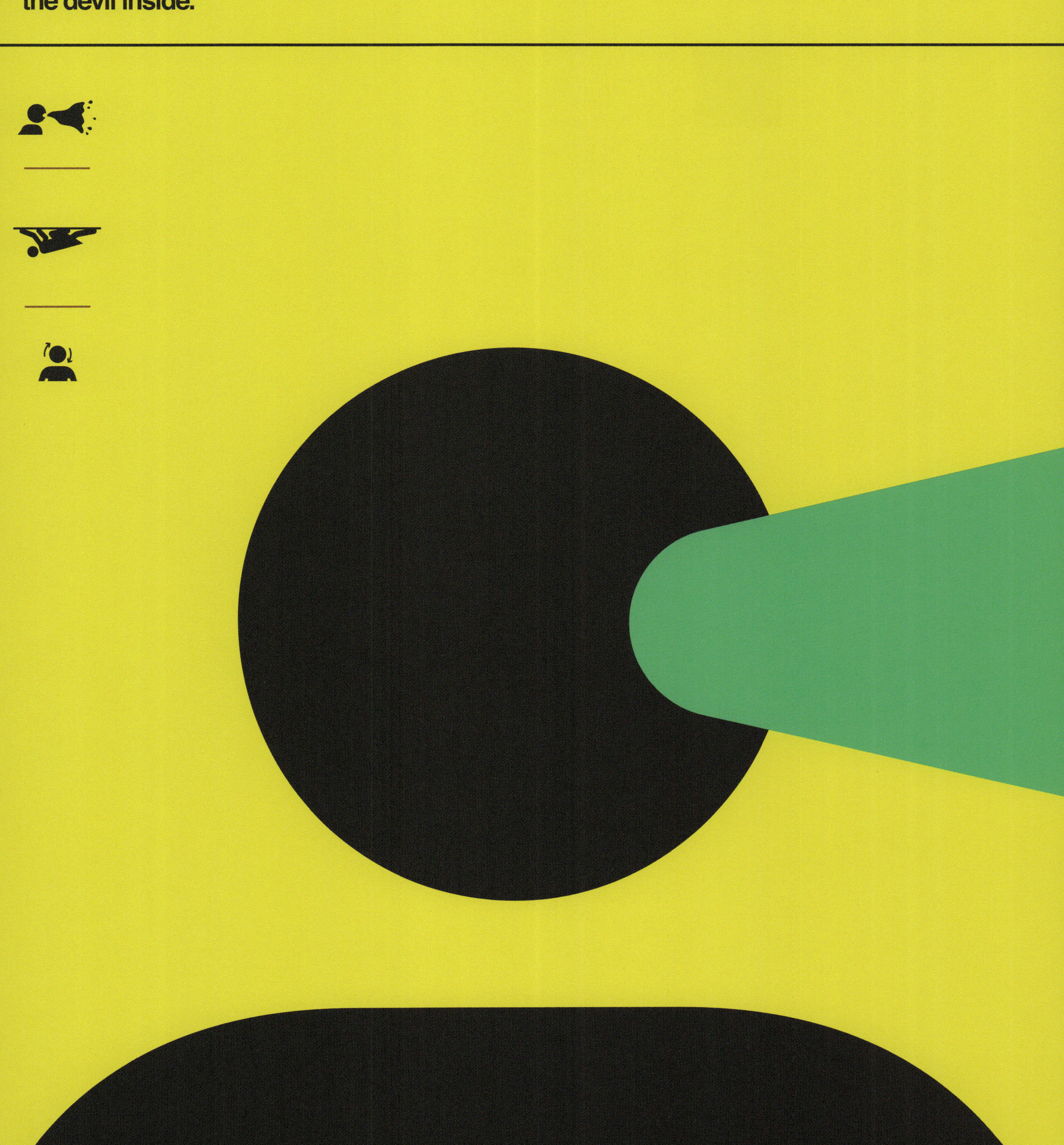

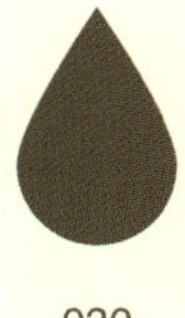

030

014

C 036
M 001
Y 022
K 000

024

C 046
M 095
Y 056
K 056

psycho

exploring the blackness of the subconscious man.

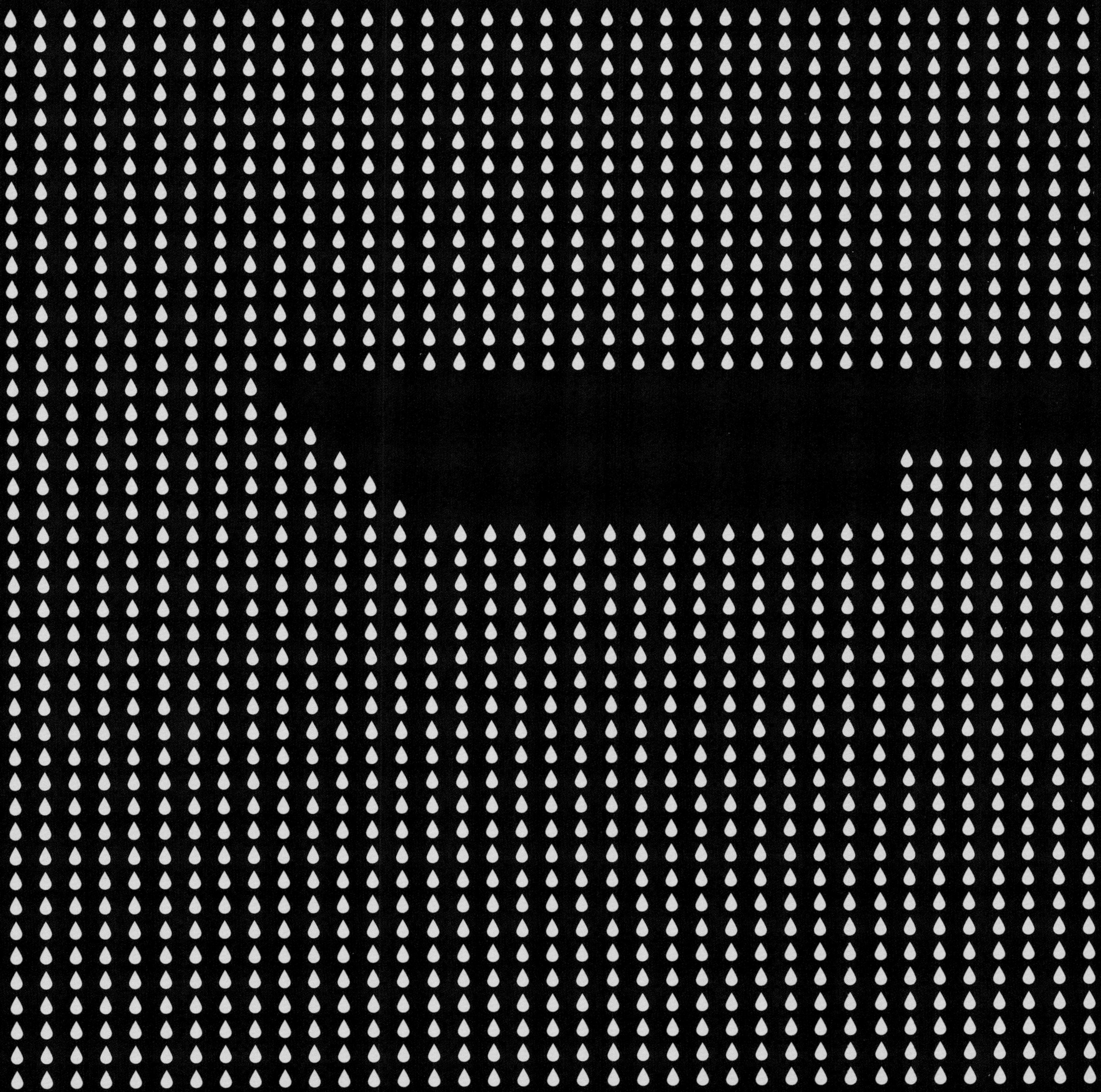

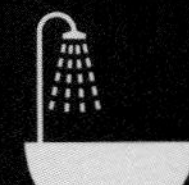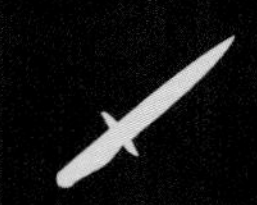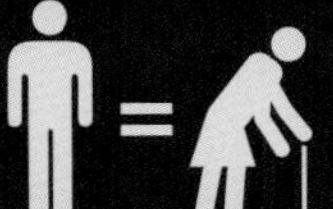

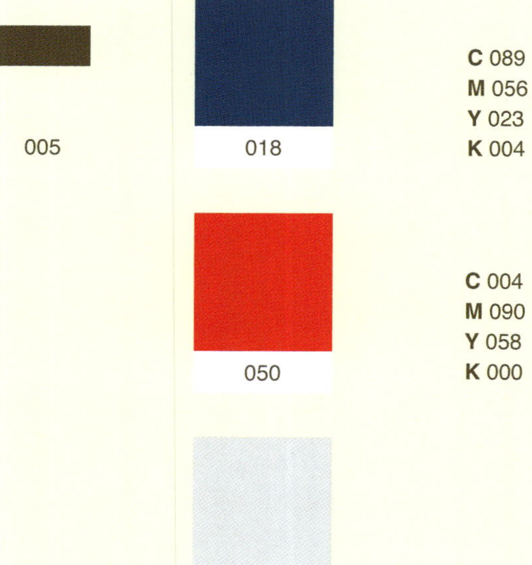

005

018

C 089
M 056
Y 023
K 004

050

C 004
M 090
Y 058
K 000

012

the
matrix

free your mind.

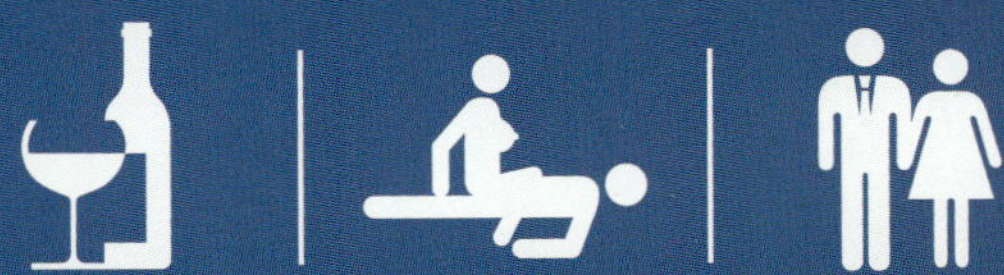
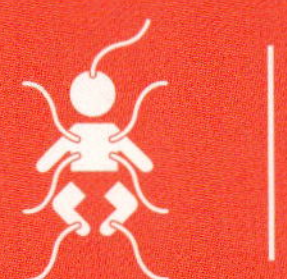
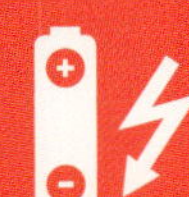
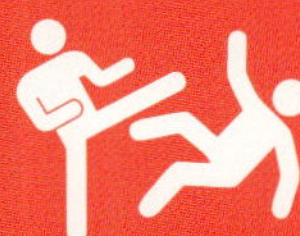

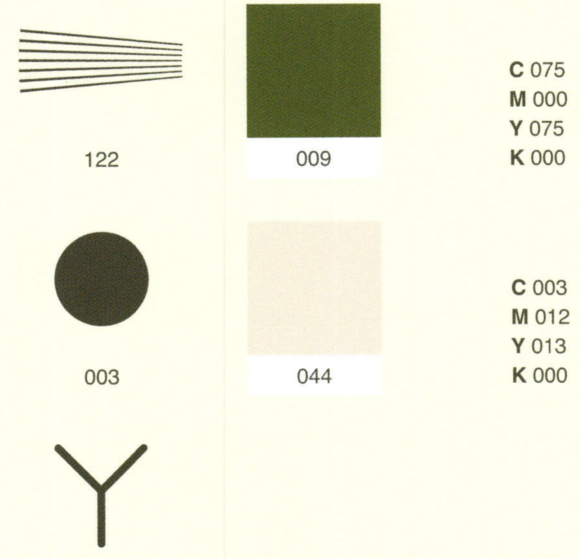

122

009

C 075
M 000
Y 075
K 000

003

044

C 003
M 012
Y 013
K 000

018

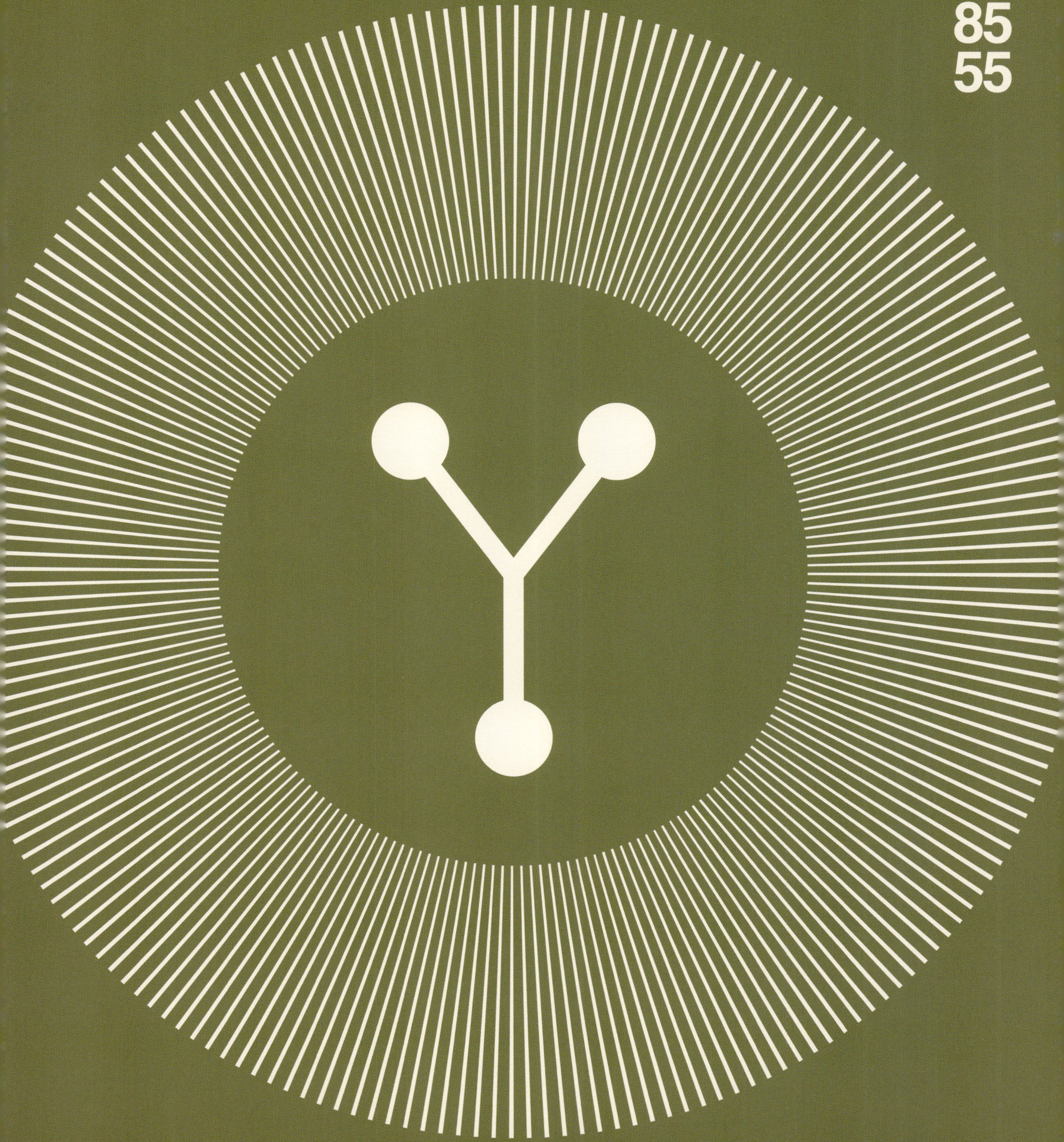

back to the future

he was never in time for his classes... then one day he wasn't in his time at all.

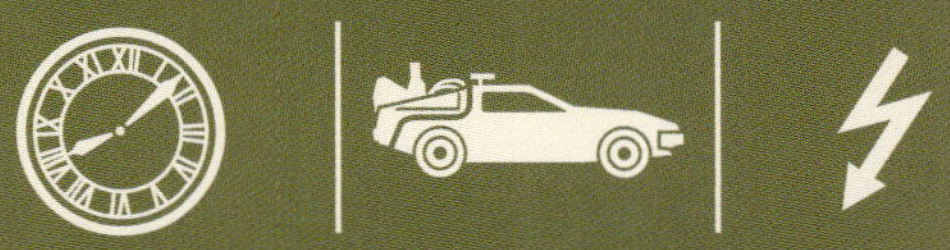

 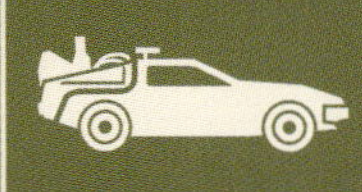

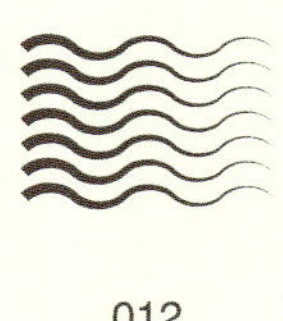

012

014

C 036
M 001
Y 022
K 000

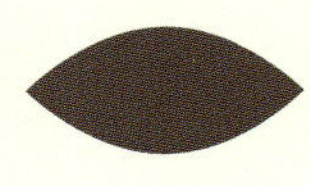

025

013

C 003
M 000
Y 013
K 000

003

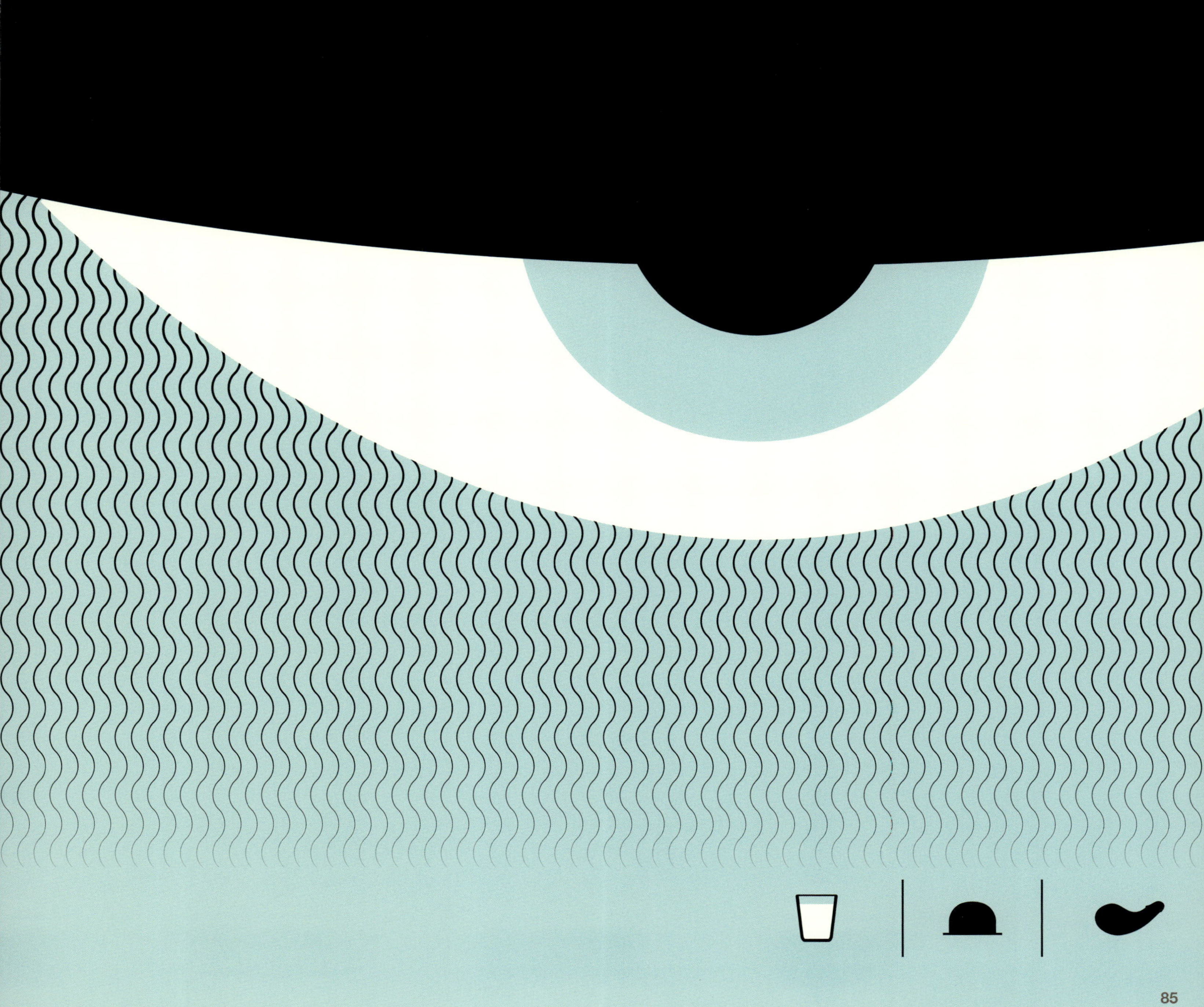

56
71
a clockwork orange
being the adventures of a young man whose principal interests are rape, ultra-violence and beethoven.
85

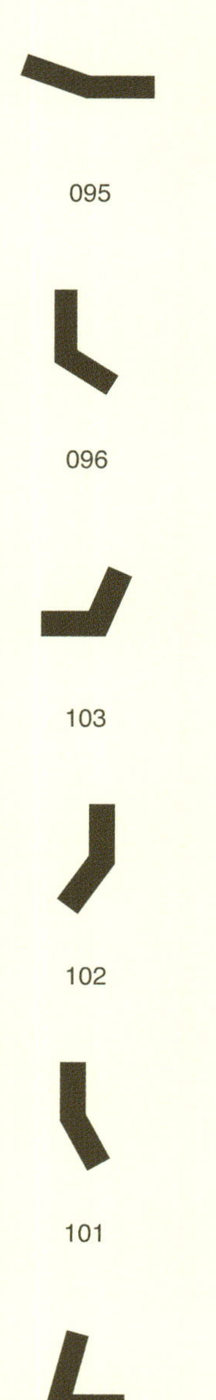

095

096

103

102

101

100

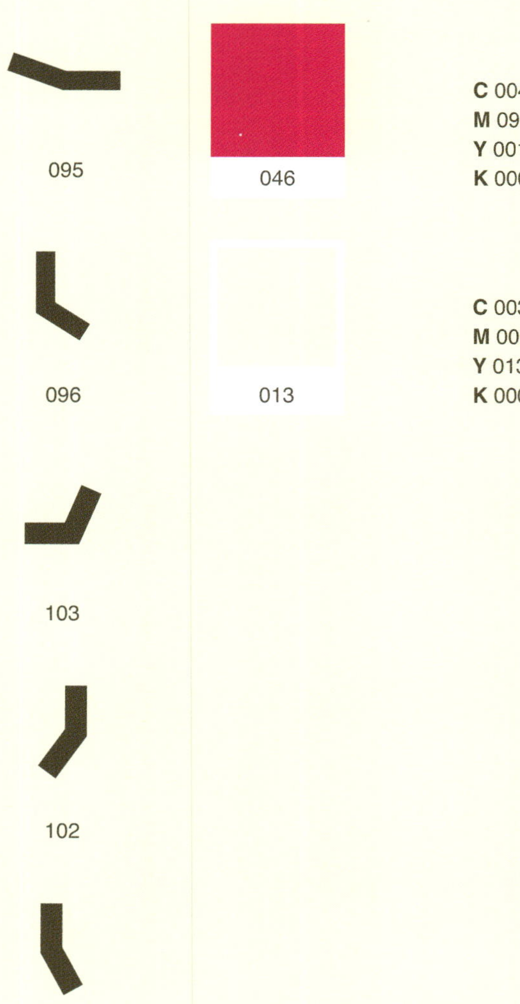

046

C 004
M 091
Y 001
K 000

013

C 003
M 000
Y 013
K 000

eyes wide shut

cruise. kidman. kubrick.

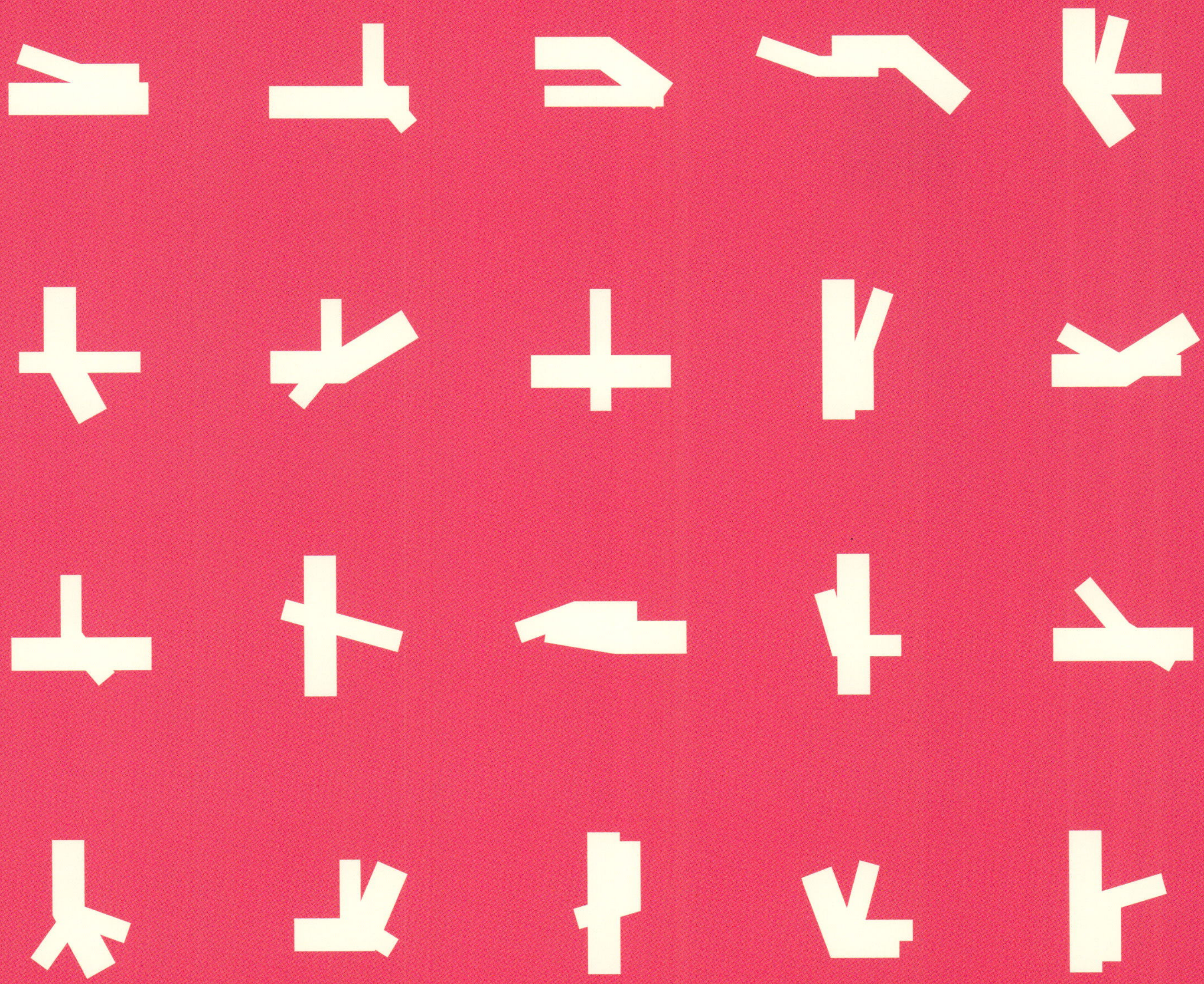

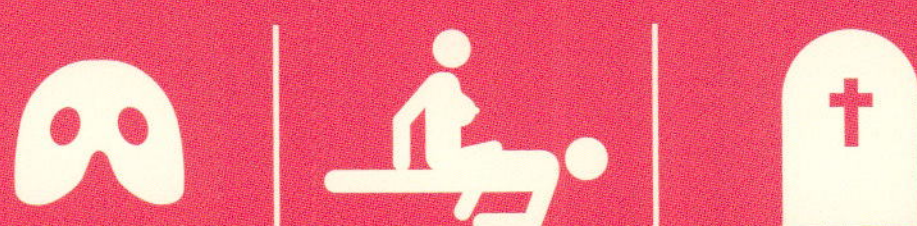

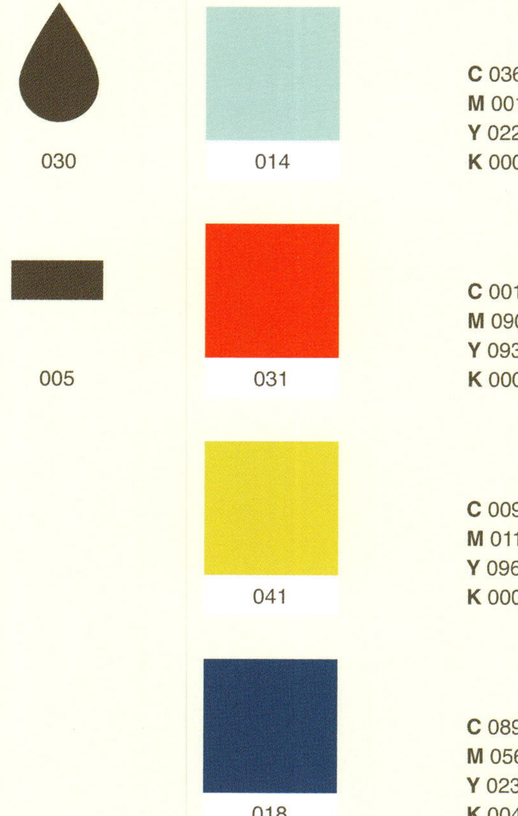

030

005

014

C 036
M 001
Y 022
K 000

031

C 001
M 090
Y 093
K 000

041

C 009
M 011
Y 096
K 000

018

C 089
M 056
Y 023
K 004

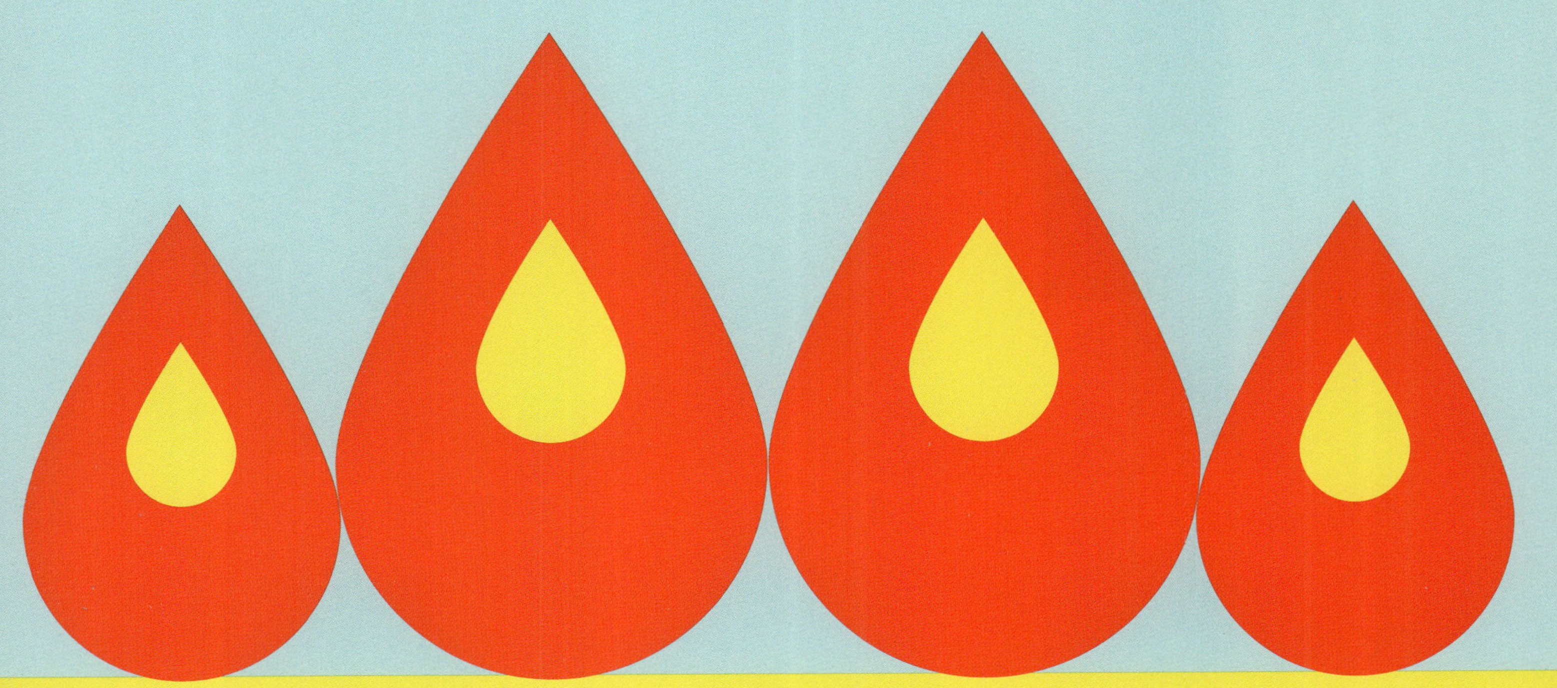

apocalypse now

the horror... the horror...

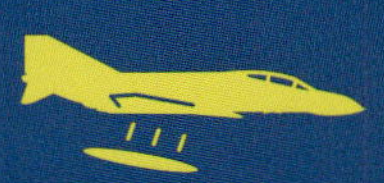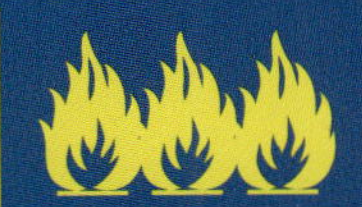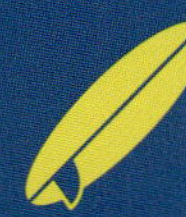

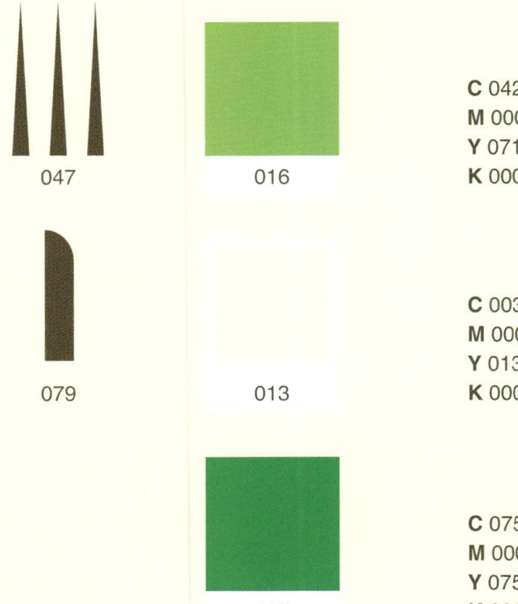

047

079

016

013

017

C 042
M 000
Y 071
K 000

C 003
M 000
Y 013
K 000

C 075
M 000
Y 075
K 000

edward scissorhands

his scars run deep.

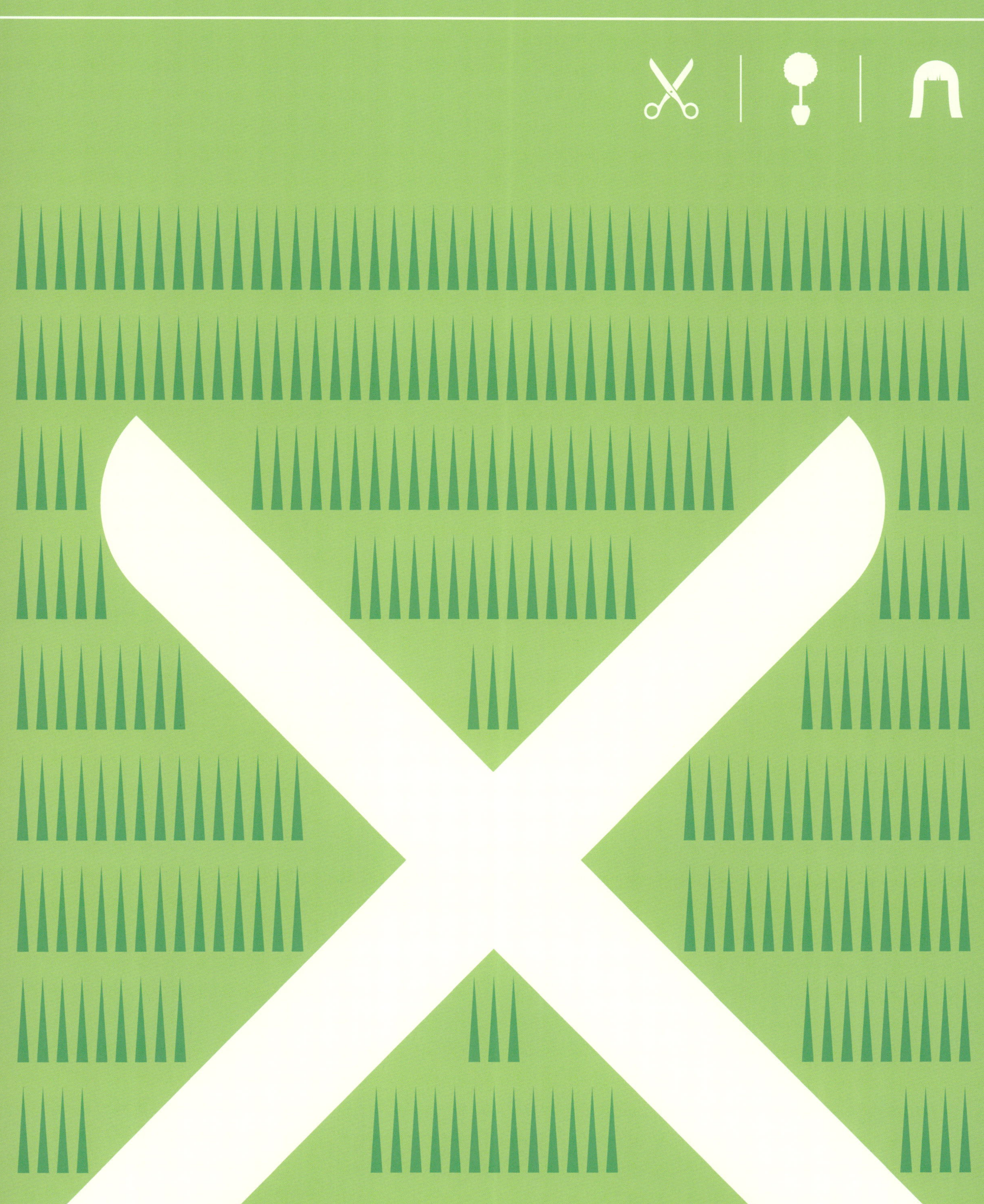

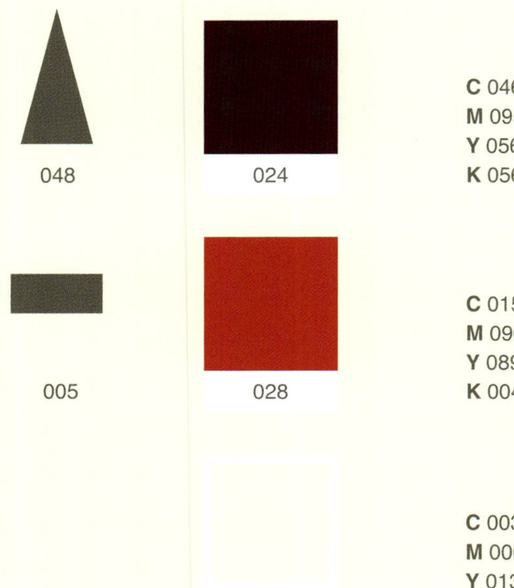

048

005

024

028

013

C 046
M 095
Y 056
K 056

C 015
M 096
Y 089
K 004

C 003
M 000
Y 013
K 000

bram stoker's dracula

the blood is the life.

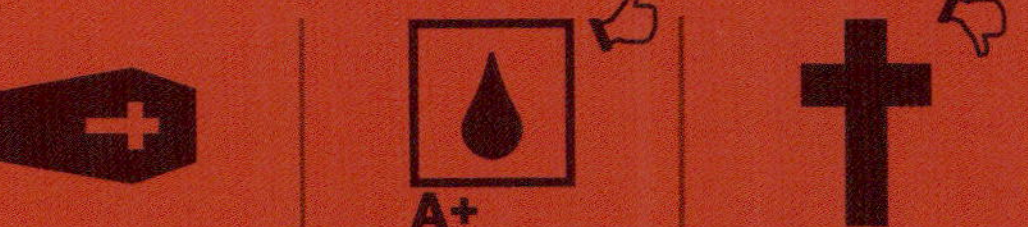

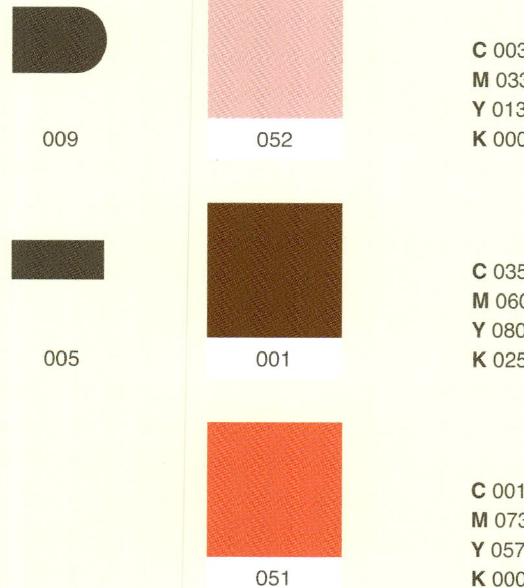

009

005

052

C 003
M 033
Y 013
K 000

001

C 035
M 060
Y 080
K 025

051

C 001
M 073
Y 057
K 000

E.T. the extra-terrestrial

he is afraid. he is totally alone. he is 3 million light years from home.

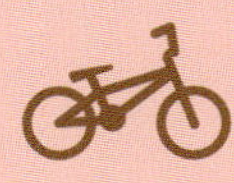
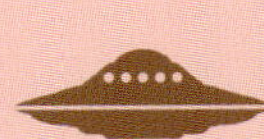

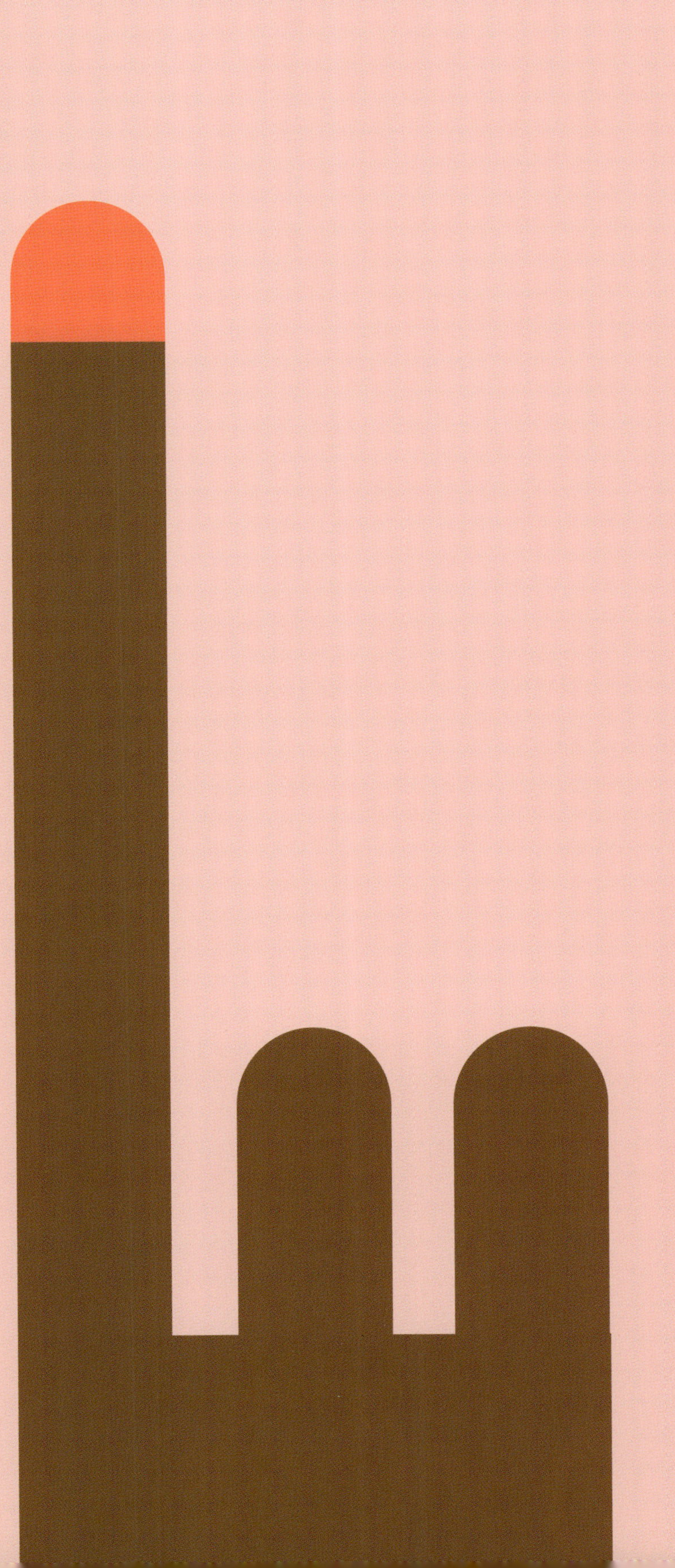

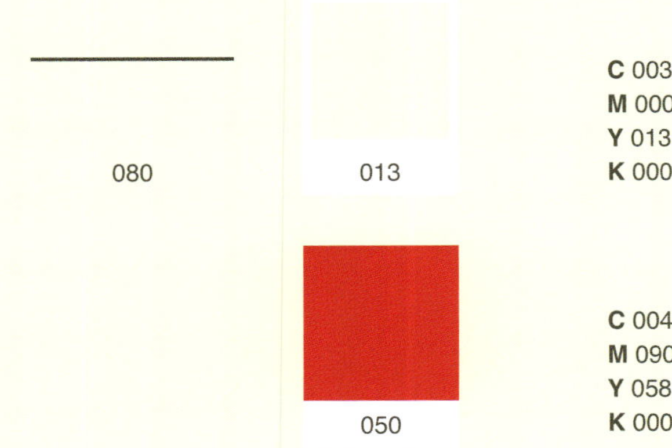

080

013

C 003
M 000
Y 013
K 000

050

C 004
M 090
Y 058
K 000

the thin red line

every man fights his own war.

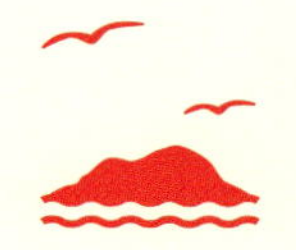

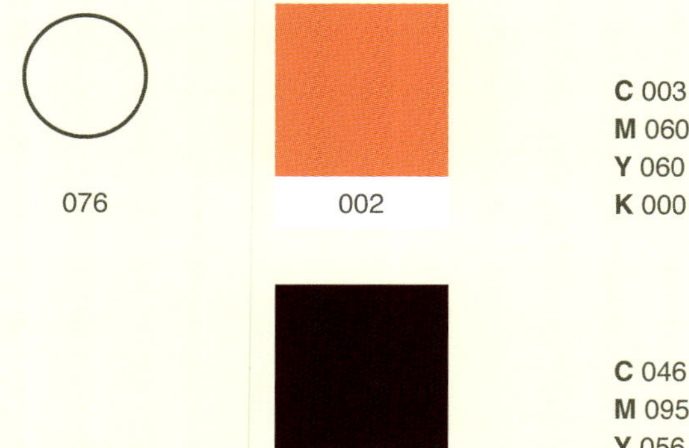

076

002

C 003
M 060
Y 060
K 000

024

C 046
M 095
Y 056
K 056

the hudsucker proxy

they took him for a fall guy... but he threw them for a hoop.

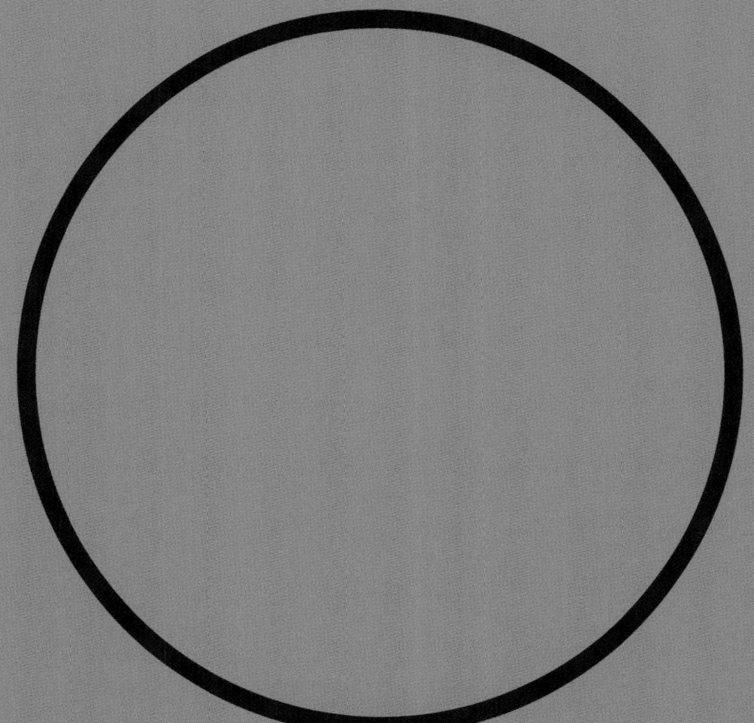

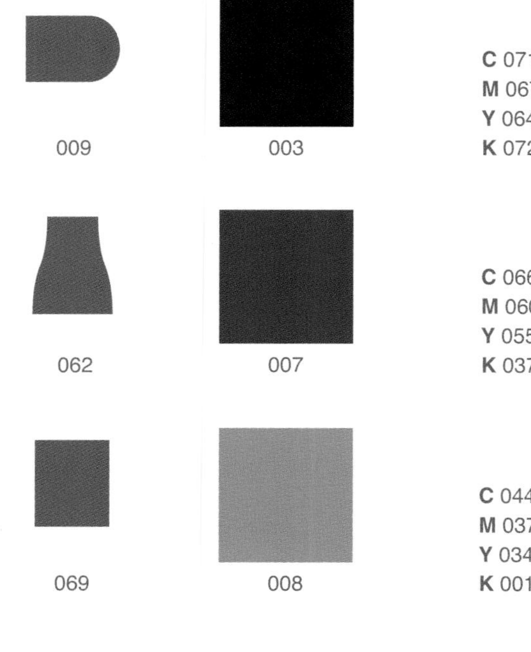

009

003

C 071
M 067
Y 064
K 072

062

007

C 066
M 060
Y 055
K 037

069

008

C 044
M 037
Y 034
K 001

065

ghost

a love that will last forever.

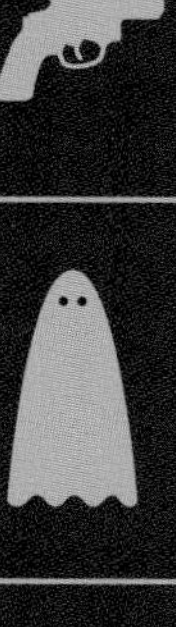

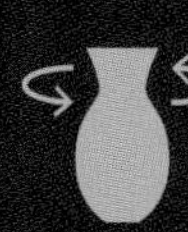

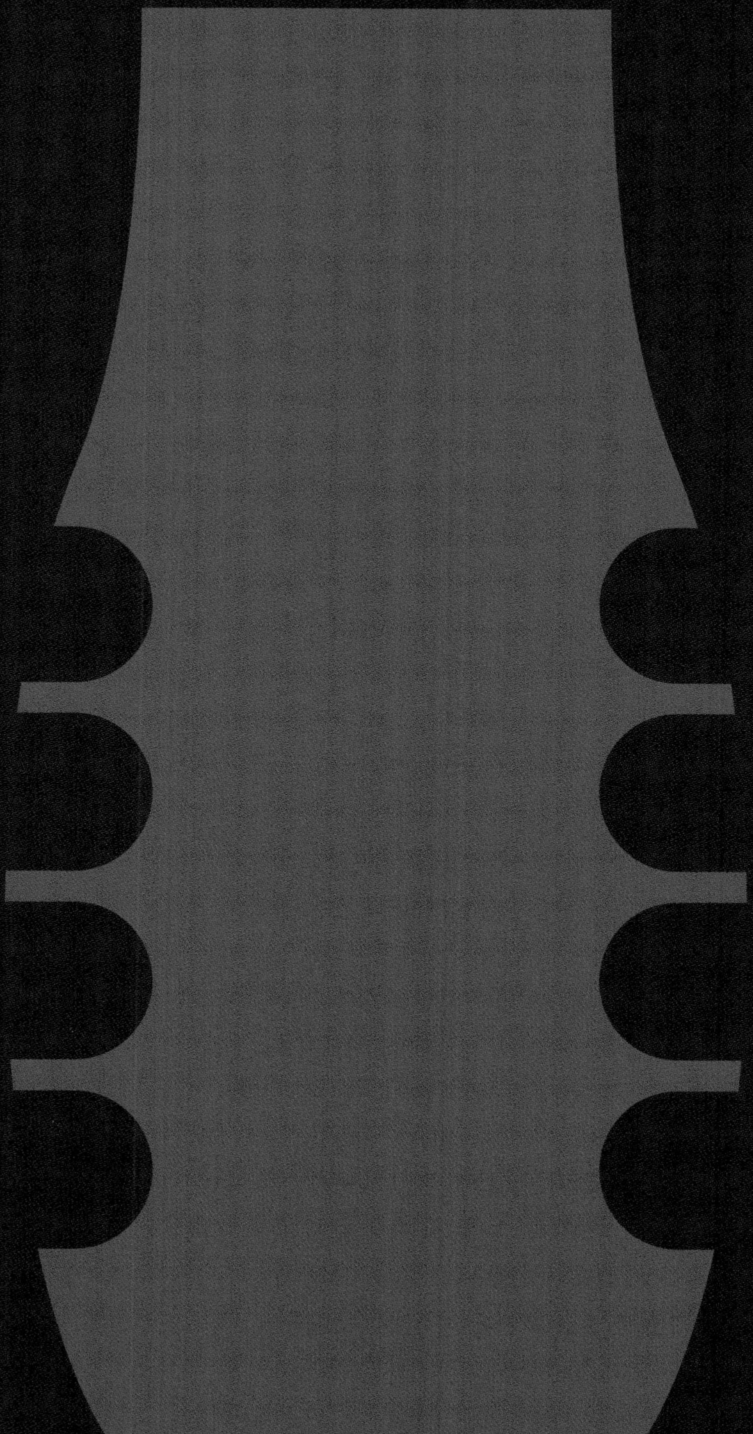

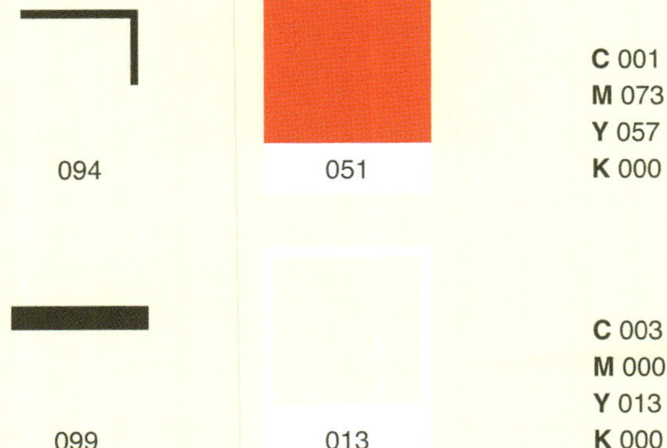

094

051

C 001
M 073
Y 057
K 000

099

013

C 003
M 000
Y 013
K 000

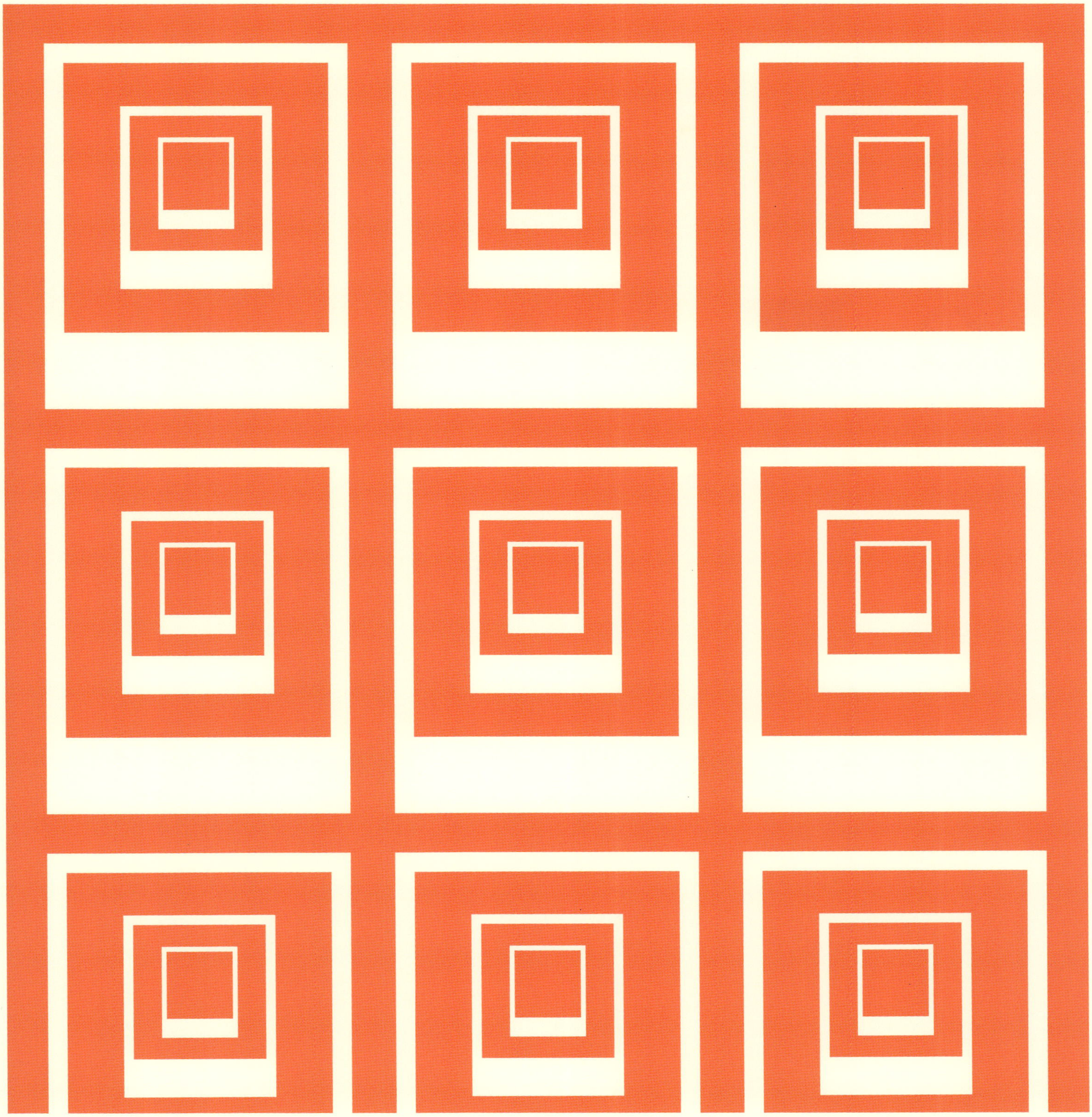

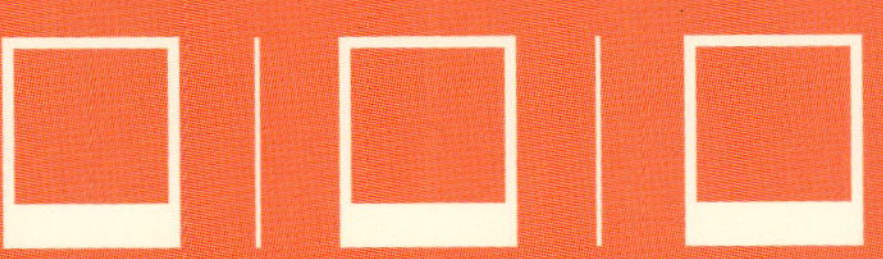

01
34

memento

some memories are best forgotten.

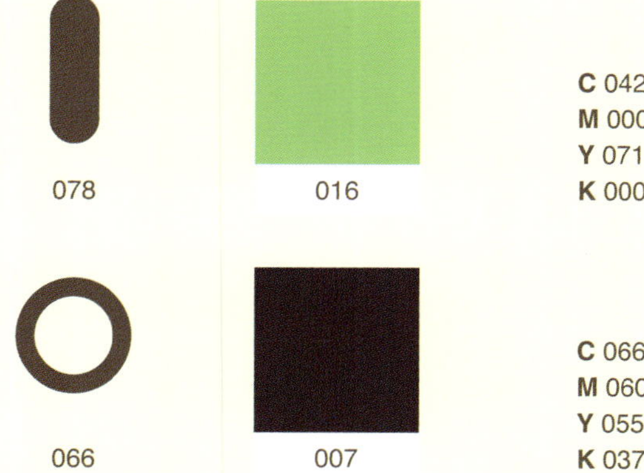

078

016

C 042
M 000
Y 071
K 000

066

007

C 066
M 060
Y 055
K 037

match point

there are no little secrets.

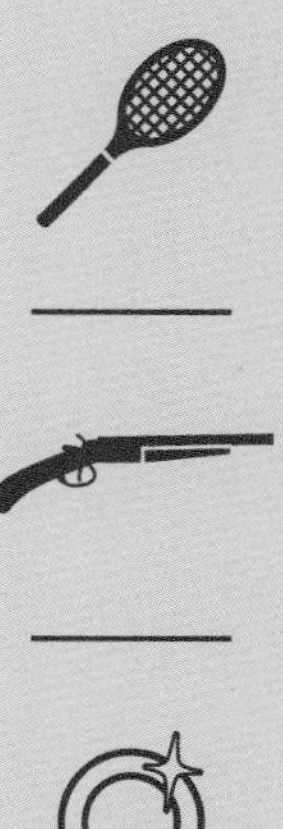

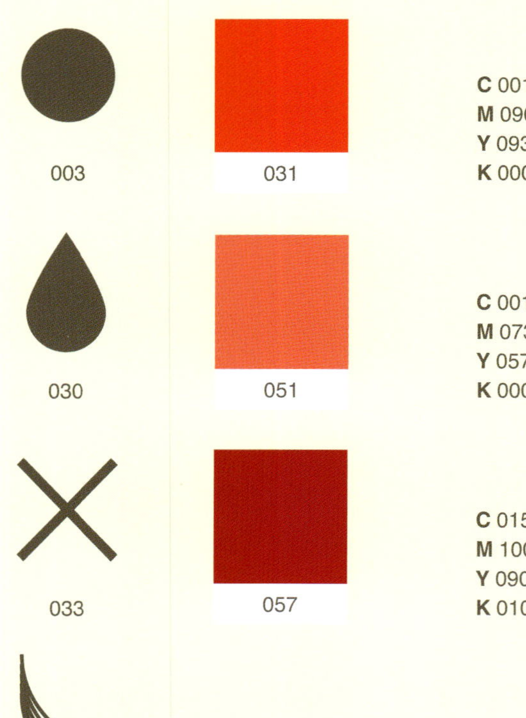

003

030

033

035

031

C 001
M 090
Y 093
K 000

051

C 001
M 073
Y 057
K 000

057

C 015
M 100
Y 090
K 010

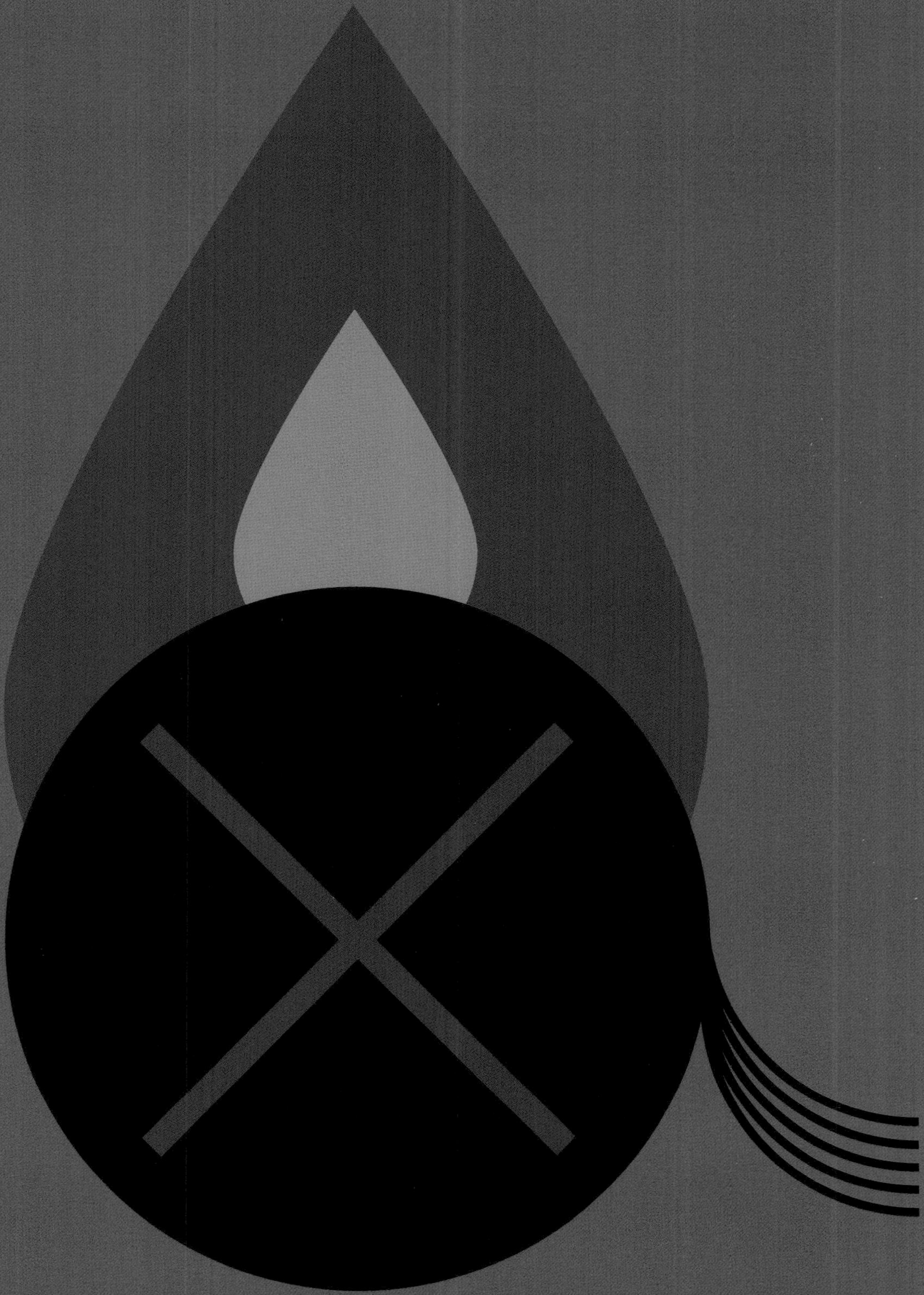

inglourious basterds

an inglorious, uproarious thrill-ride of vengeance.

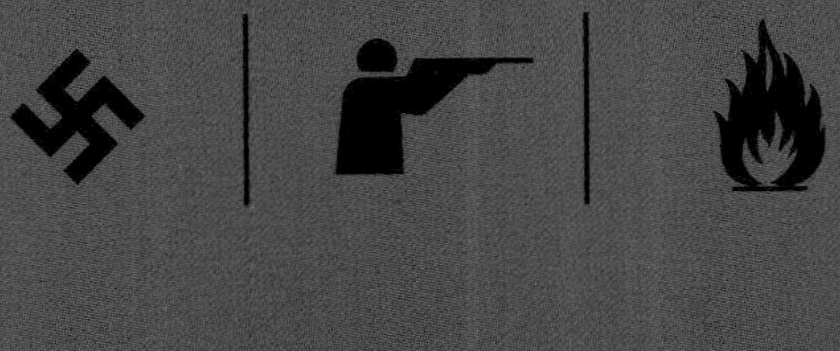

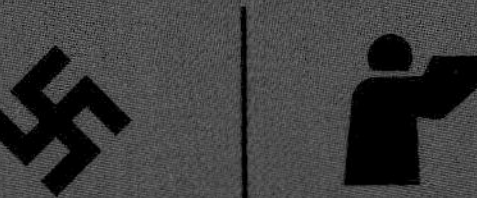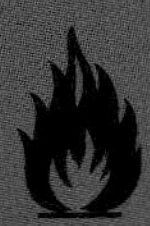

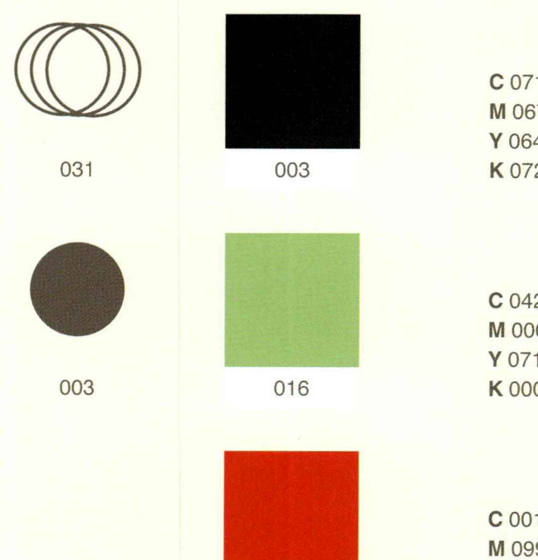

031

003

003

C 071
M 067
Y 064
K 072

016

C 042
M 000
Y 071
K 000

030

C 001
M 099
Y 094
K 000

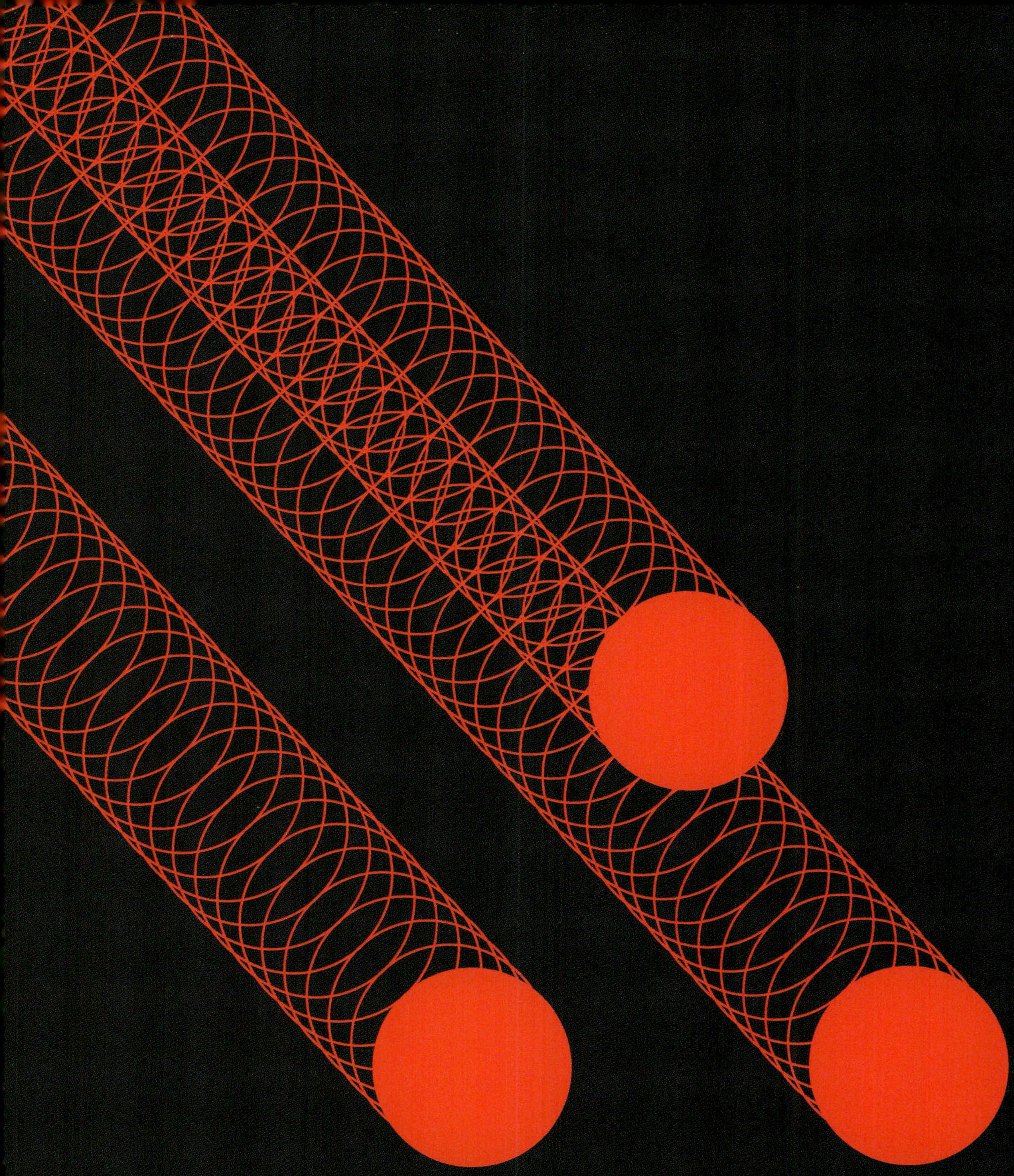

predator

if it bleeds, we can kill it.

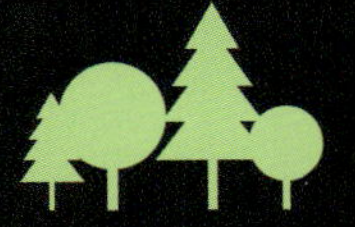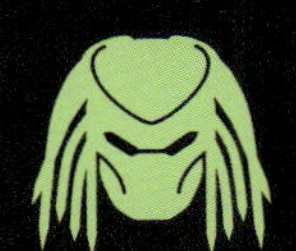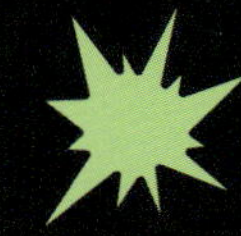

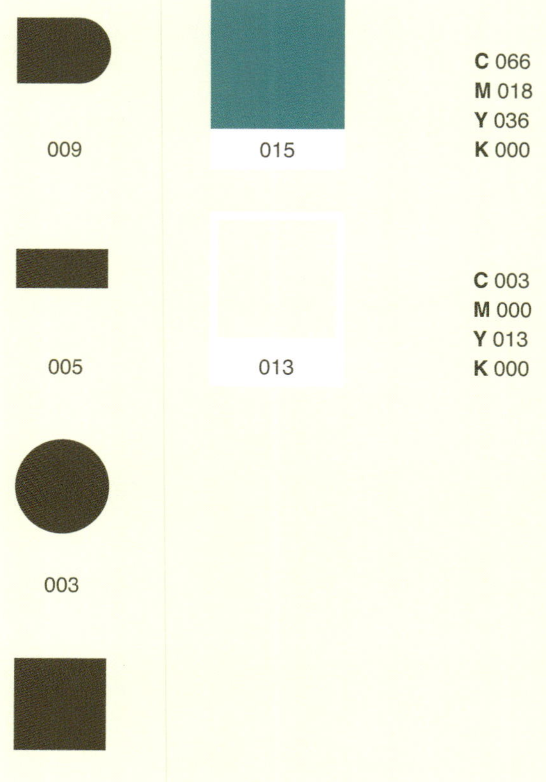

009

015

C 066
M 018
Y 036
K 000

005

013

C 003
M 000
Y 013
K 000

003

002

city of god / / /

if you run, the beast will get you. if you stay, the beast will eat you.

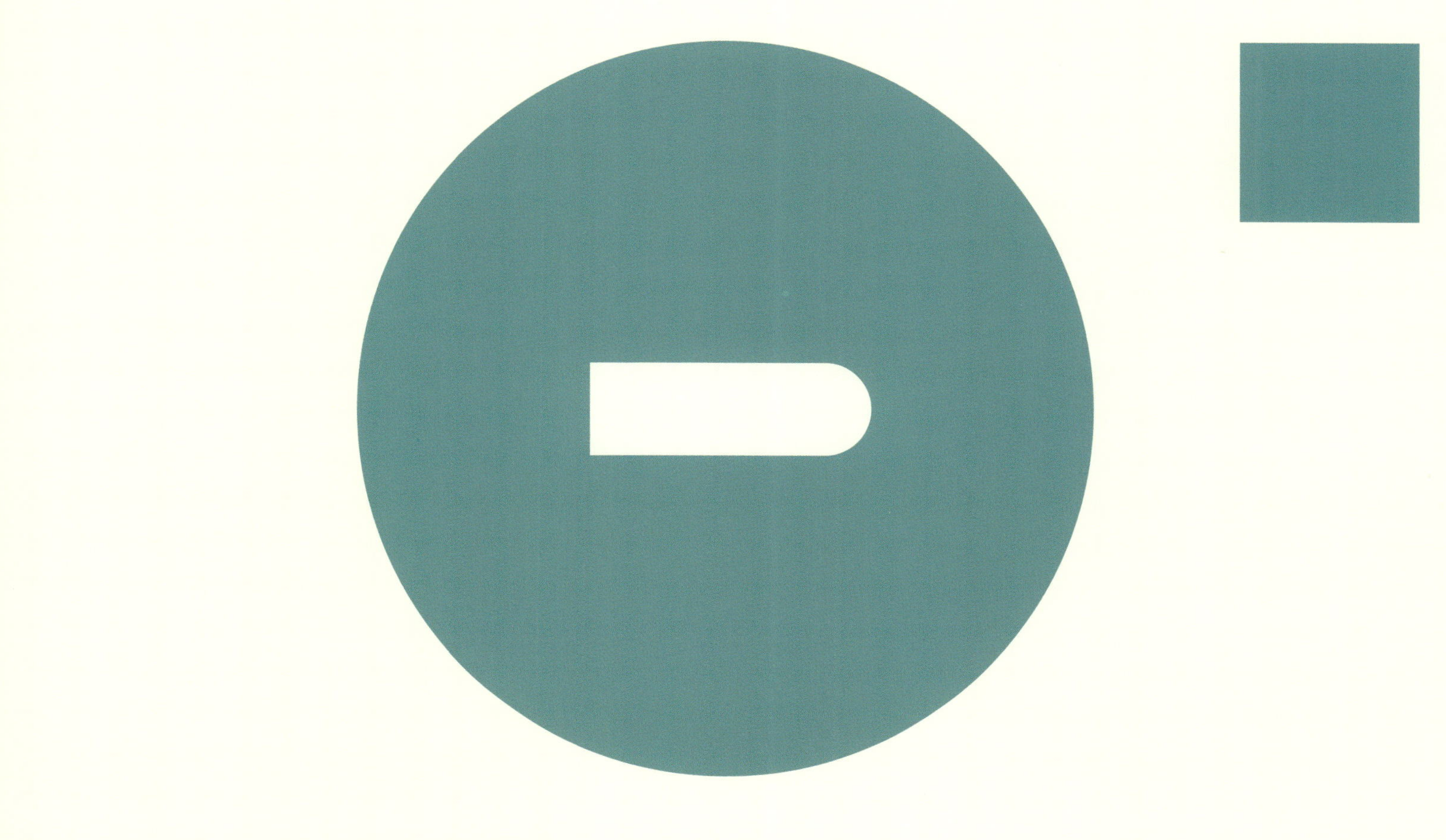

cidade de deus

se correr o bicho pega. se ficar o bicho come.

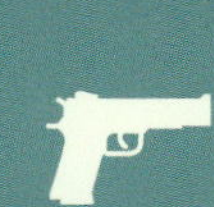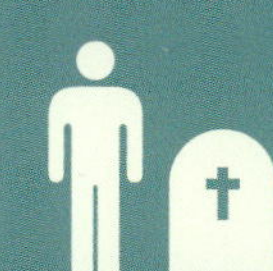

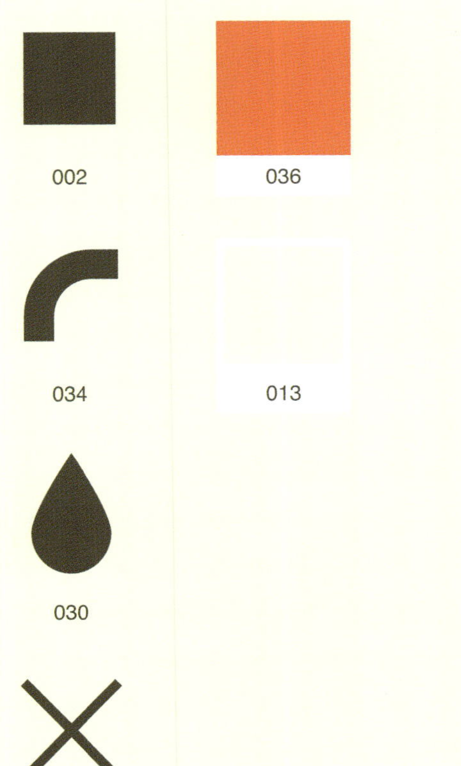

002

036

C 003
M 060
Y 060
K 000

034

013

C 003
M 000
Y 013
K 000

030

033

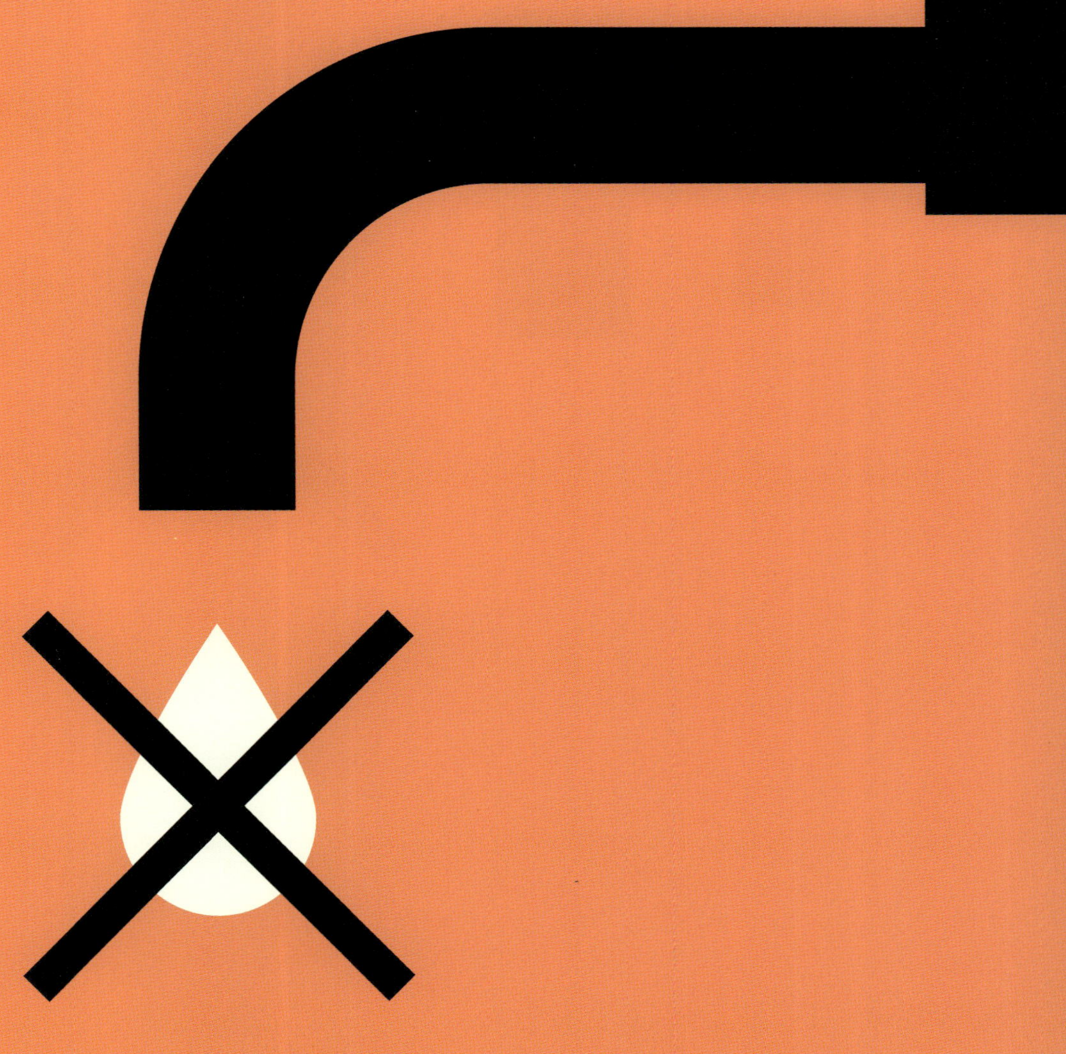

mad max: fury road

only the mad survive.

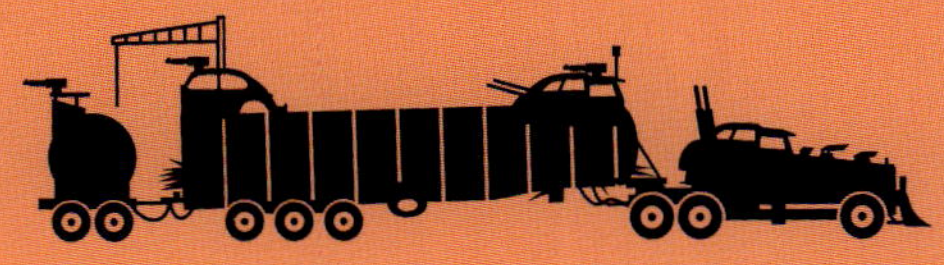

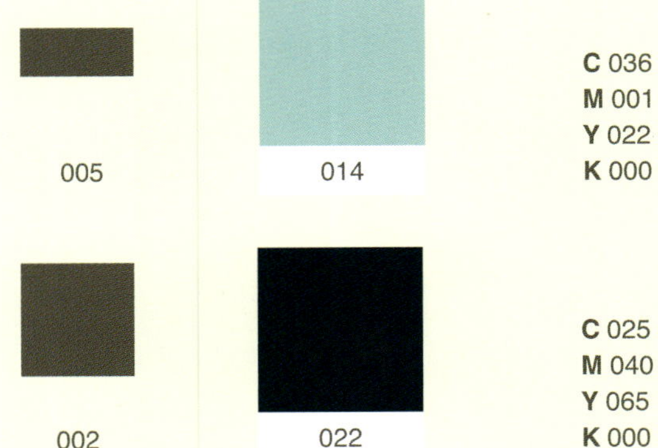

005

014

C 036
M 001
Y 022
K 000

002

022

C 025
M 040
Y 065
K 000

rear window

in deadly danger... because they saw too much!

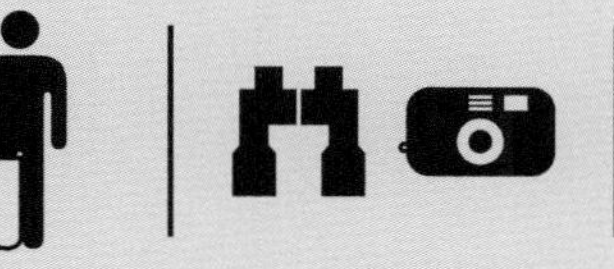

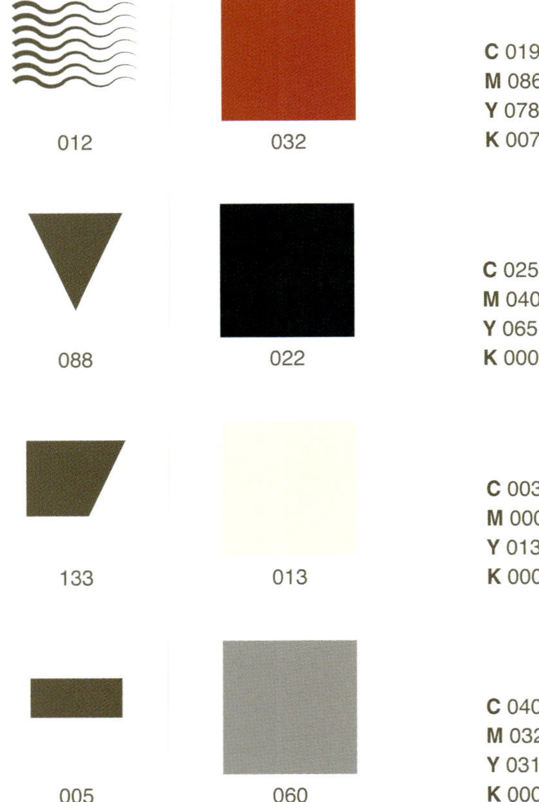

012 032

C 019
M 086
Y 078
K 007

088 022

C 025
M 040
Y 065
K 000

133 013

C 003
M 000
Y 013
K 000

005 060

C 040
M 032
Y 031
K 000

titanic

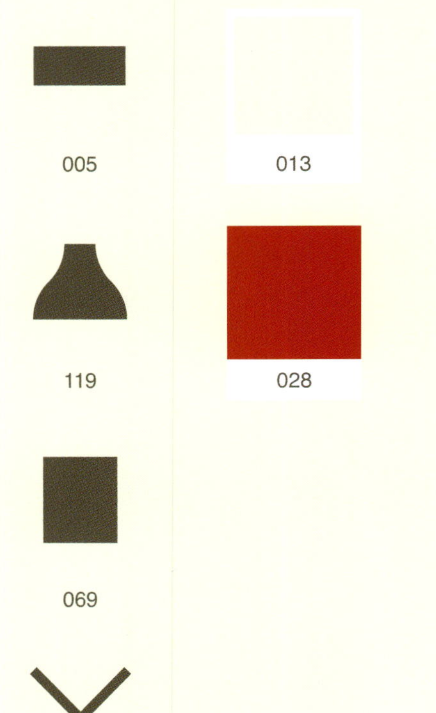

005

013

C 003
M 000
Y 013
K 000

119

028

C 015
M 096
Y 089
K 004

069

033

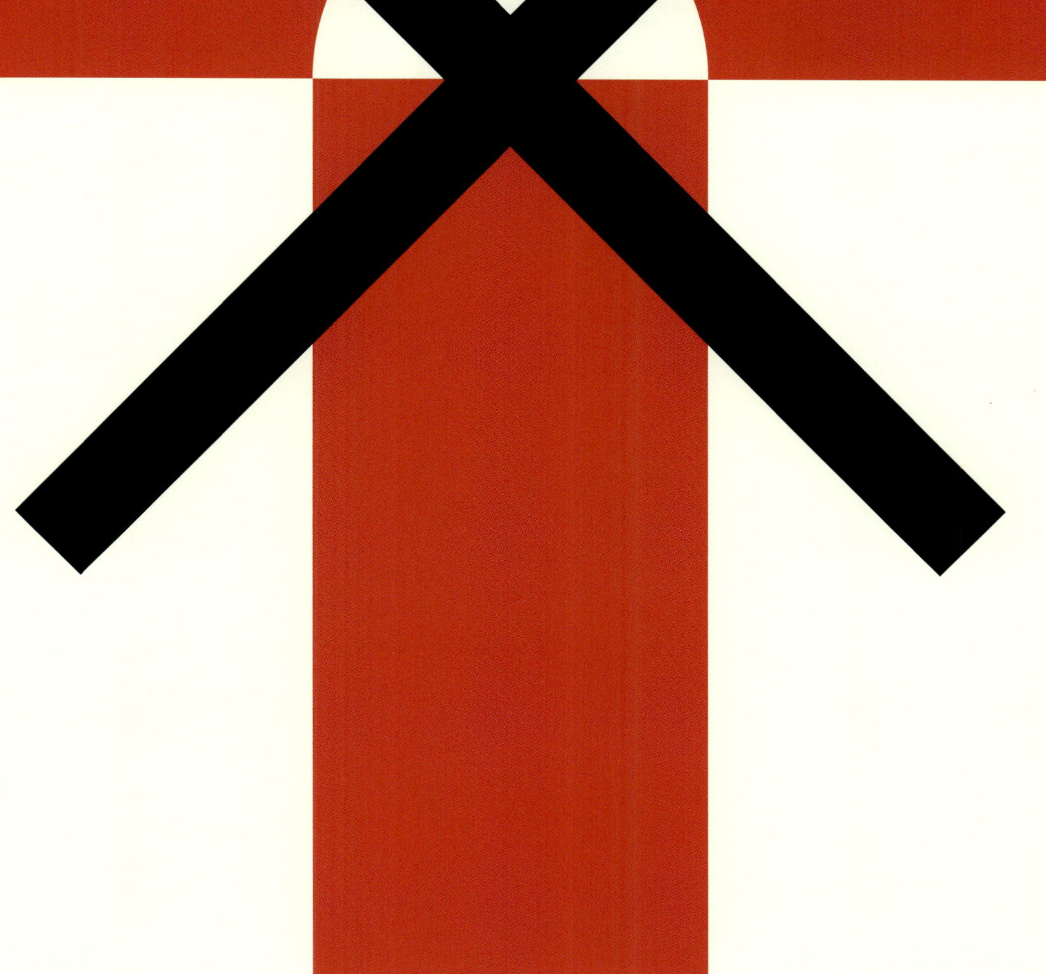

19
33
the untouchables
what are you prepared to do?

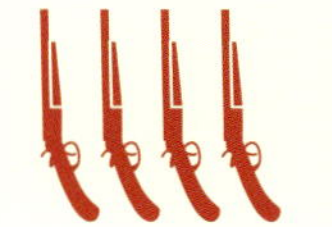
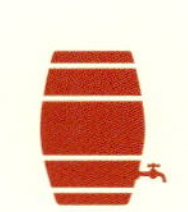

BLAH BLAH BLAH

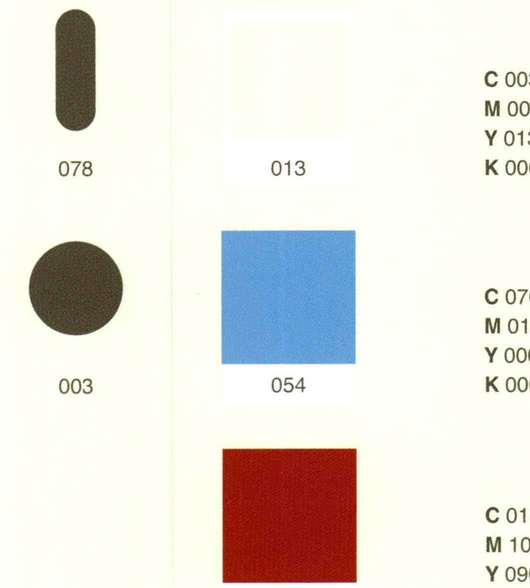

078

003

013

054

057

C 003
M 000
Y 013
K 000

C 070
M 015
Y 000
K 000

C 015
M 100
Y 090
K 010

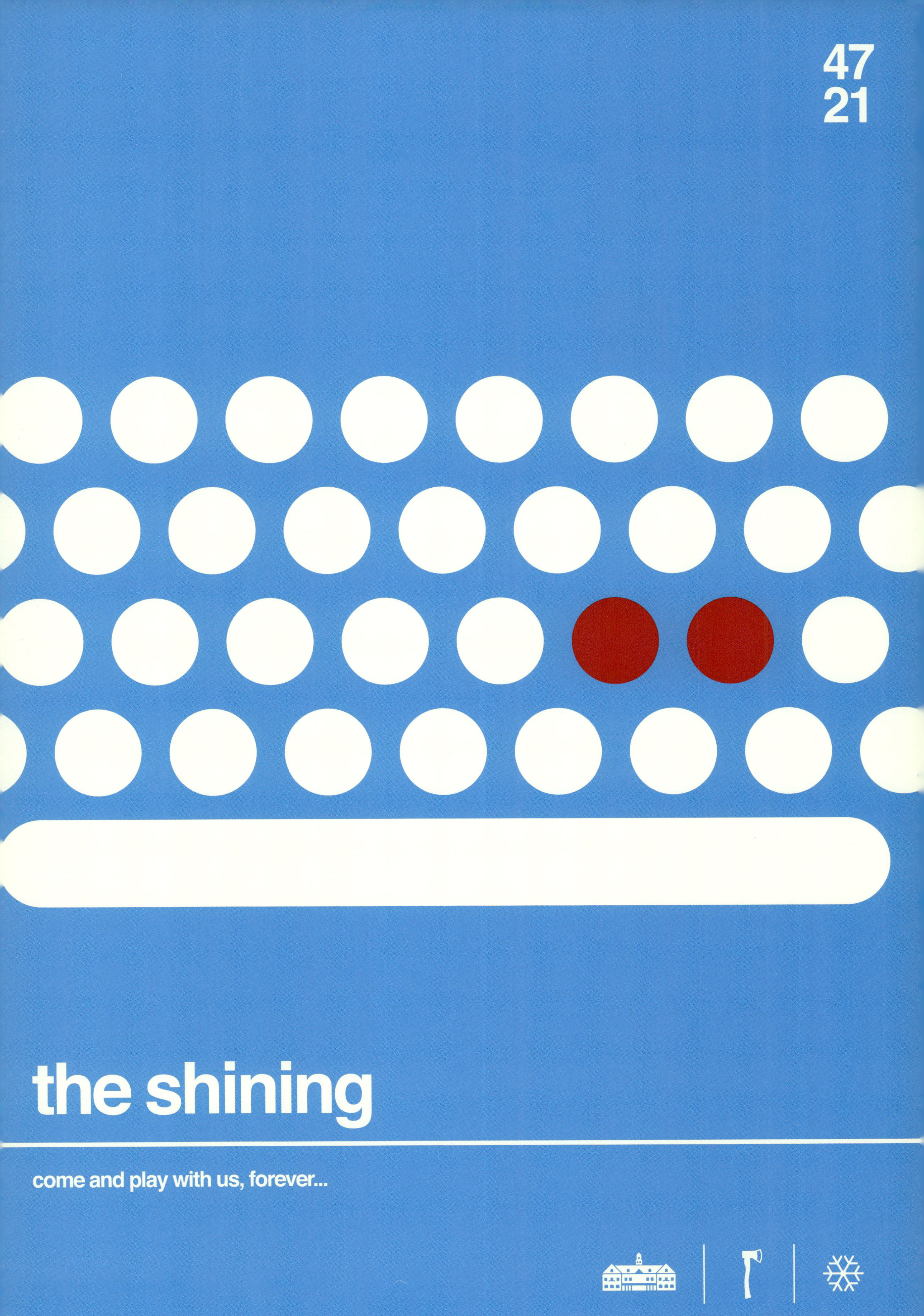

the shining

come and play with us, forever...

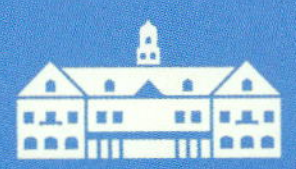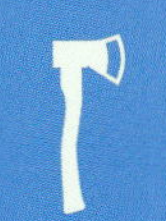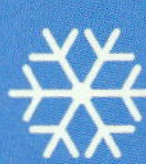

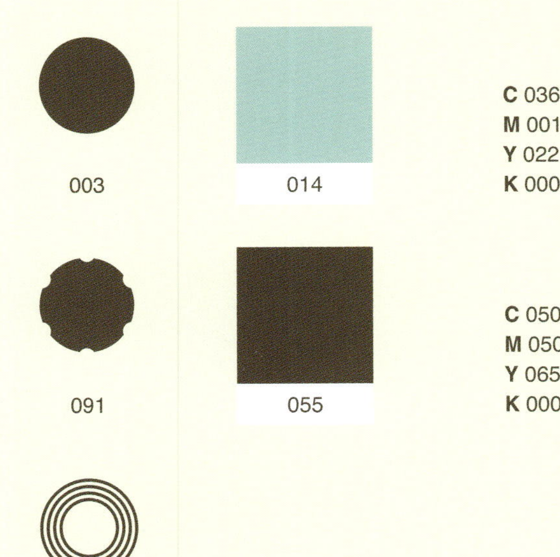

003

091

036

014

055

C 036
M 001
Y 022
K 000

C 050
M 050
Y 065
K 000

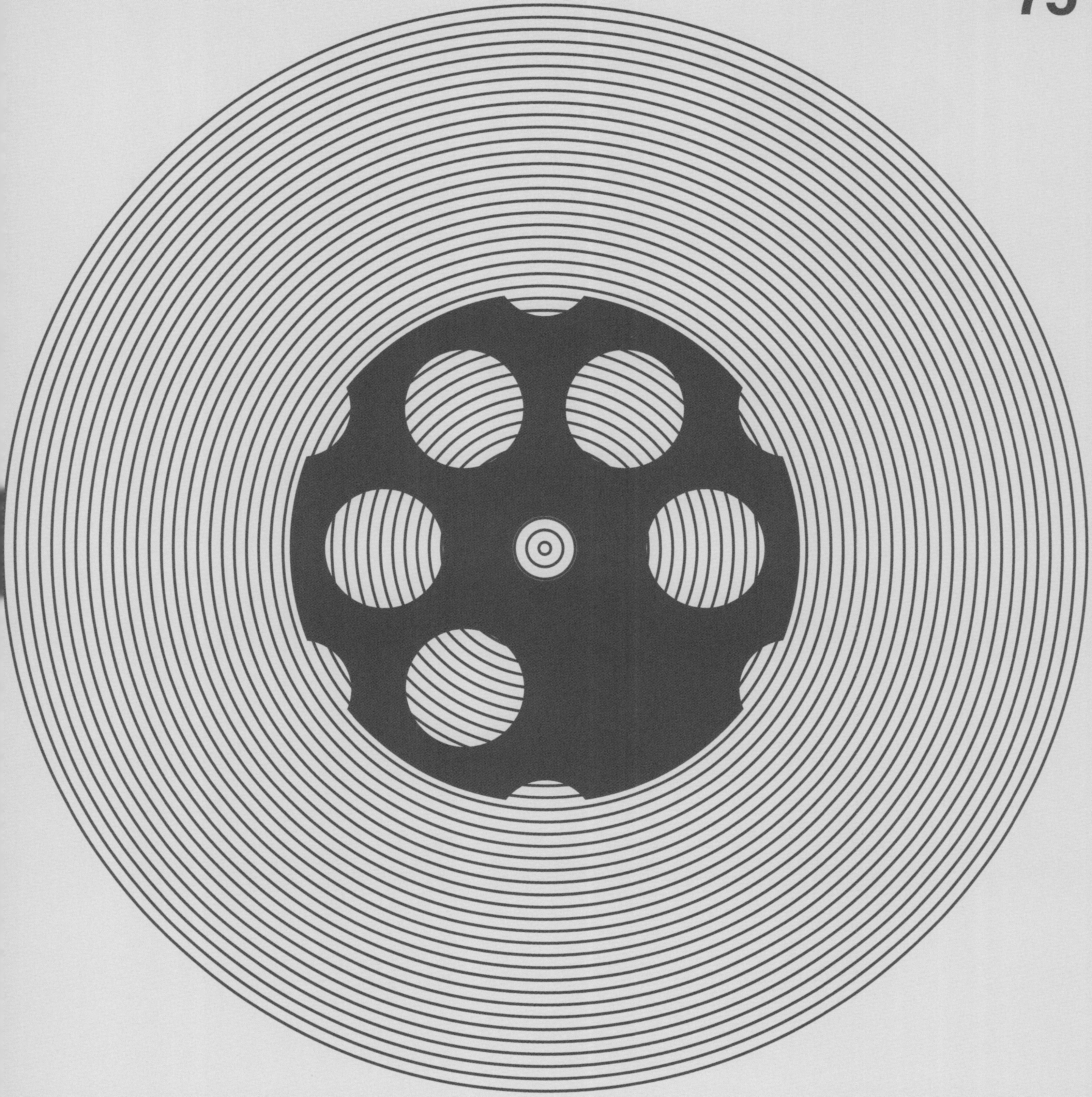

the deer hunter

we gotta play with more bullets.

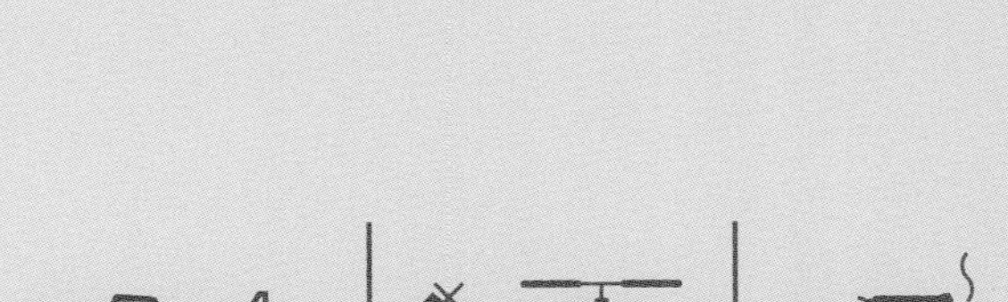

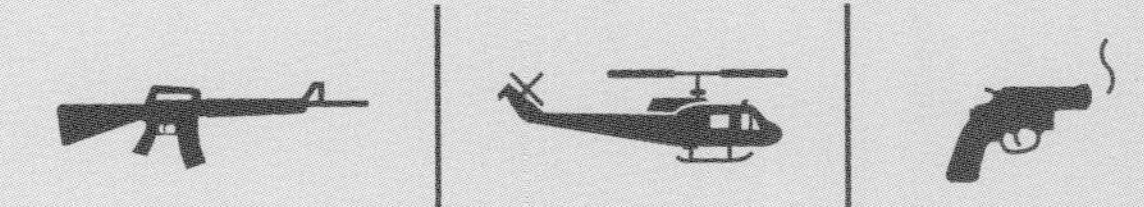

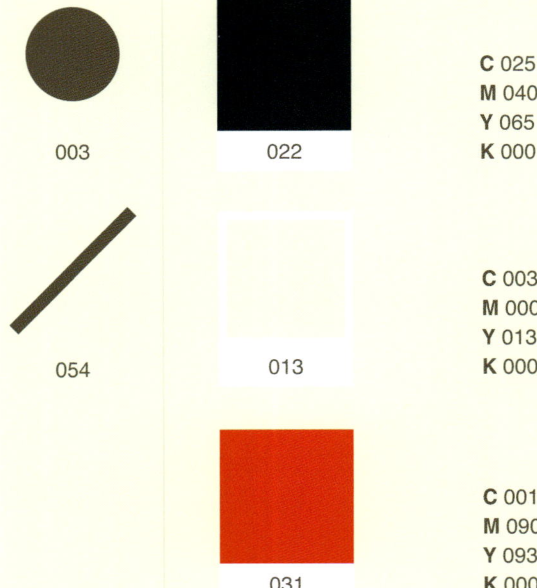

003

054

022

013

031

C 025
M 040
Y 065
K 000

C 003
M 000
Y 013
K 000

C 001
M 090
Y 093
K 000

star wars

may the force be with you.

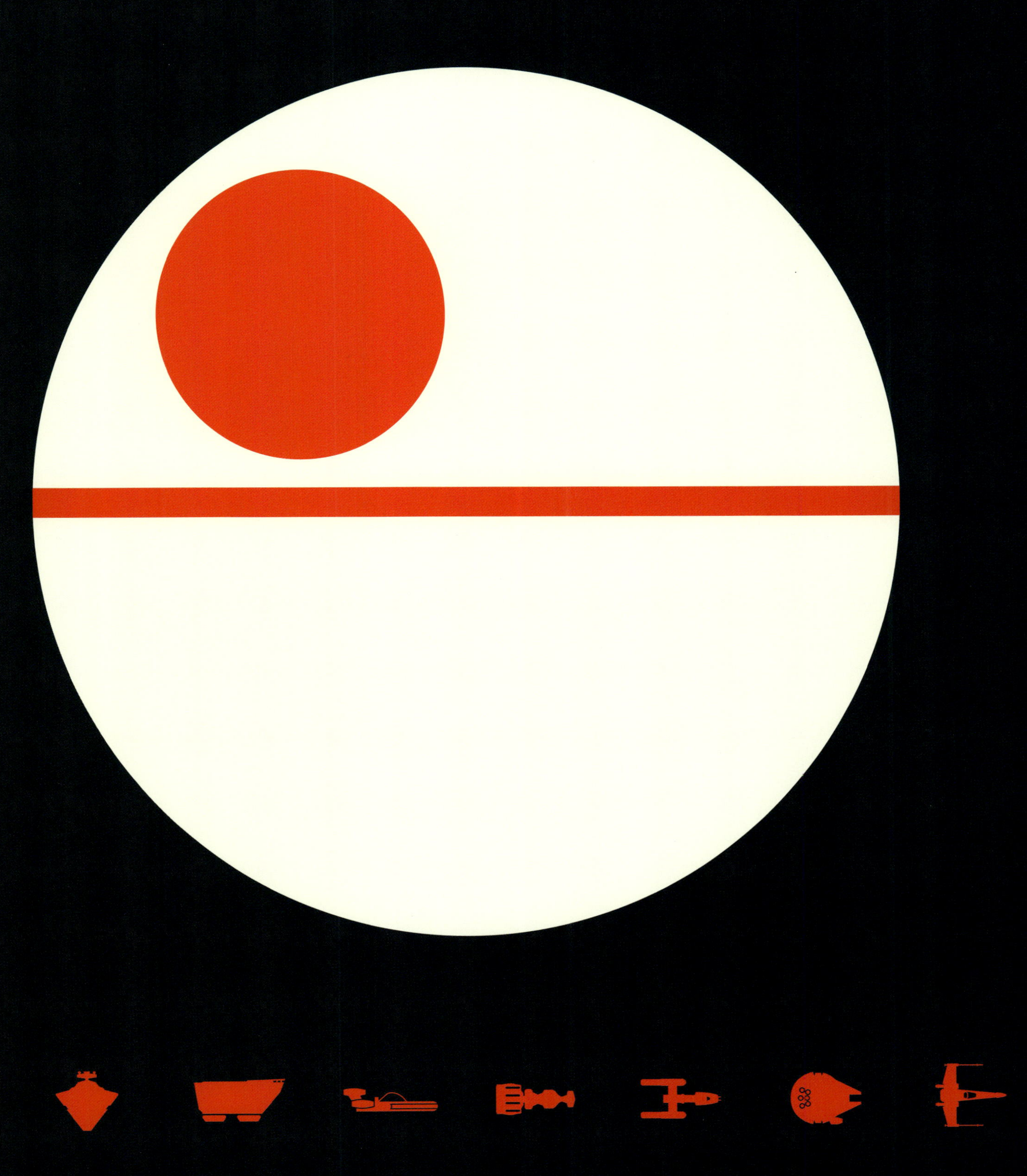

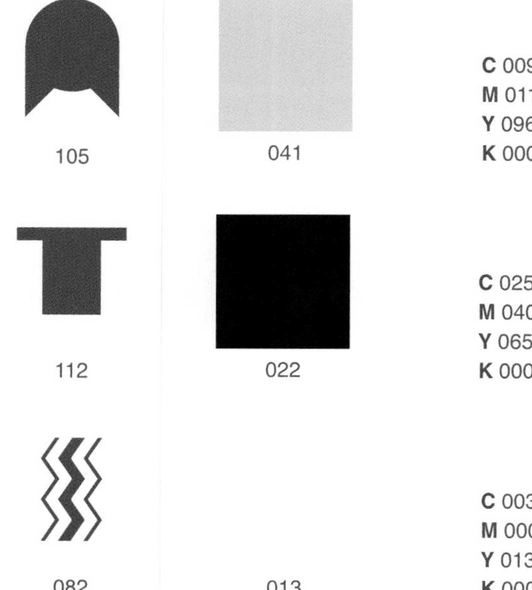

105   041

C 009
M 011
Y 096
K 000

112   022

C 025
M 040
Y 065
K 000

082   013

C 003
M 000
Y 013
K 000

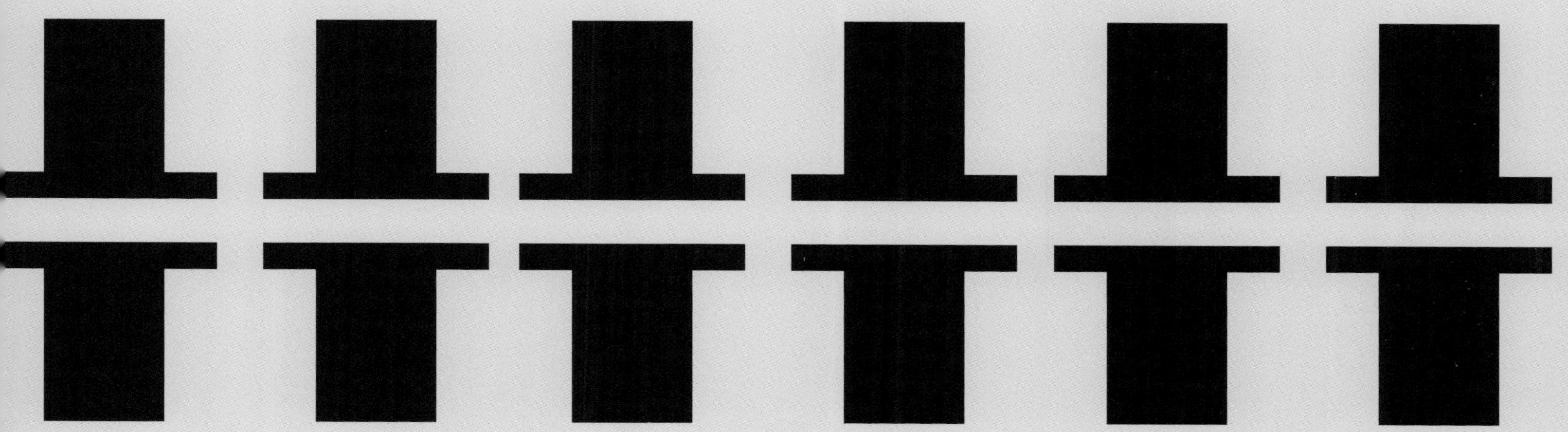

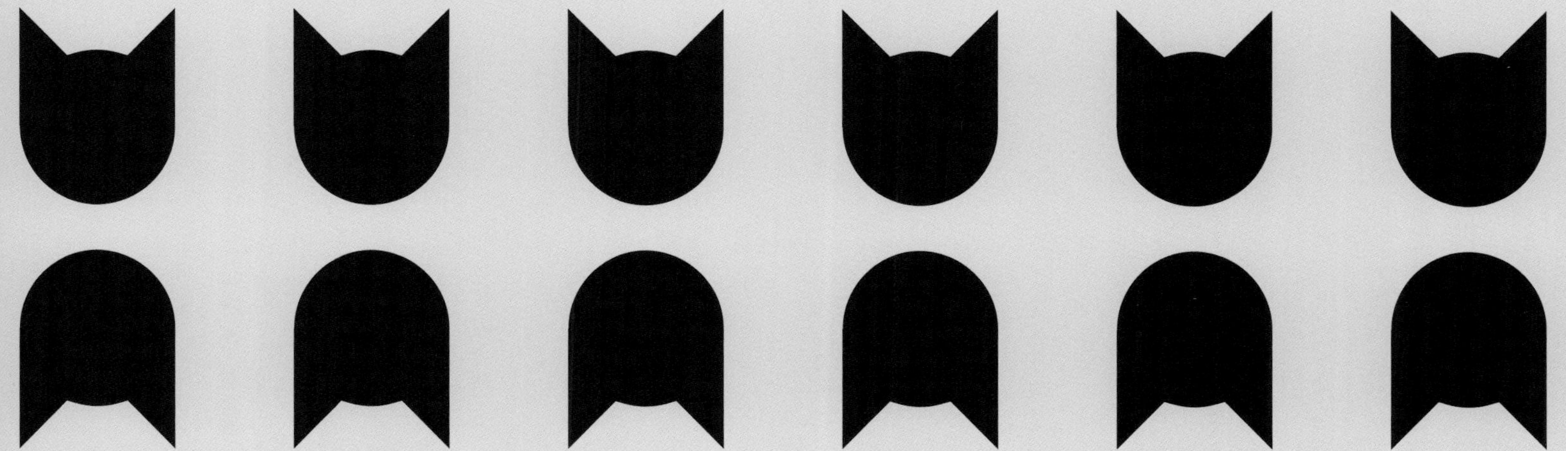

the prestige

are you watching closely?

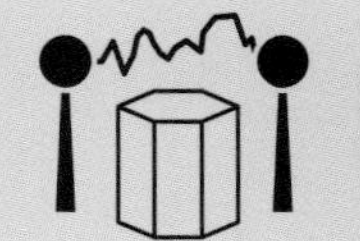 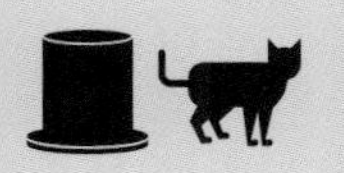 

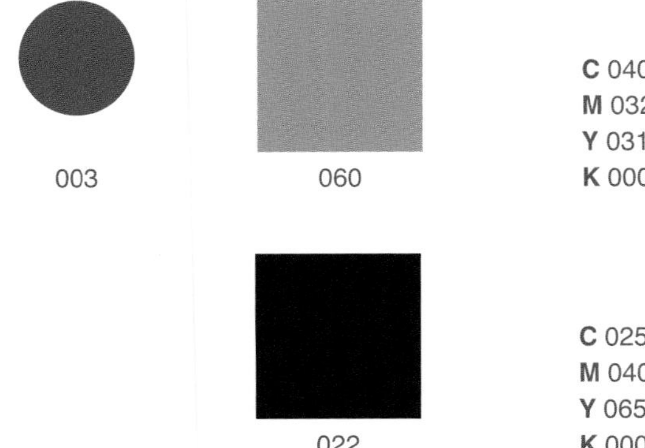

003

060

022

C 040
M 032
Y 031
K 000

C 025
M 040
Y 065
K 000

pulp fiction

you won't know the facts until you've seen the fiction.

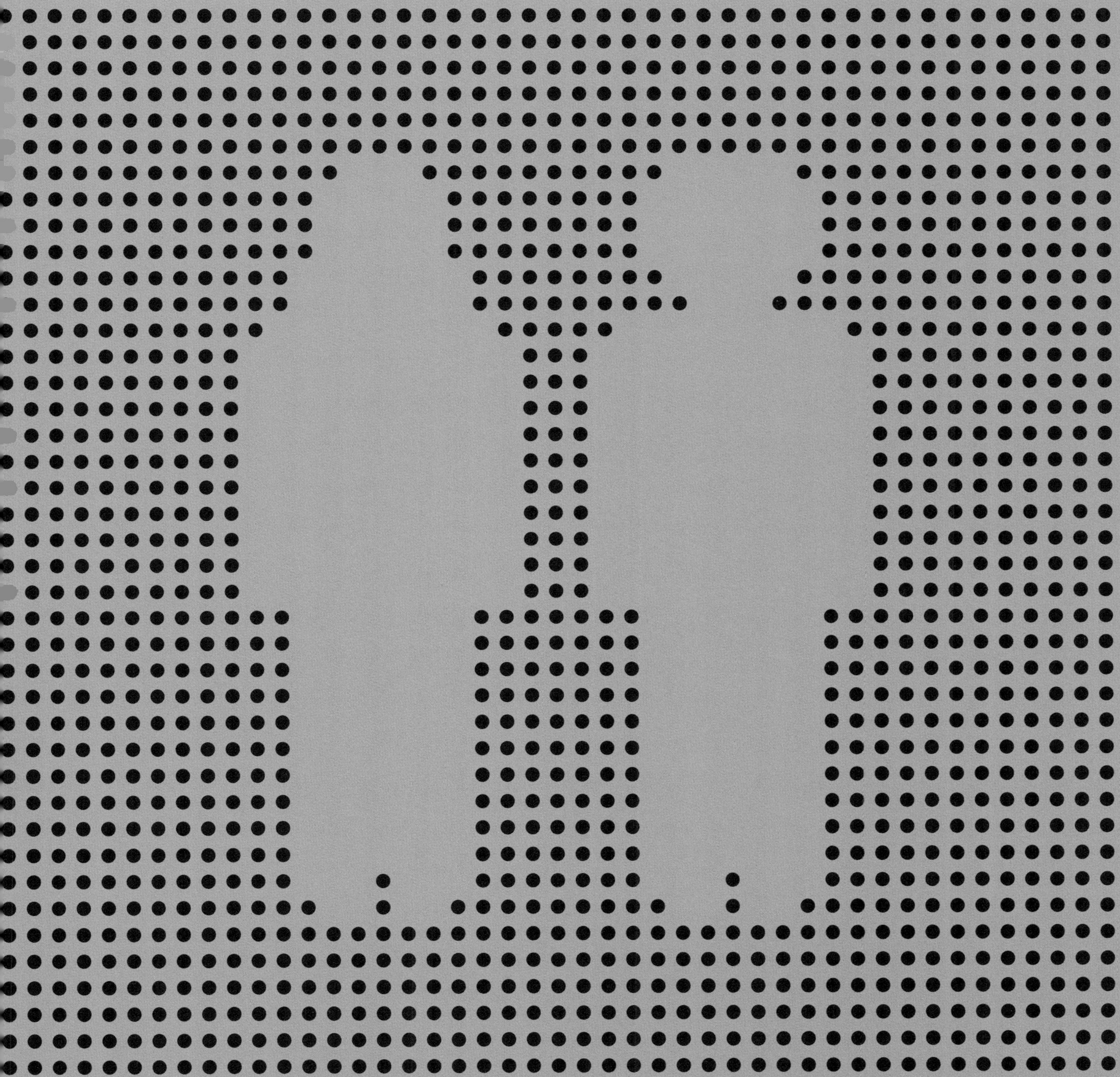

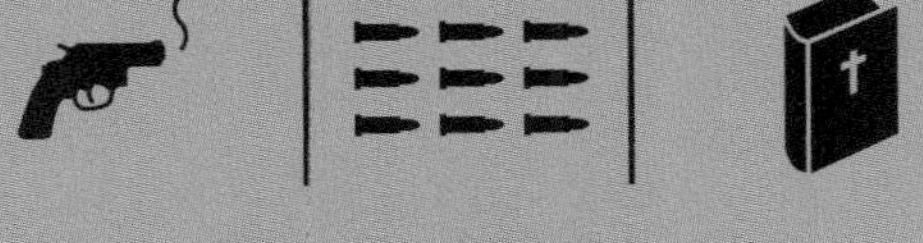

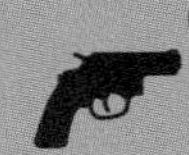 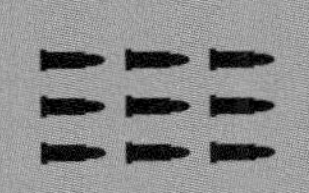 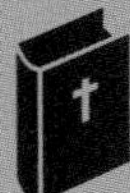

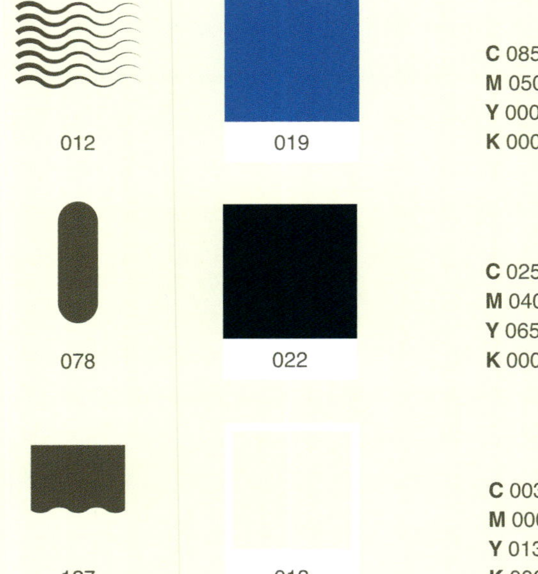

012

019

C 085
M 050
Y 000
K 000

078

022

C 025
M 040
Y 065
K 000

127

013

C 003
M 000
Y 013
K 000

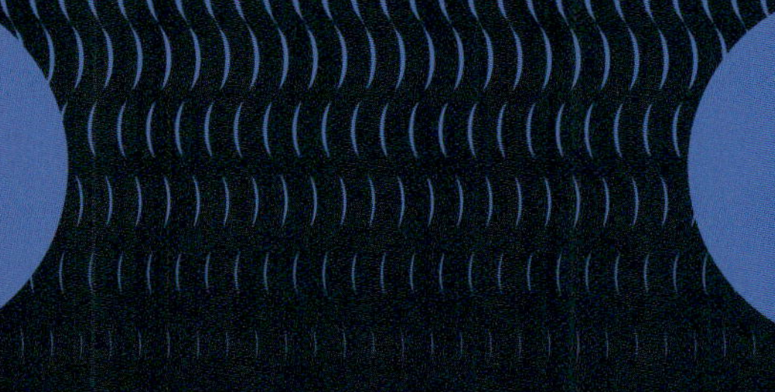

10
17
the hunt for red october
invisible. silent. stolen.

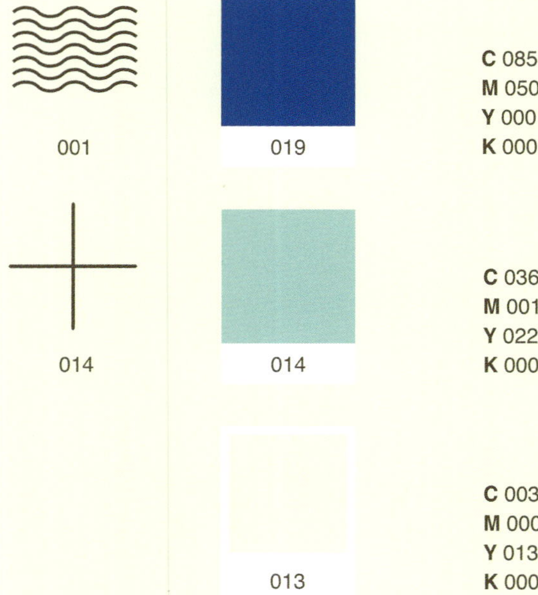

001

014

019

C 085
M 050
Y 000
K 000

014

C 036
M 001
Y 022
K 000

013

C 003
M 000
Y 013
K 000

a clockwork orange

being the adventures of a young man whose principal interests are rape, ultra-violence and beethoven.

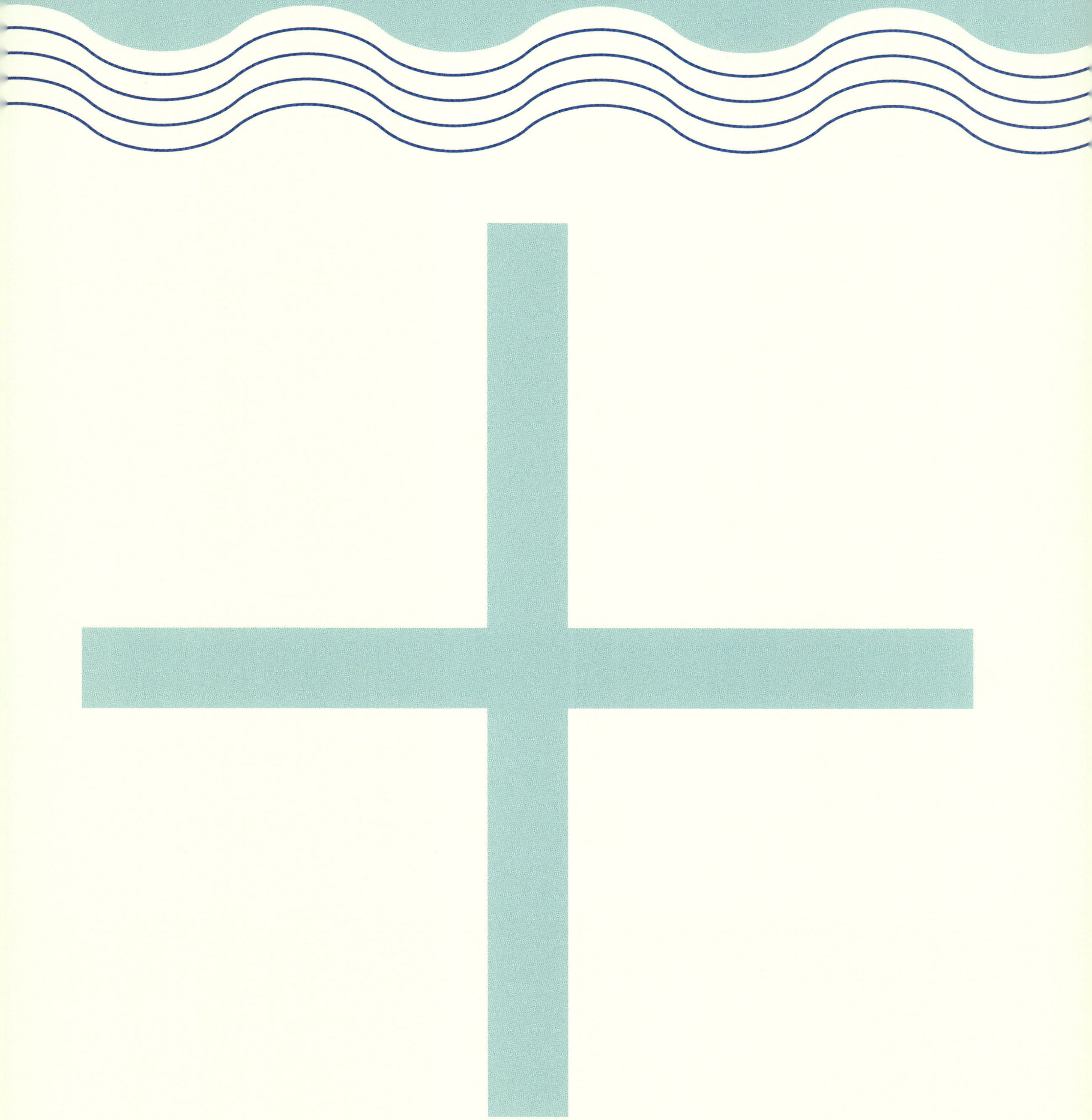

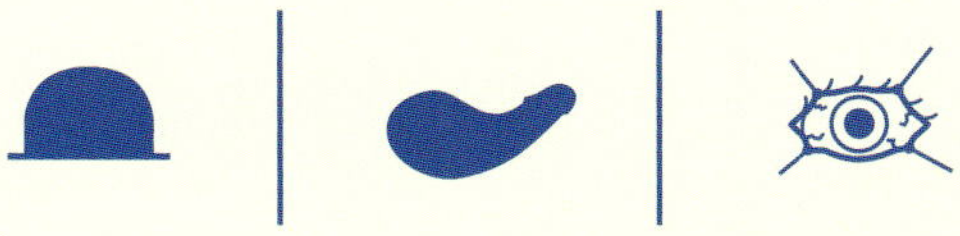

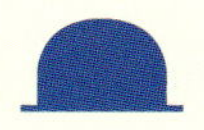  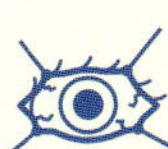

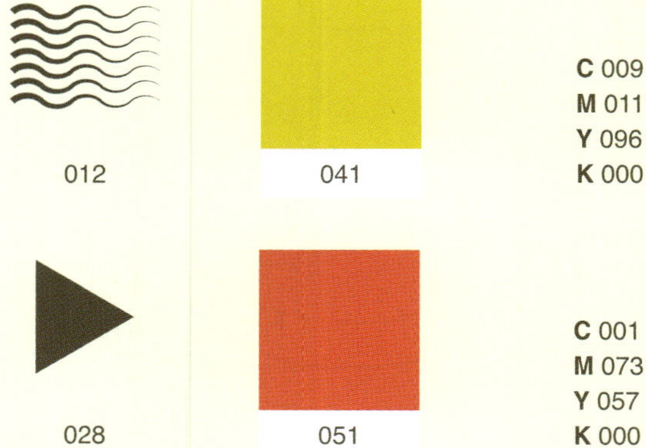

012

041

C 009
M 011
Y 096
K 000

028

051

C 001
M 073
Y 057
K 000

01
50
game of thrones
five kings, one throne.

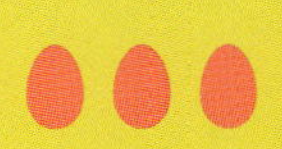
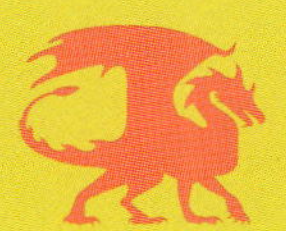

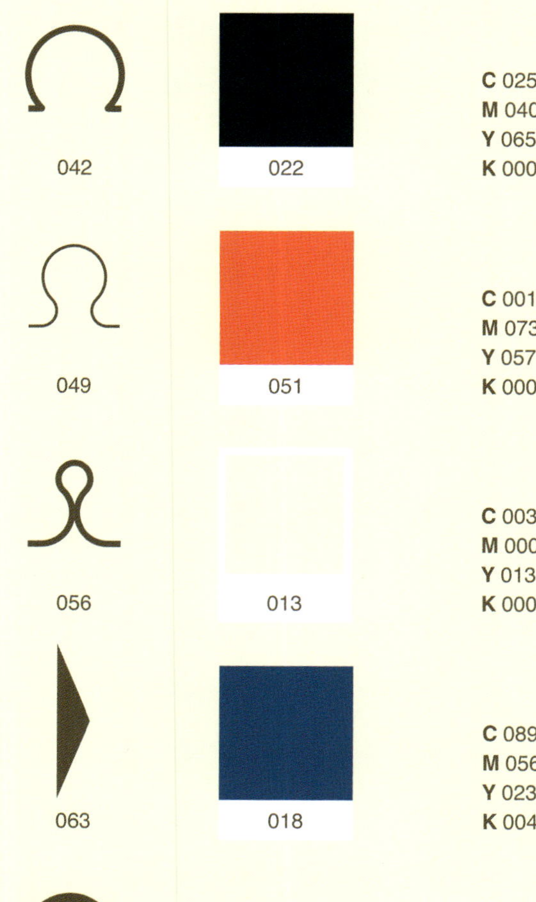

042

049

056

063

003

022

051

013

018

C 025
M 040
Y 065
K 000

C 001
M 073
Y 057
K 000

C 003
M 000
Y 013
K 000

C 089
M 056
Y 023
K 004

interstellar

---

the end of earth will not be the end of us.

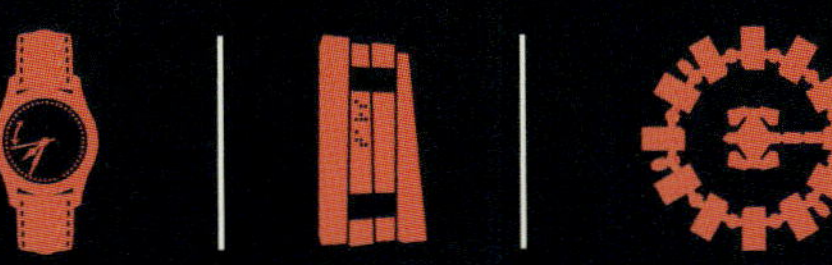

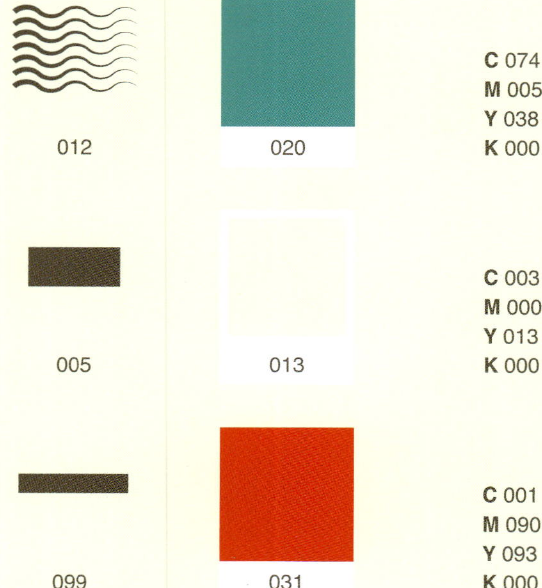

012

020

C 074
M 005
Y 038
K 000

005

013

C 003
M 000
Y 013
K 000

099

031

C 001
M 090
Y 093
K 000

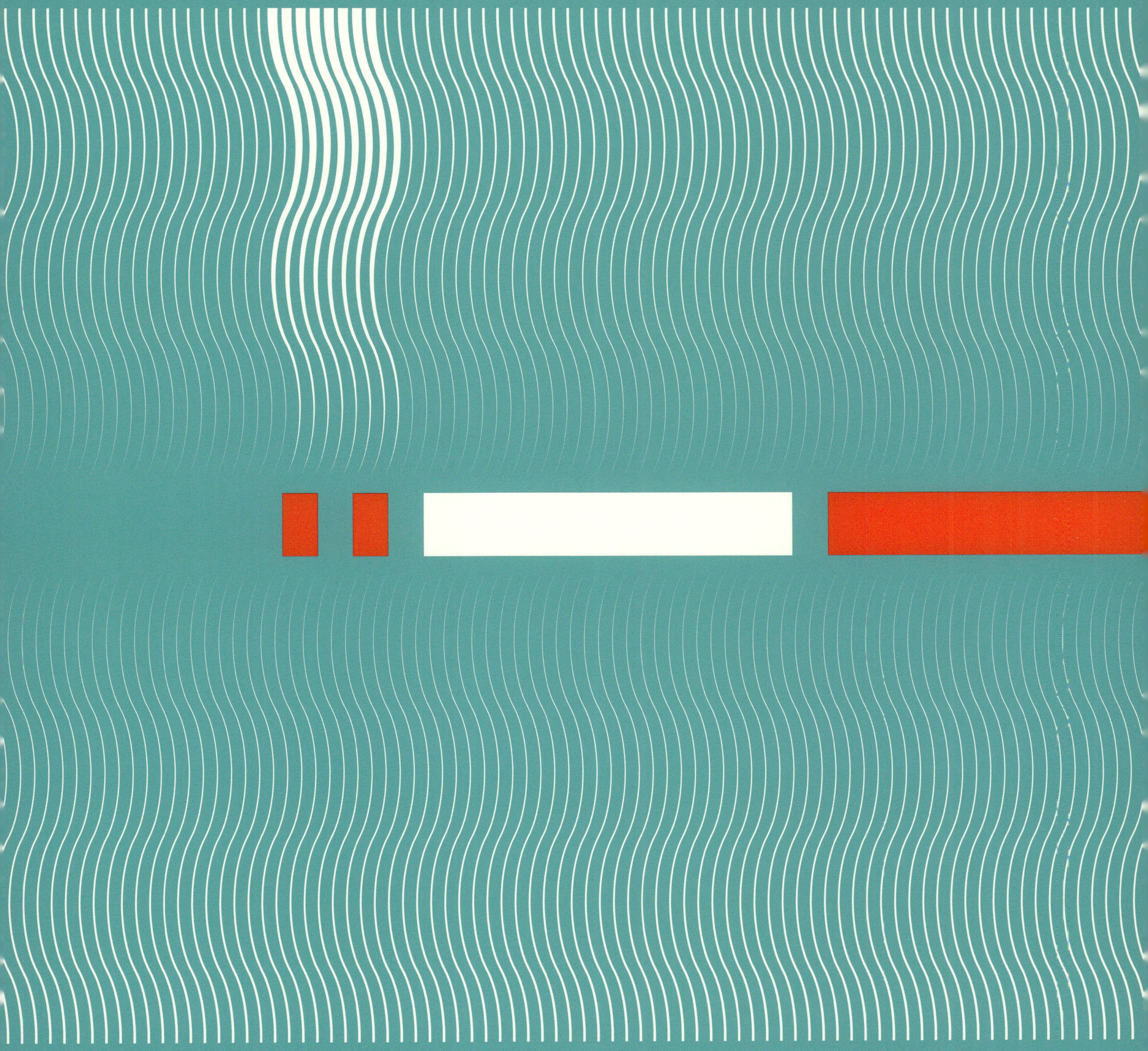

breakfast at tiffany's

the fairest lady of all.

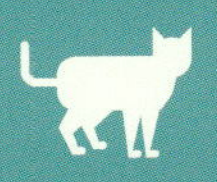

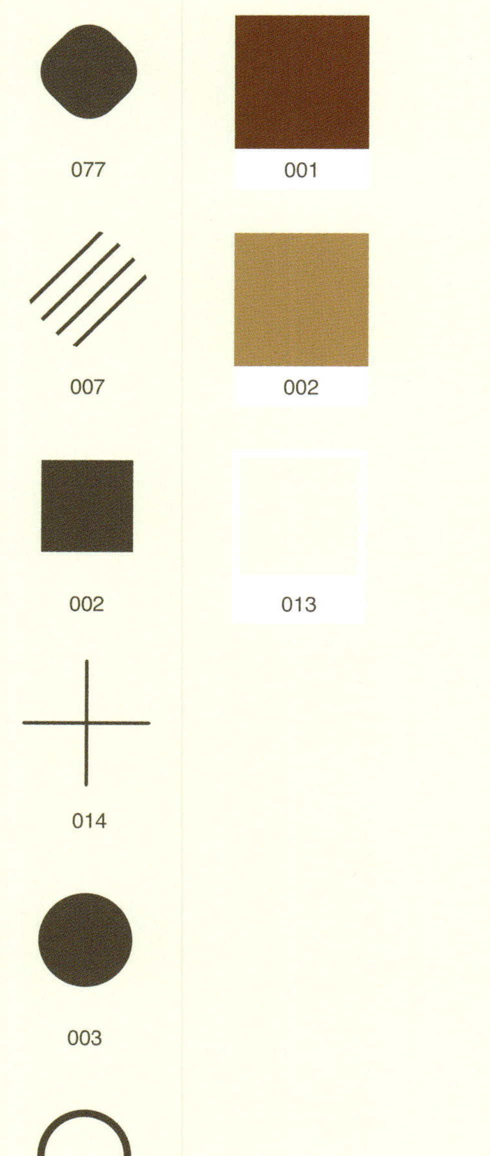

077

007

002

014

003

027

001

002

013

C 035
M 060
Y 080
K 025

C 025
M 040
Y 065
K 000

C 003
M 000
Y 013
K 000

forrest gump

you never know what you're gonna get.

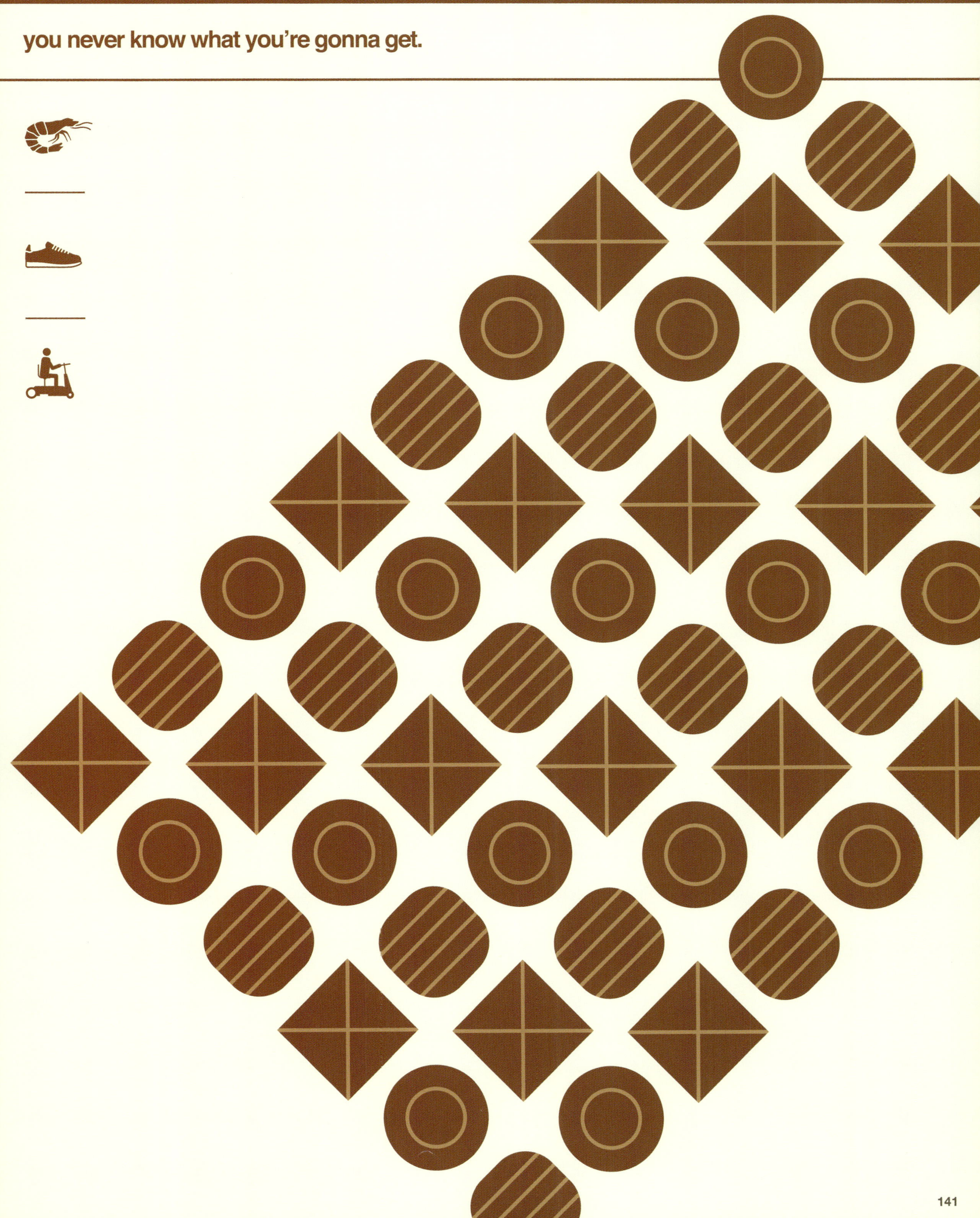

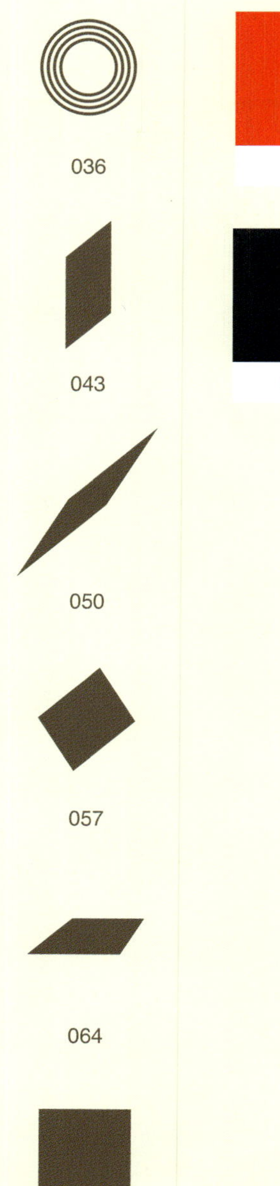

036

043

050

057

064

002

031

C 001
M 090
Y 093
K 000

022

C 025
M 040
Y 065
K 000

se7en

seven deadly sins. seven ways to die.

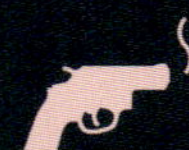

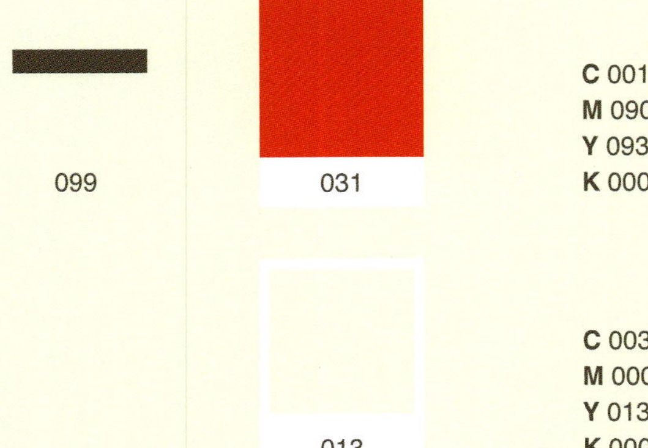

099

031

C 001
M 090
Y 093
K 000

013

C 003
M 000
Y 013
K 000

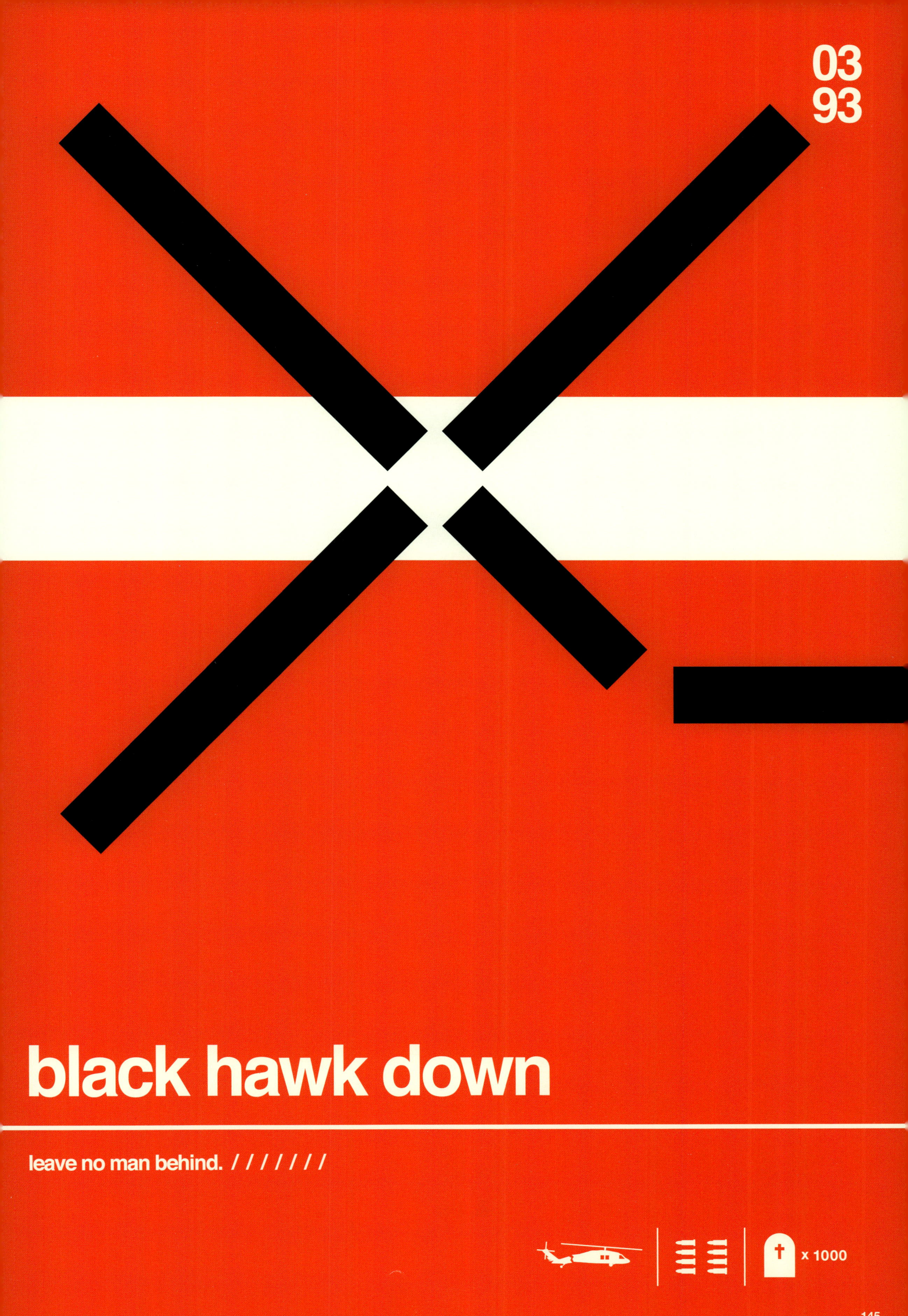

black hawk down

leave no man behind. / / / / / / /

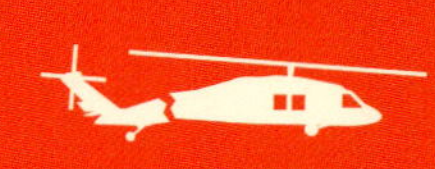 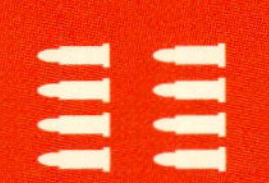 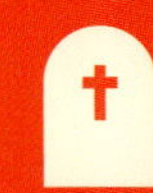 x 1000

003

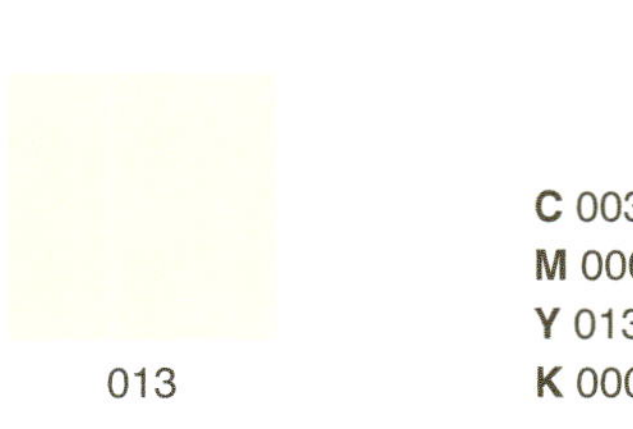

060

C 040
M 032
Y 031
K 000

029

013

C 003
M 000
Y 013
K 000

005

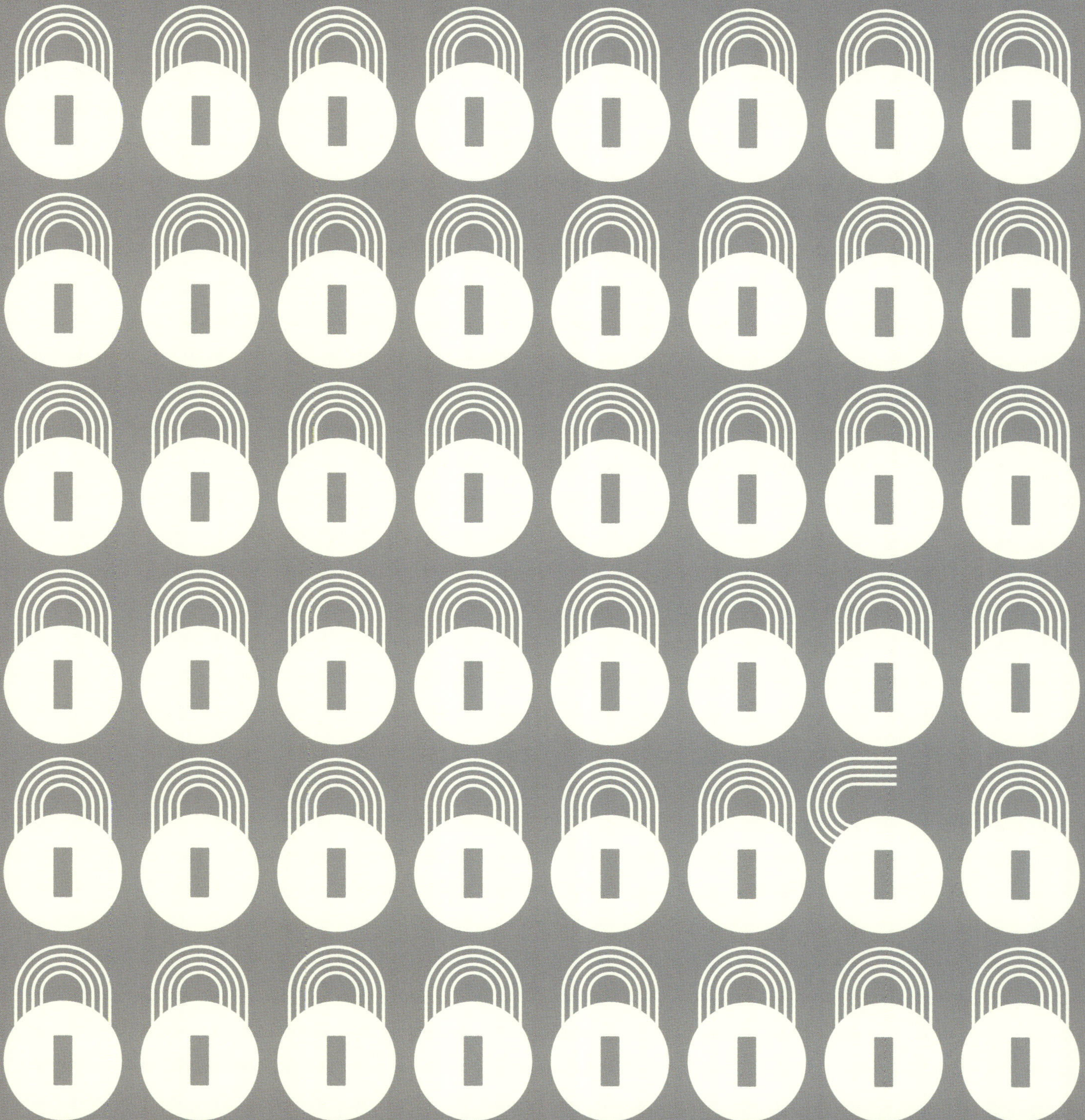

the shawshank redemption

fear can hold you prisoner. hope can set you free.

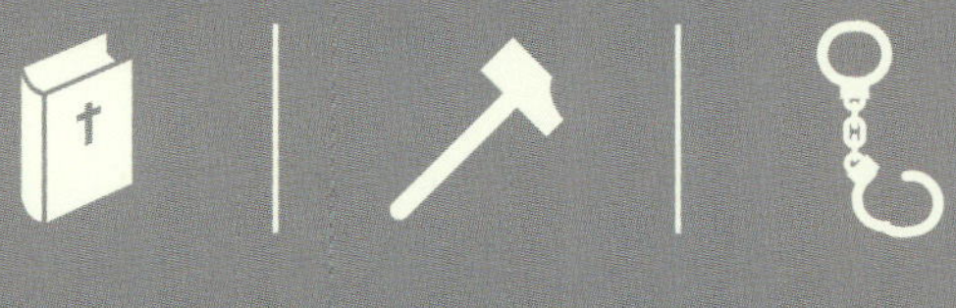

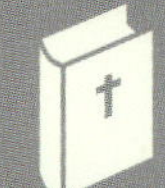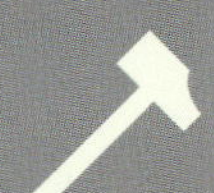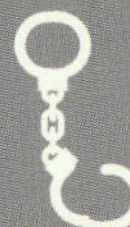

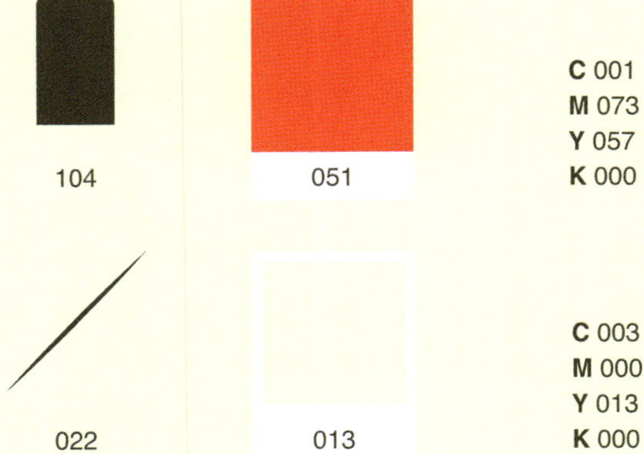

104

051

C 001
M 073
Y 057
K 000

022

013

C 003
M 000
Y 013
K 000

ratatouille

he's dying to become a chef.

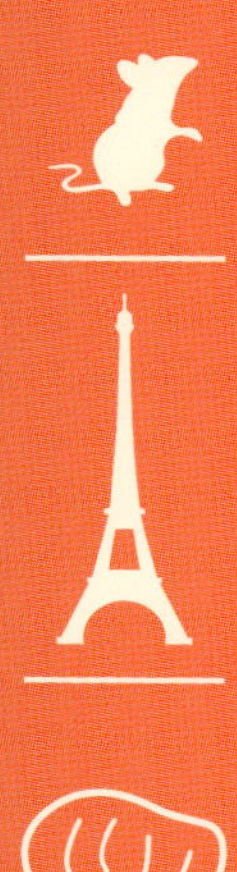

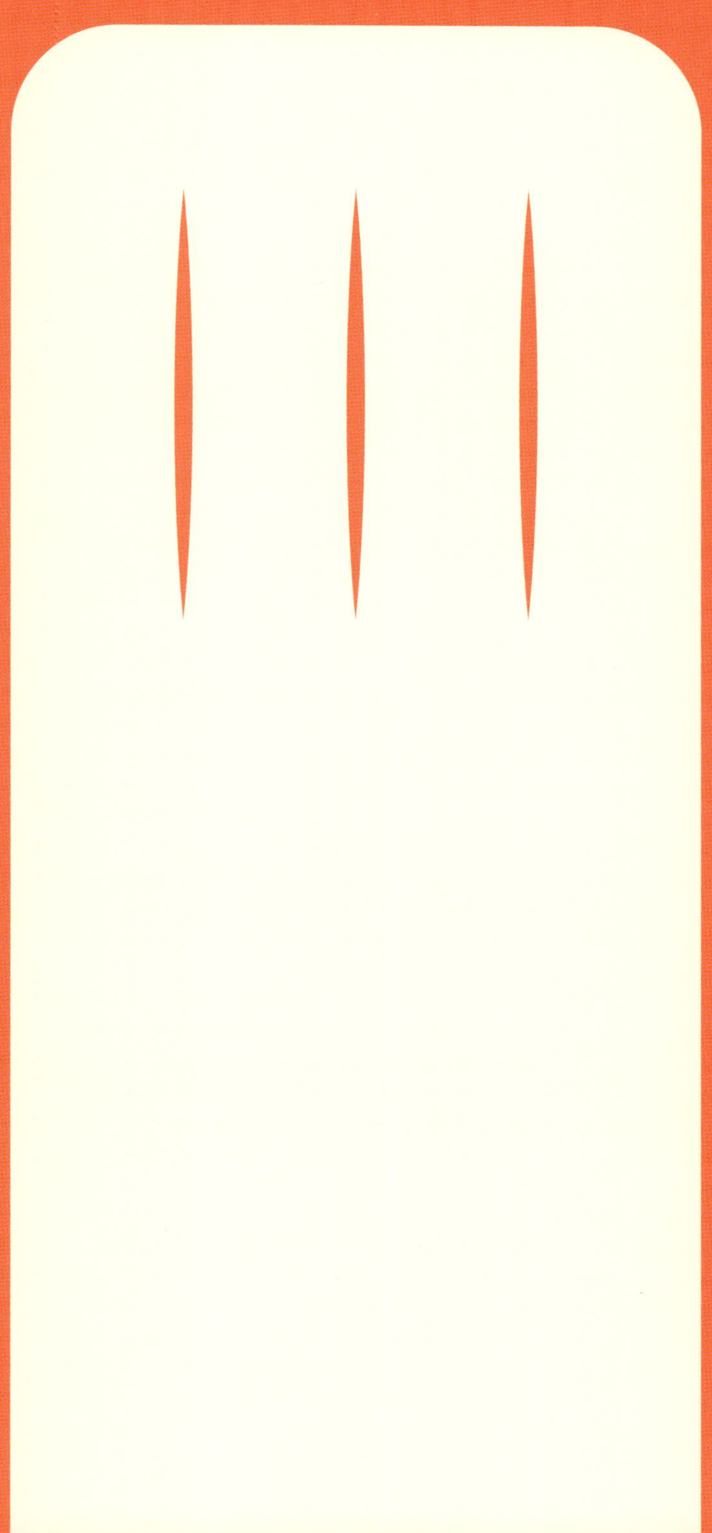

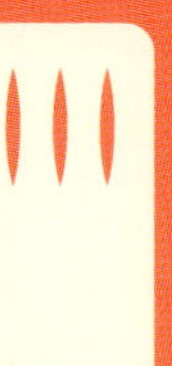

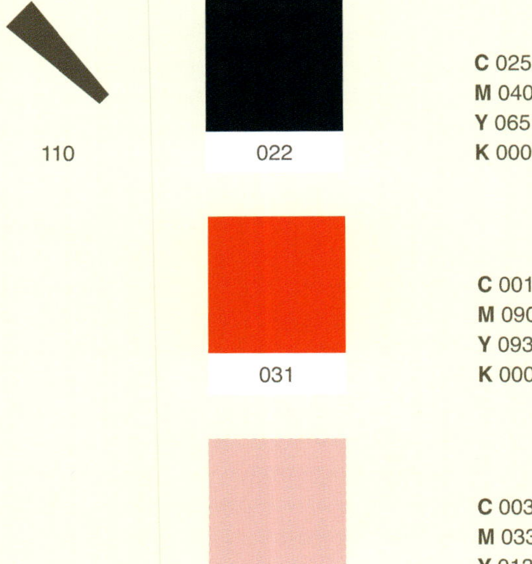

110

022

C 025
M 040
Y 065
K 000

031

C 001
M 090
Y 093
K 000

052

C 003
M 033
Y 013
K 000

moulin rouge
no laws. no limits. one rule. never fall in love.

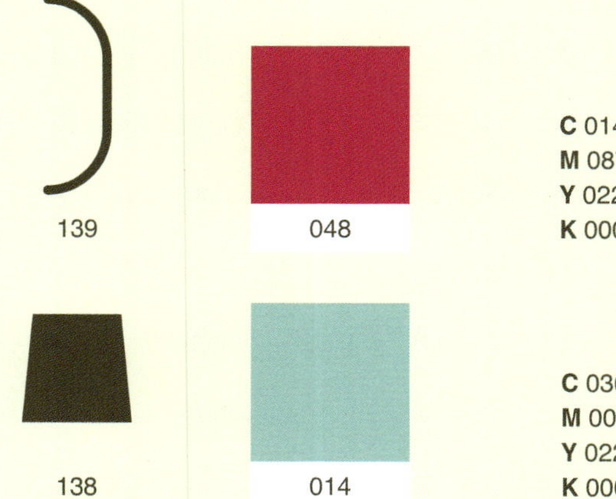

139

138

048

014

C 014
M 087
Y 022
K 000

C 036
M 001
Y 022
K 000

brokeback mountain

love is a force of nature.

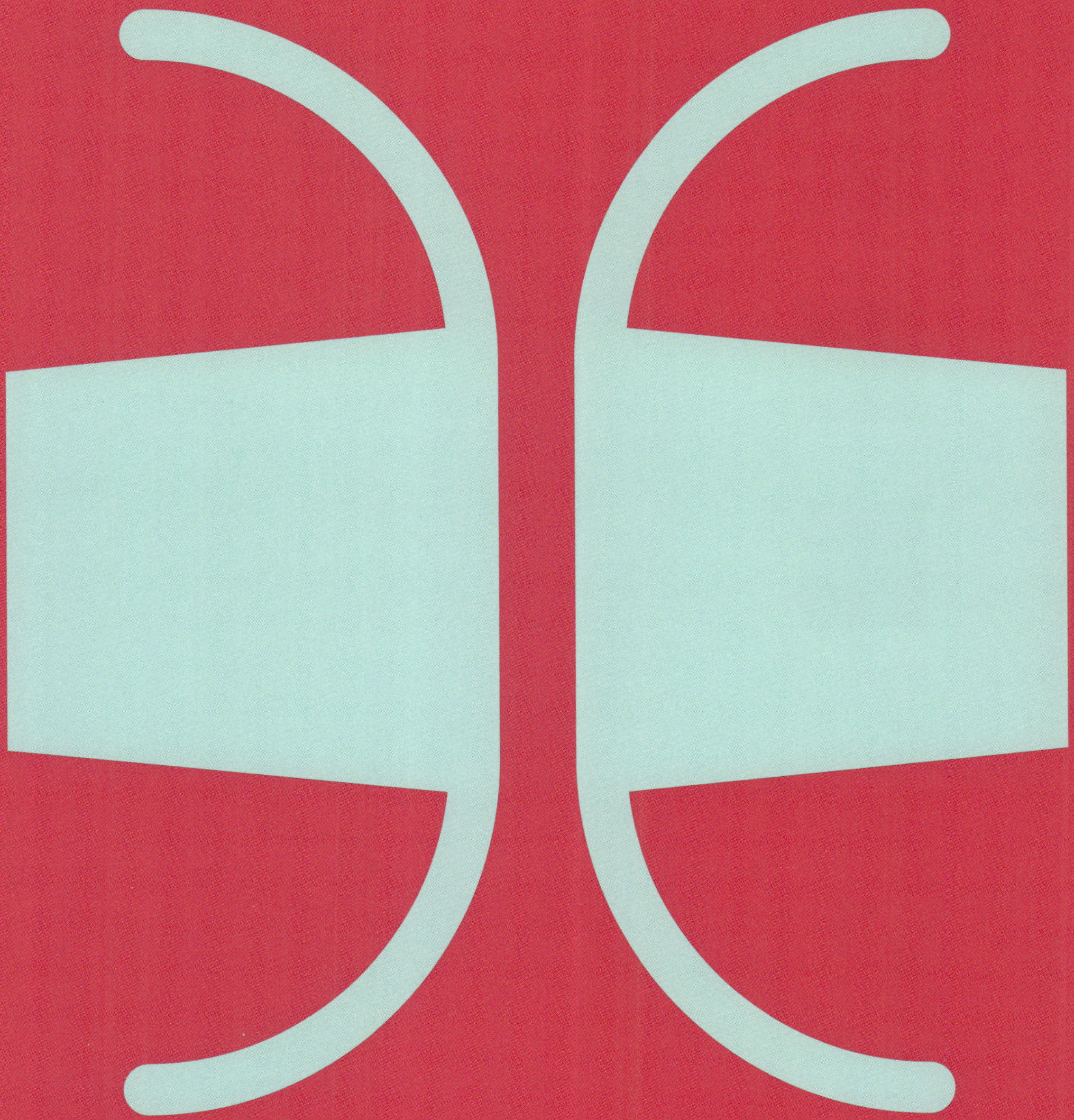

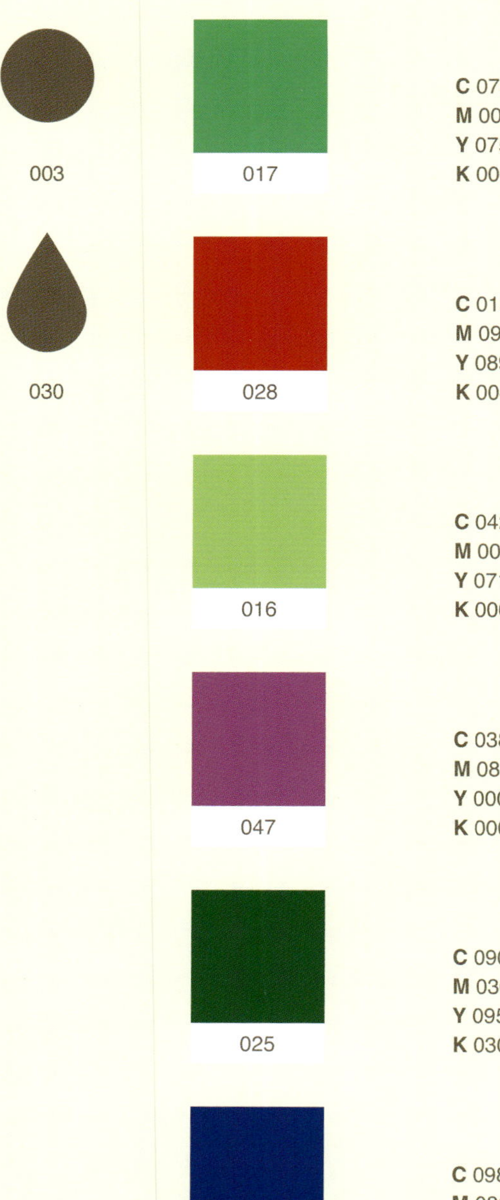

003

030

017

C 075
M 000
Y 075
K 000

028

C 015
M 096
Y 089
K 004

016

C 042
M 000
Y 071
K 000

047

C 038
M 081
Y 000
K 000

025

C 090
M 030
Y 095
K 030

023

C 098
M 086
Y 007
K 000

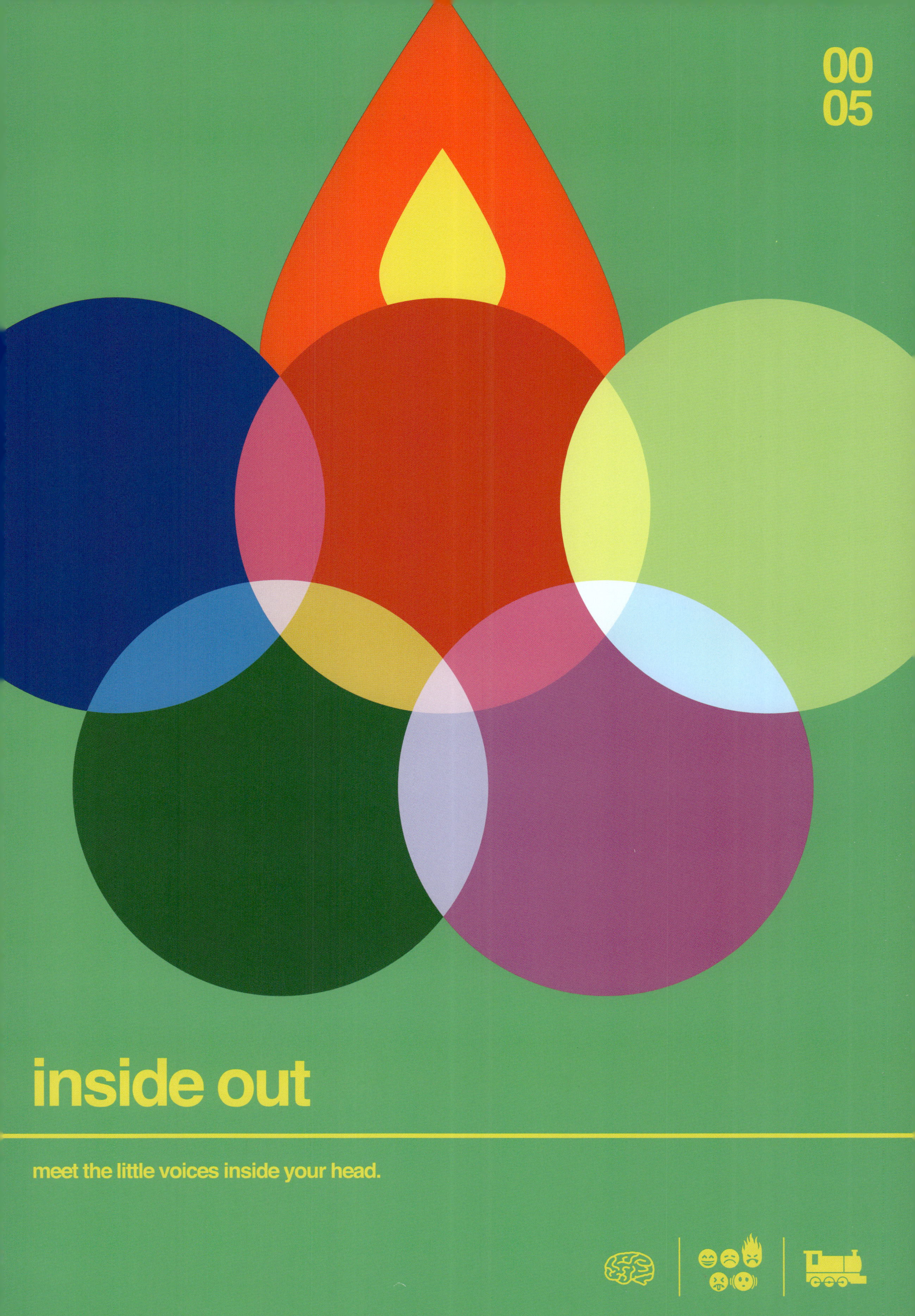

inside out

meet the little voices inside your head.

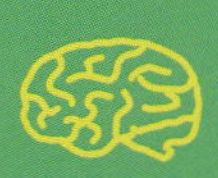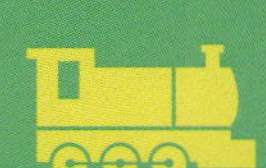

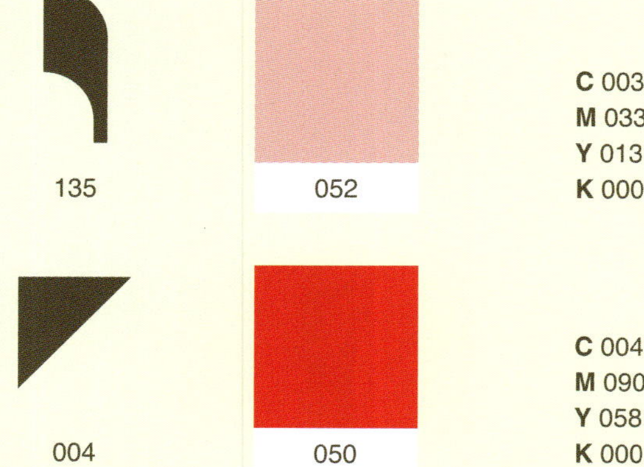

135 052

C 003
M 033
Y 013
K 000

004 050

C 004
M 090
Y 058
K 000

157

the elephant man

i am not an animal! i am a human being! i am a man!

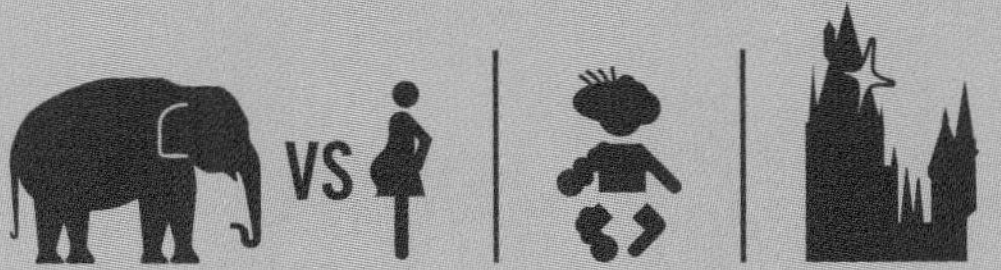

070

022

127

014

C 025
M 040
Y 065
K 000

C 036
M 001
Y 022
K 000

the shape of water

a fairy tale for troubled times.

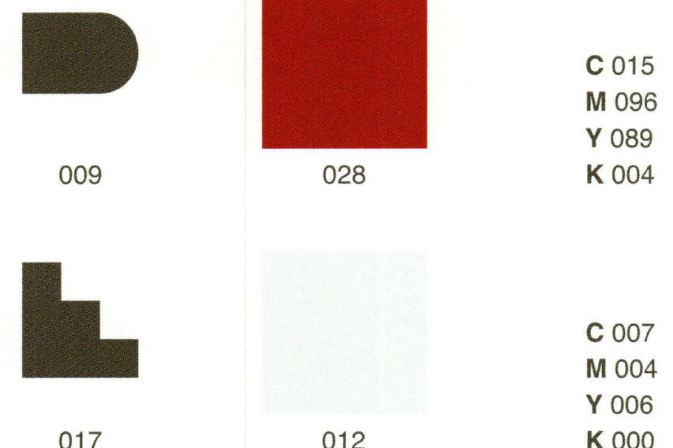

009

028

C 015
M 096
Y 089
K 004

017

012

C 007
M 004
Y 006
K 000

battleship potemkin

revolution is the only lawful, equal, effectual war. it was in russia that this war was declared and begun.

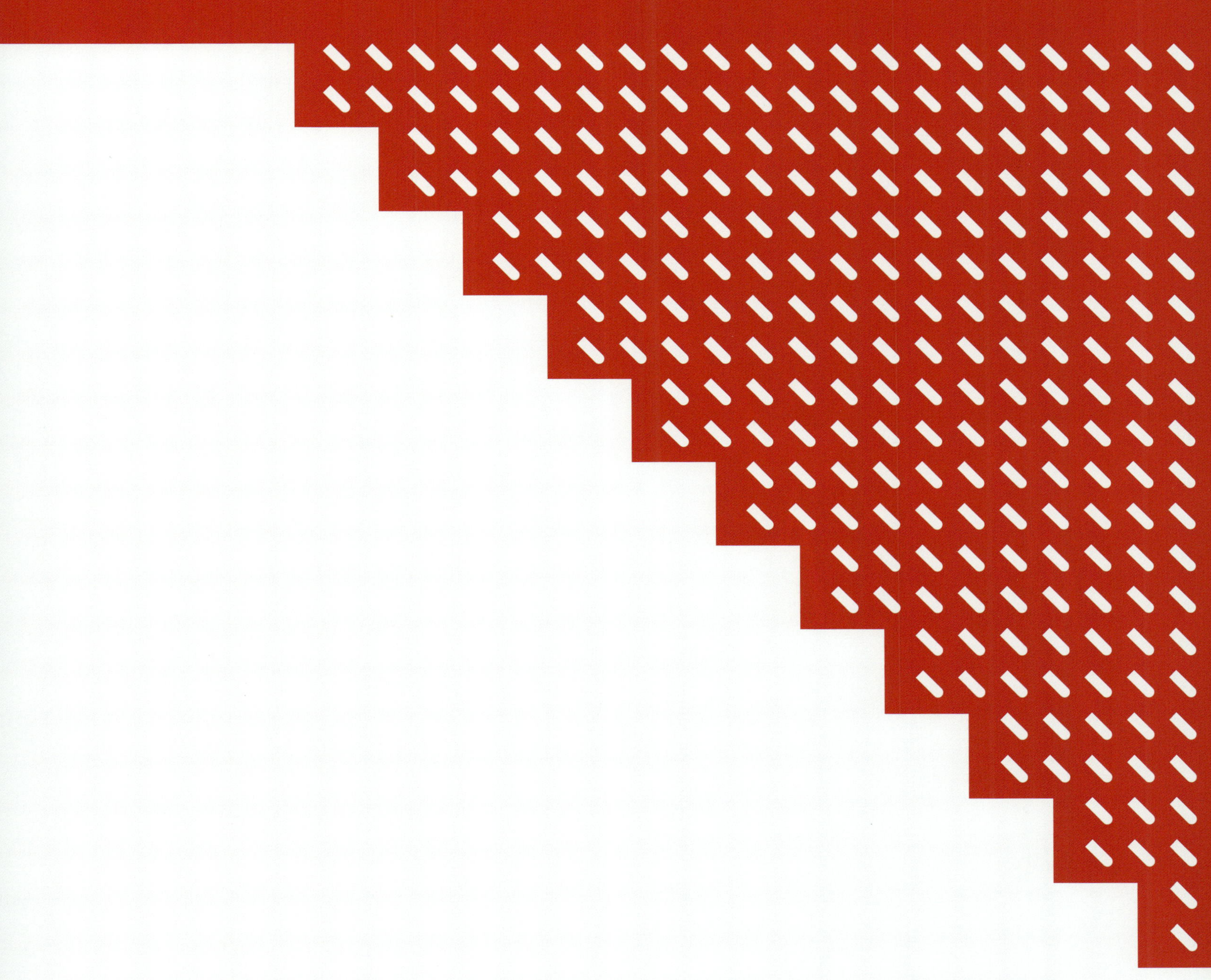

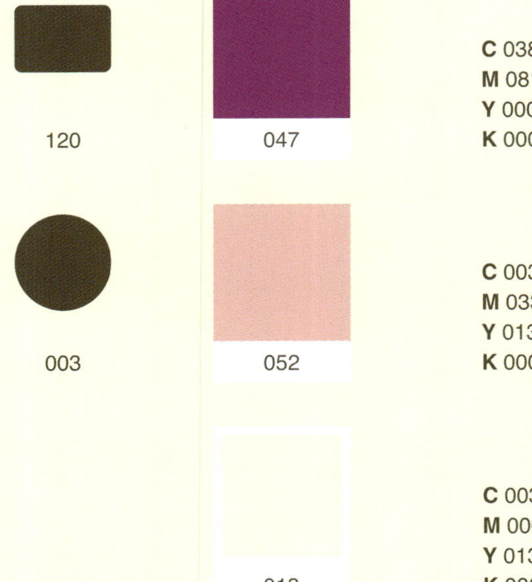

120

003

047

C 038
M 081
Y 000
K 000

052

C 003
M 033
Y 013
K 000

013

C 003
M 000
Y 013
K 000

inception

the dream is real.

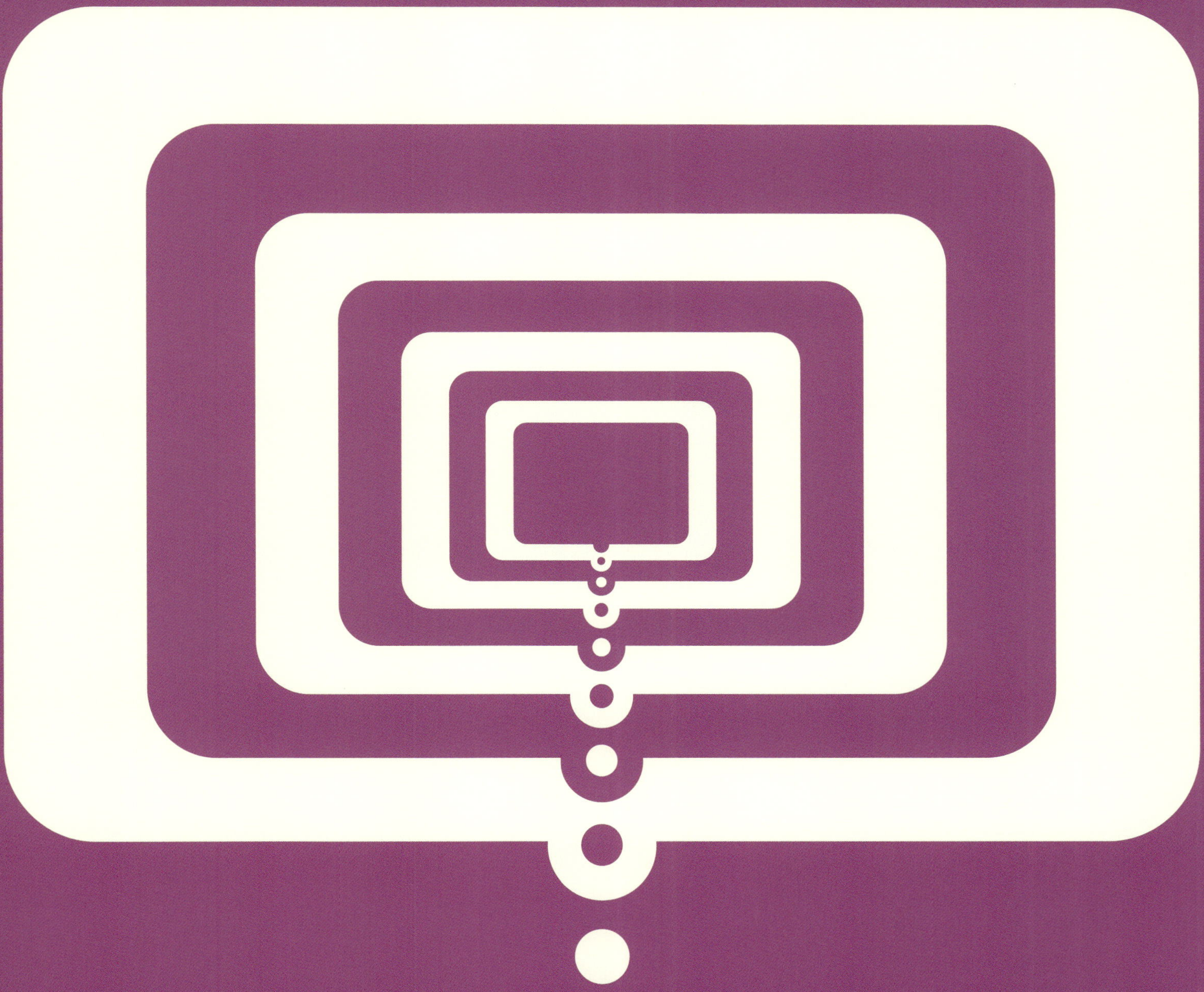

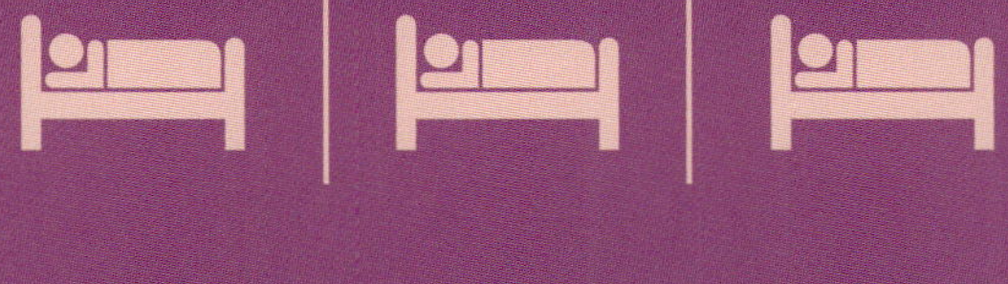

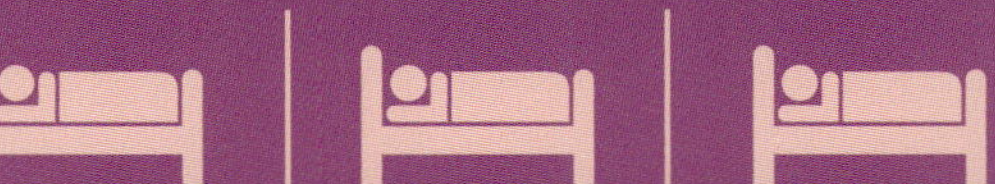

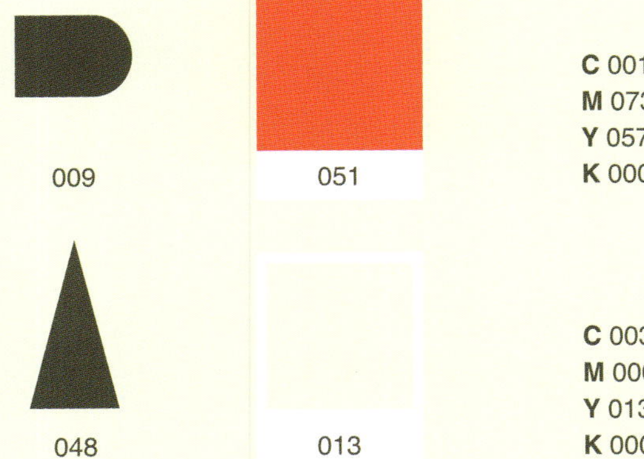

009

051

C 001
M 073
Y 057
K 000

048

013

C 003
M 000
Y 013
K 000

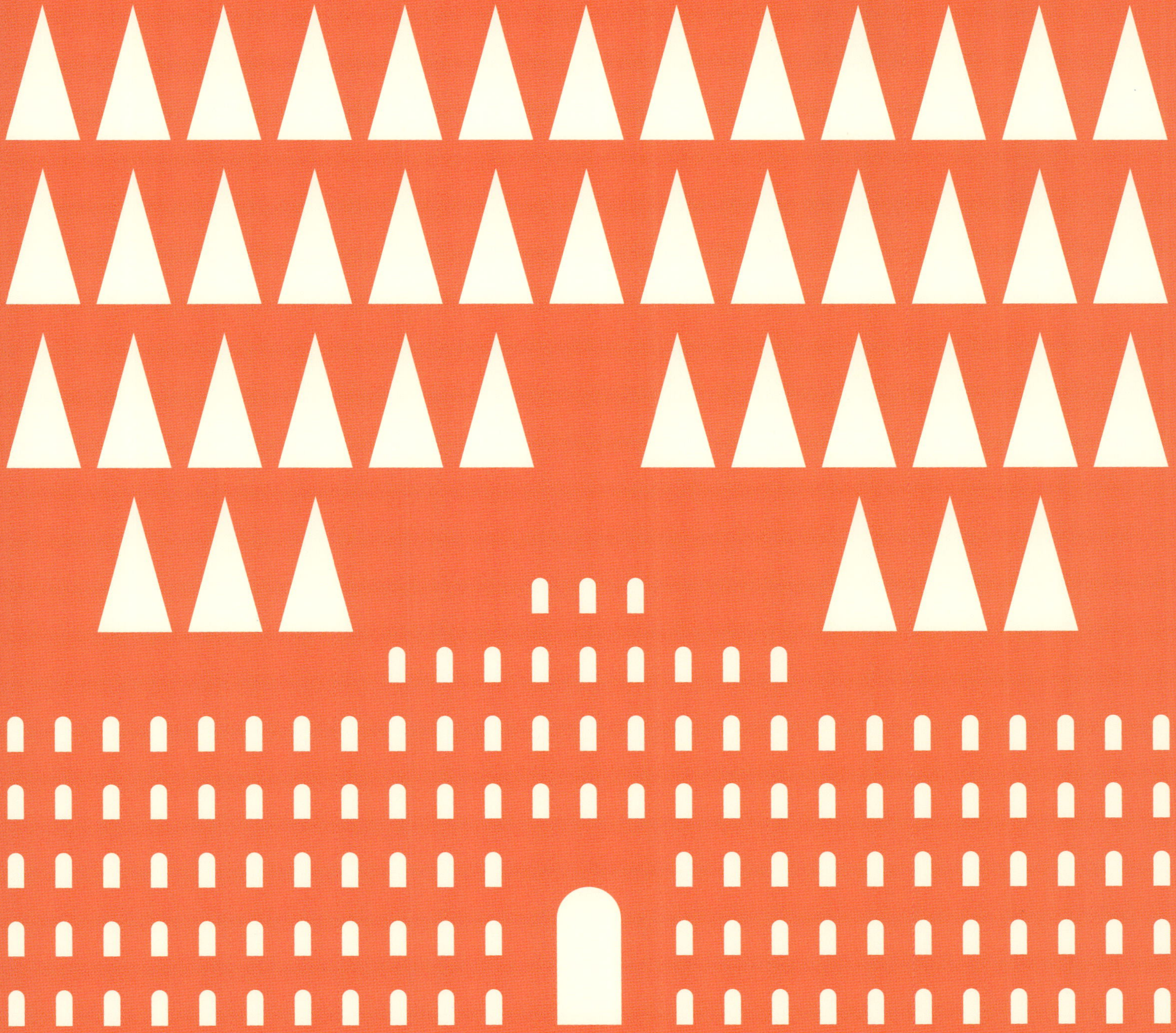

the grand budapest hotel

a murder case of madame d. with enormous wealth and the most outrageous events surrounding her sudden death.

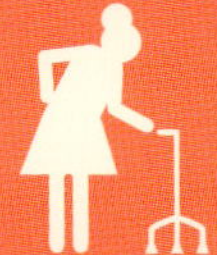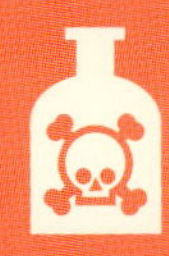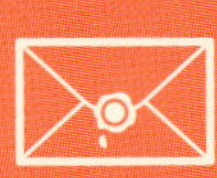

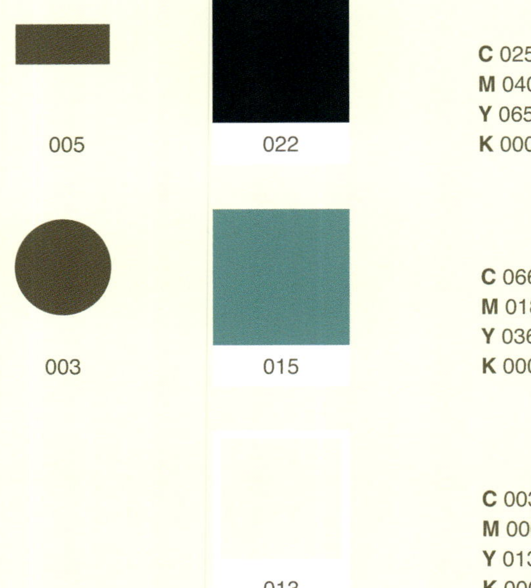

005

003

022

015

013

C 025
M 040
Y 065
K 000

C 066
M 018
Y 036
K 000

C 003
M 000
Y 013
K 000

cast away

at the edge of the world, his journey begins.

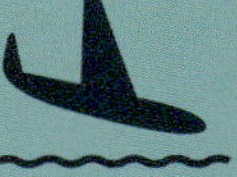 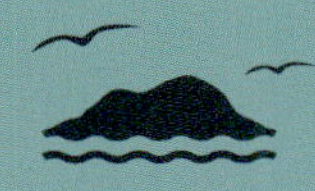 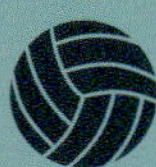

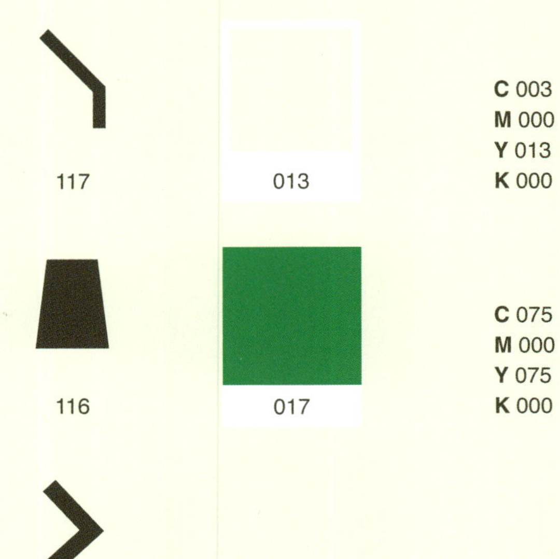

117

116

111

013

017

C 003
M 000
Y 013
K 000

C 075
M 000
Y 075
K 000

magnolia

things fall down. people look up. and when it rains, it pours.

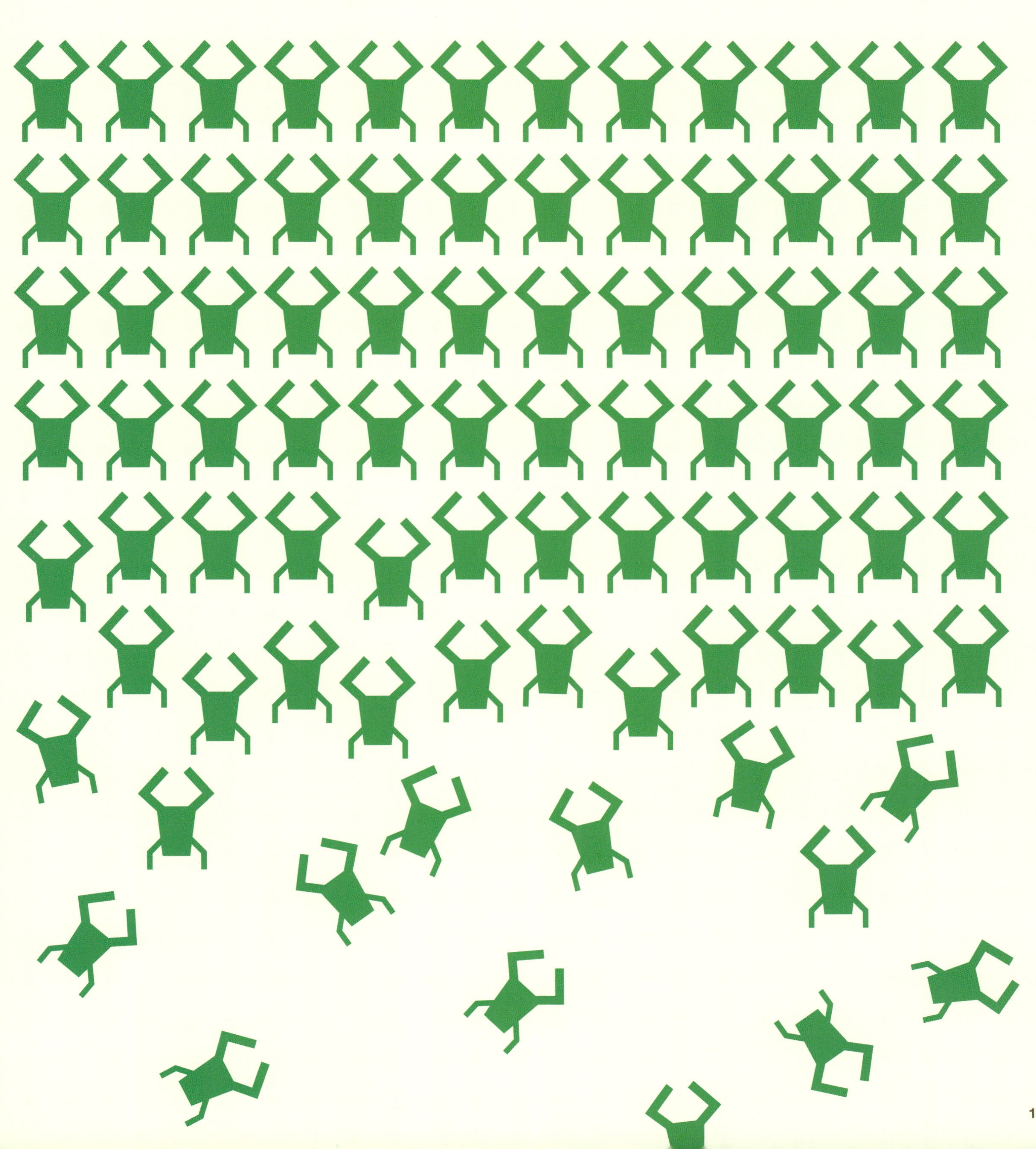

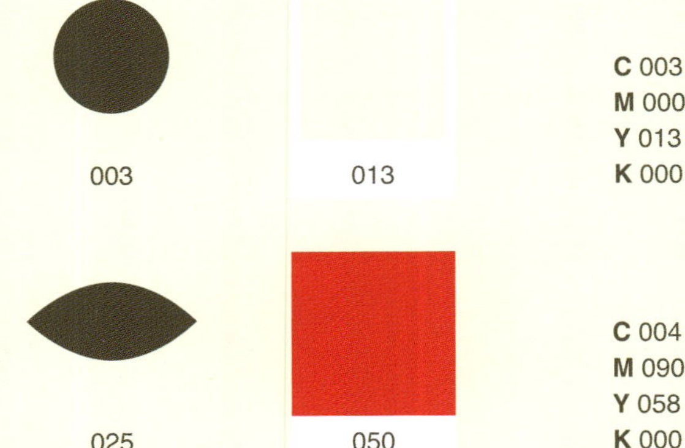

003   013   **C** 003
                          M 000
                          Y 013
                          K 000

025   050   **C** 004
                          M 090
                          Y 058
                          K 000

28 days later

the days are numbered.

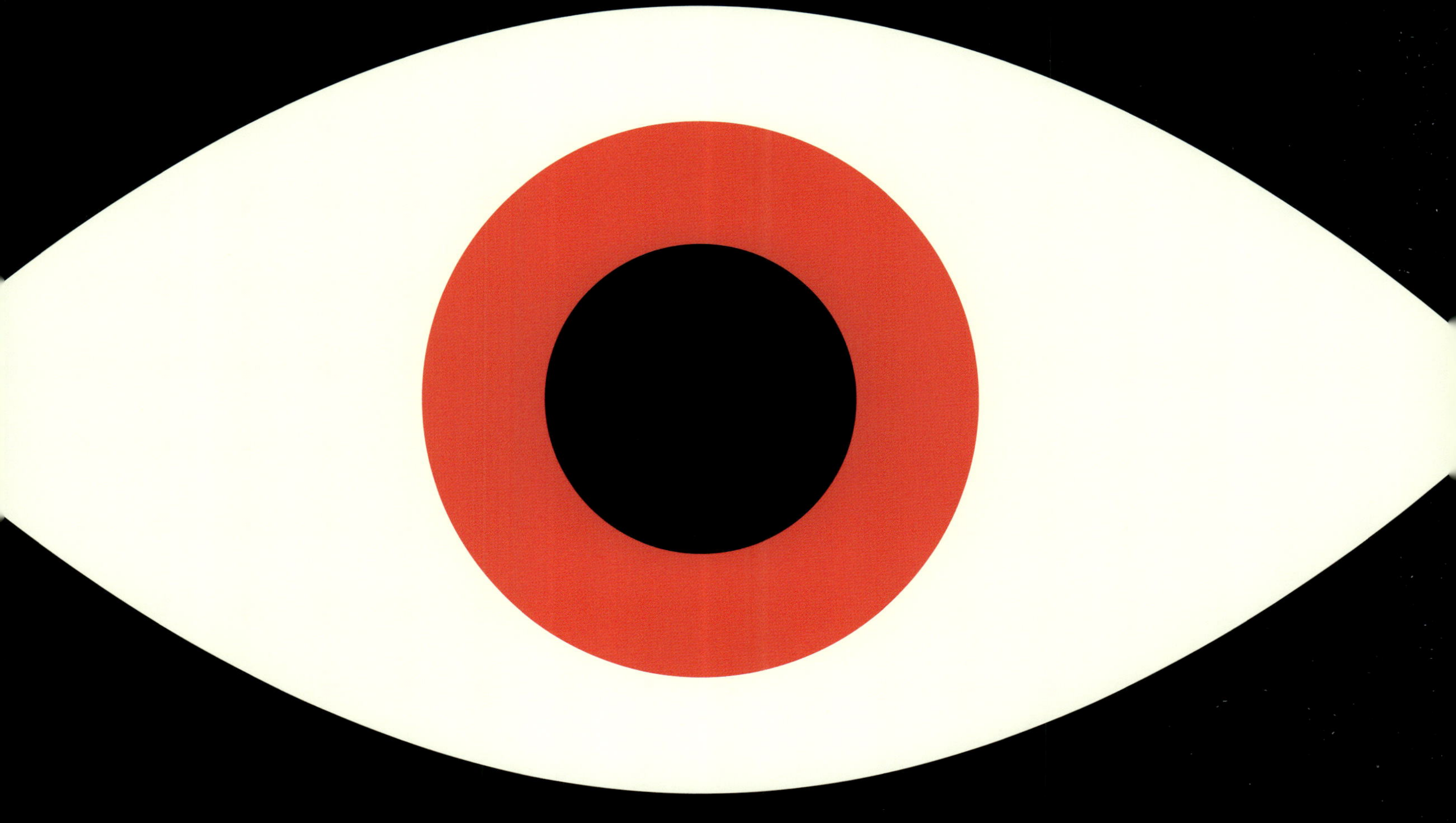

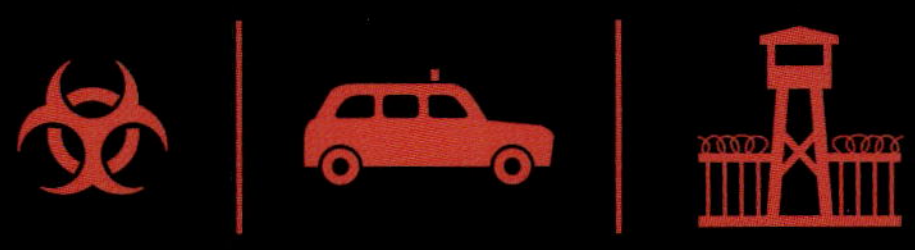

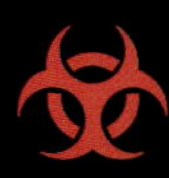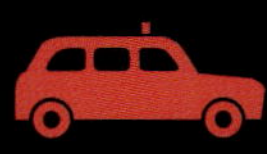

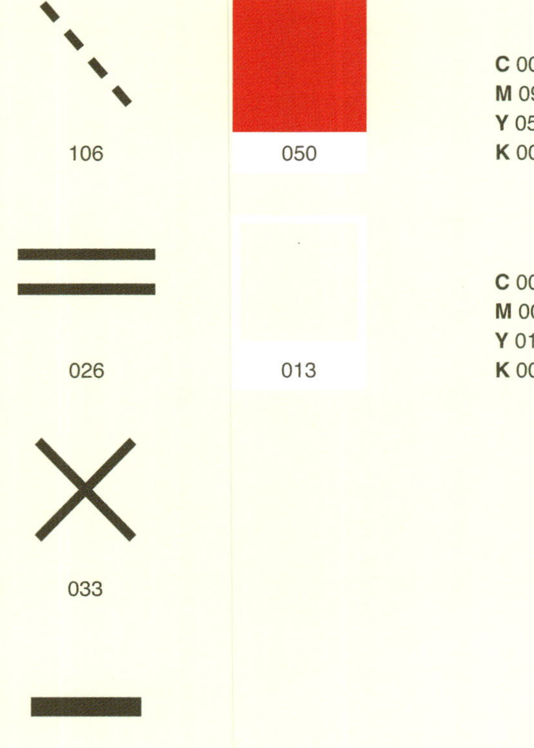

106

026

033

099

050

| C 004 |
| M 090 |
| Y 058 |
| K 000 |

013

| C 003 |
| M 000 |
| Y 013 |
| K 000 |

north by northwest

it's love and murder at first sight.

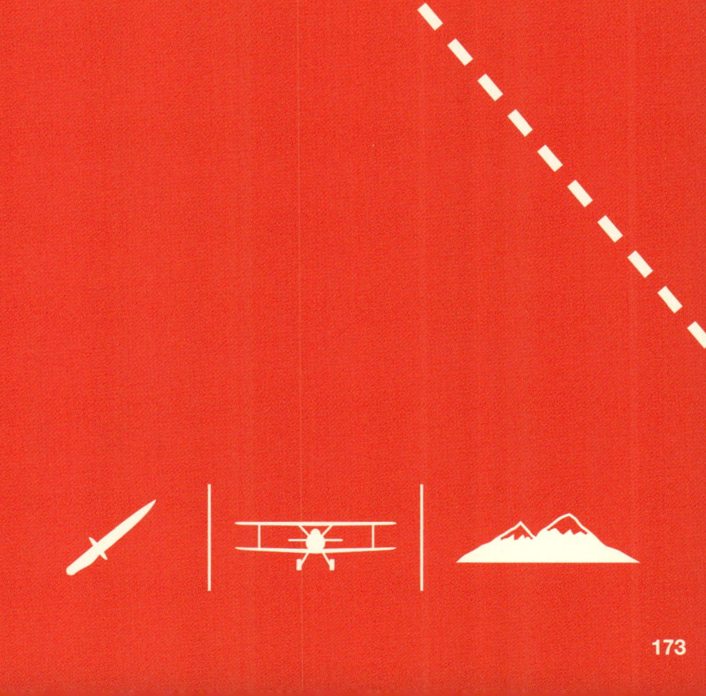

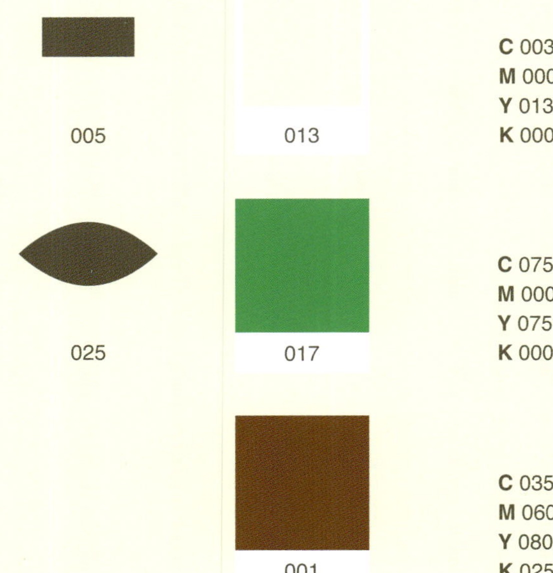

005

025

013

C 003
M 000
Y 013
K 000

017

C 075
M 000
Y 075
K 000

001

C 035
M 060
Y 080
K 025

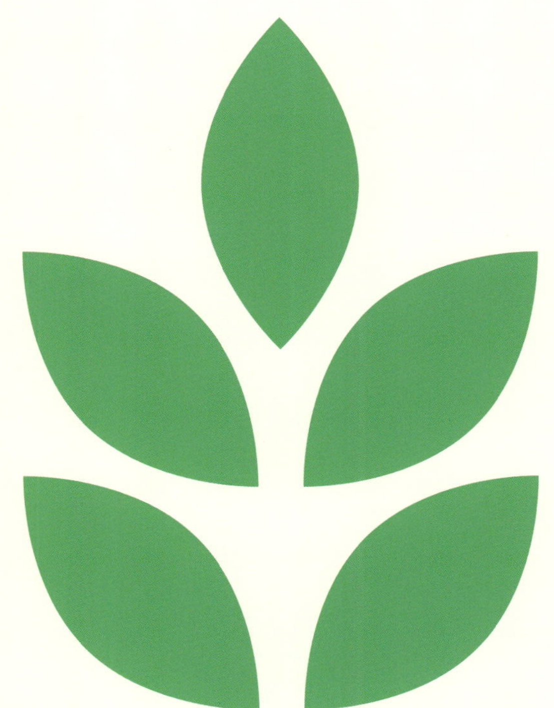

léon

if you want the job done right, hire a professional.

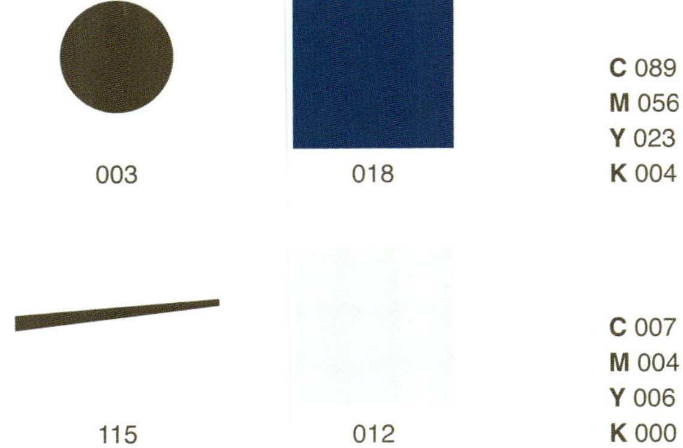

003   018   **C** 089
              M 056
              Y 023
              K 004

115   012   **C** 007
              M 004
              Y 006
              K 000

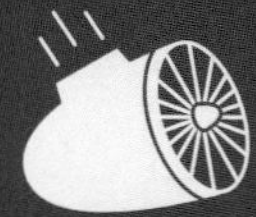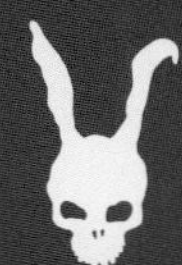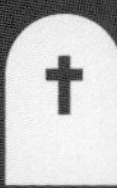

donnie darko

you can never go too far.

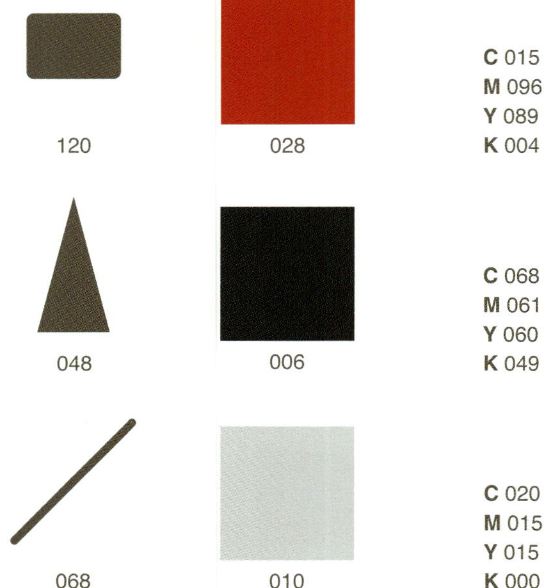

120 028

C 015
M 096
Y 089
K 004

048 006

C 068
M 061
Y 060
K 049

068 010

C 020
M 015
Y 015
K 000

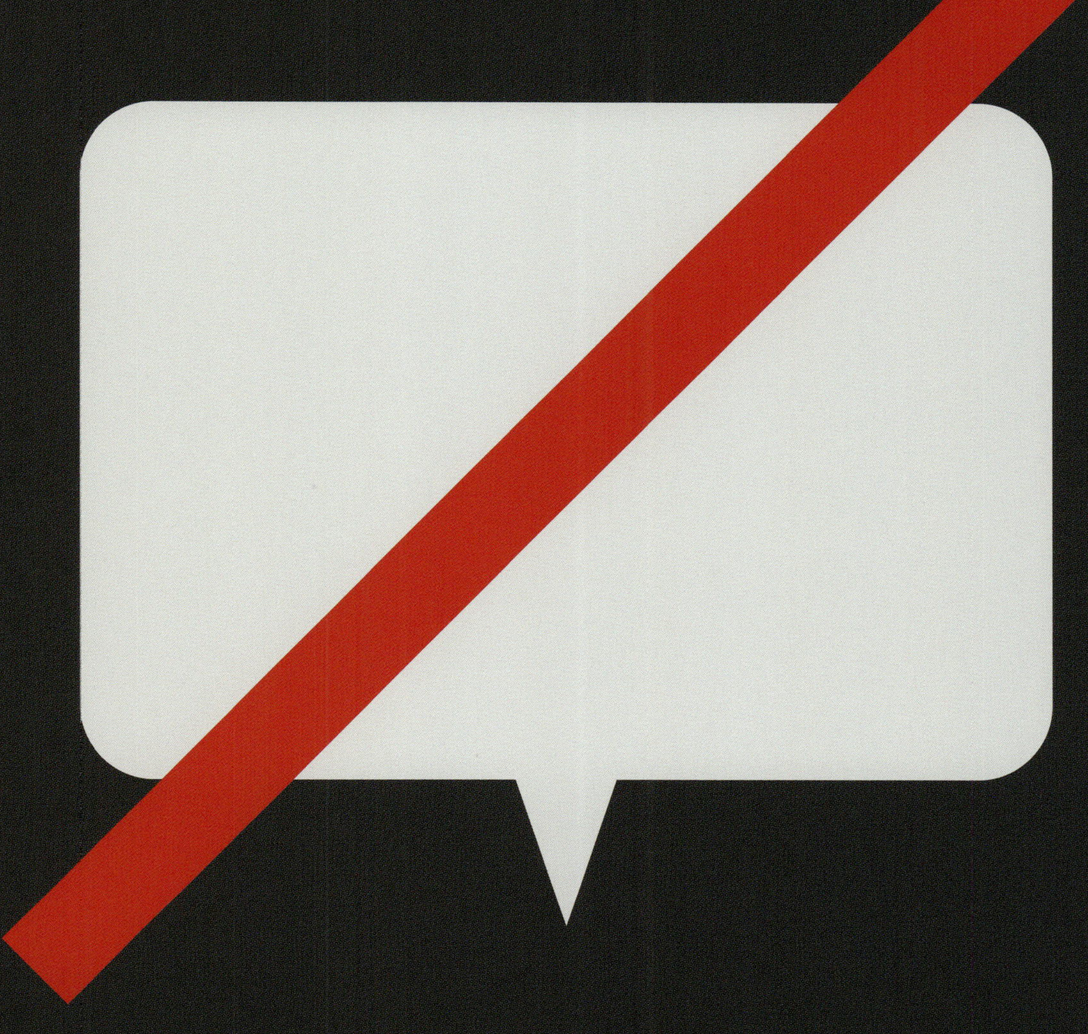

the artist

i won't talk! i won't say a word!

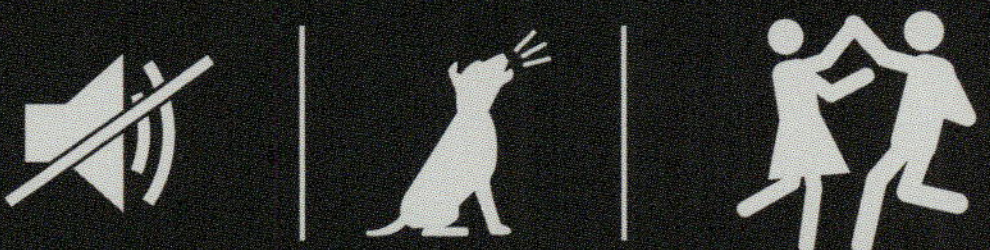

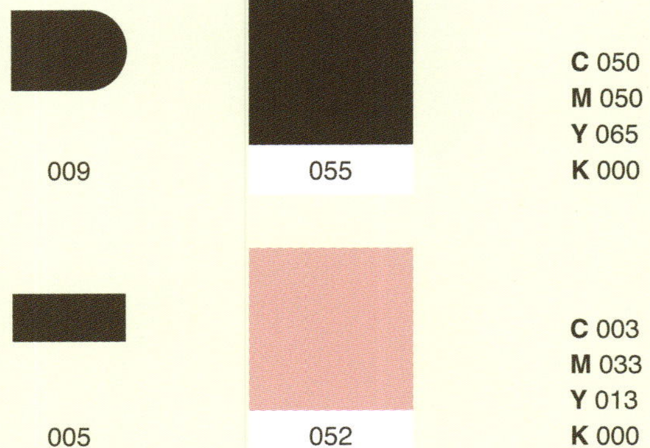

009 055

C 050
M 050
Y 065
K 000

005 052

C 003
M 033
Y 013
K 000

the big lebowski

her life was in their hands. now her toe is in the mail.

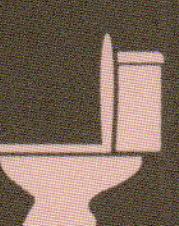
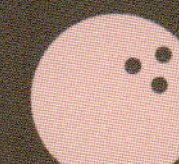
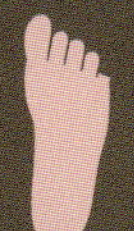

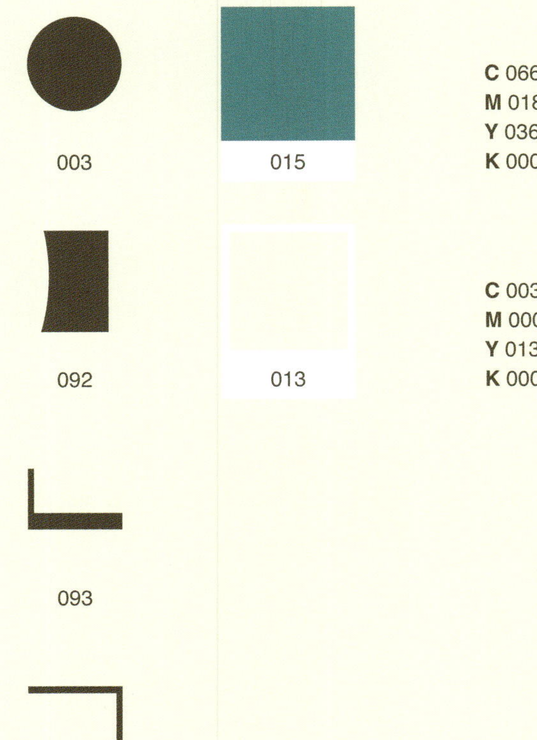

003

092

093

094

015

013

C 066
M 018
Y 036
K 000

C 003
M 000
Y 013
K 000

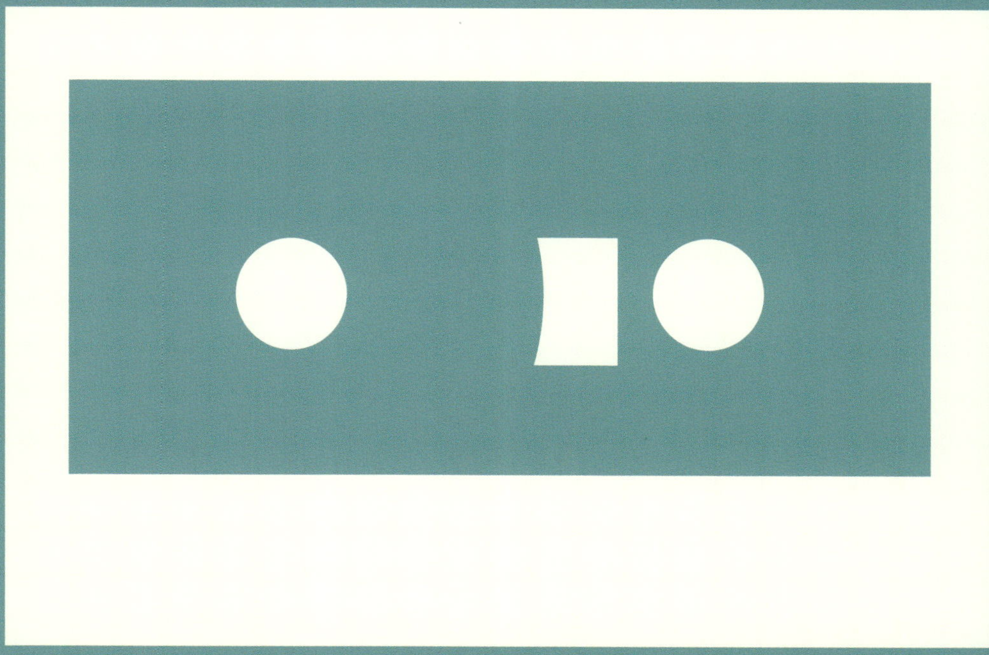

eternal sunshine
of the spotless mind

you can erase someone from your mind. getting them out of your heart is another story.

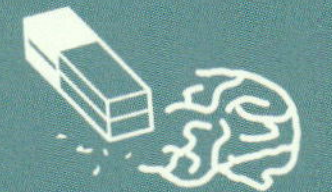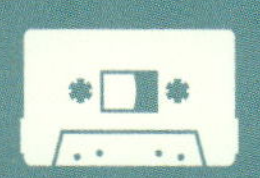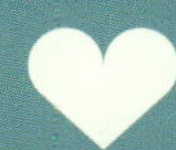

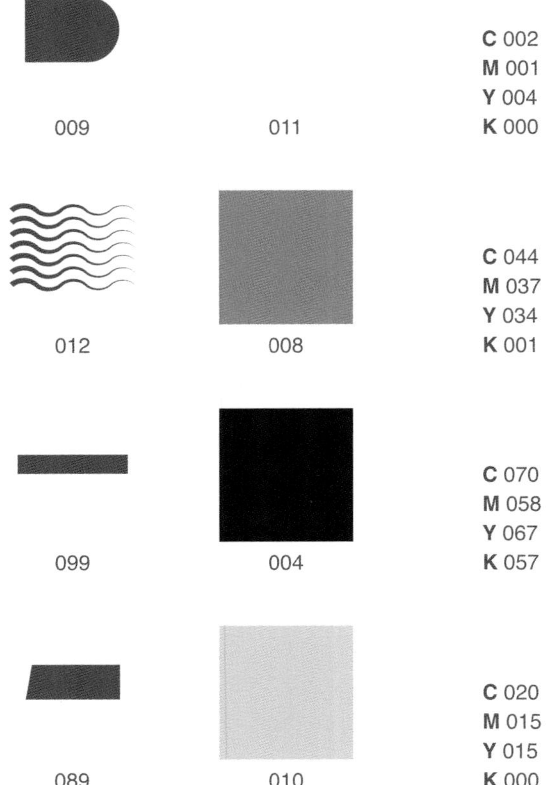

009	011	**C** 002 **M** 001 **Y** 004 **K** 000
012	008	**C** 044 **M** 037 **Y** 034 **K** 001
099	004	**C** 070 **M** 058 **Y** 067 **K** 057
089	010	**C** 020 **M** 015 **Y** 015 **K** 000

murder
on the
orient
express

12
12

everyone is a suspect.

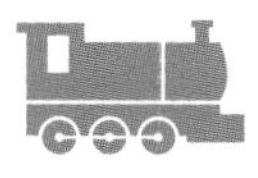

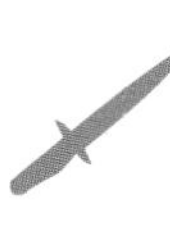

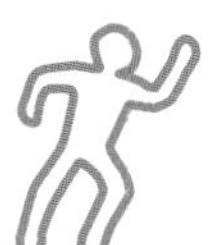

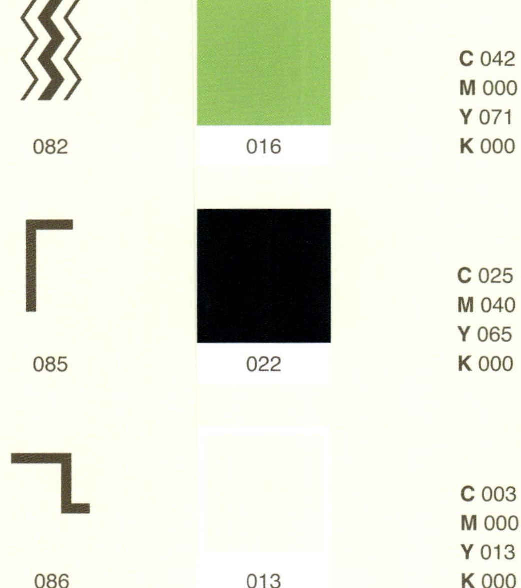

082 016

C 042
M 000
Y 071
K 000

085 022

C 025
M 040
Y 065
K 000

086 013

C 003
M 000
Y 013
K 000

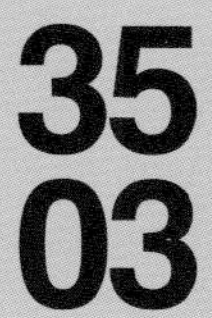

the green mile

paul edgecomb didn't believe in miracles. until the day he met one.

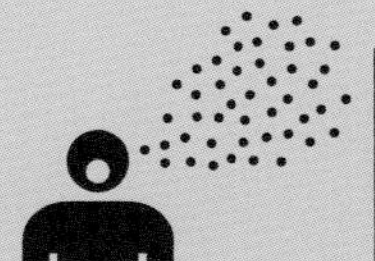 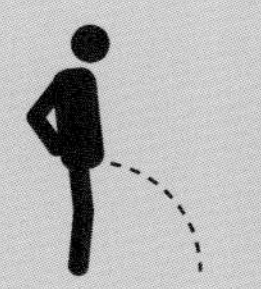 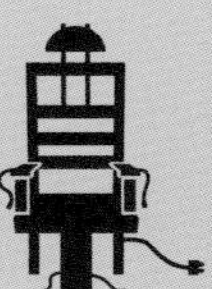

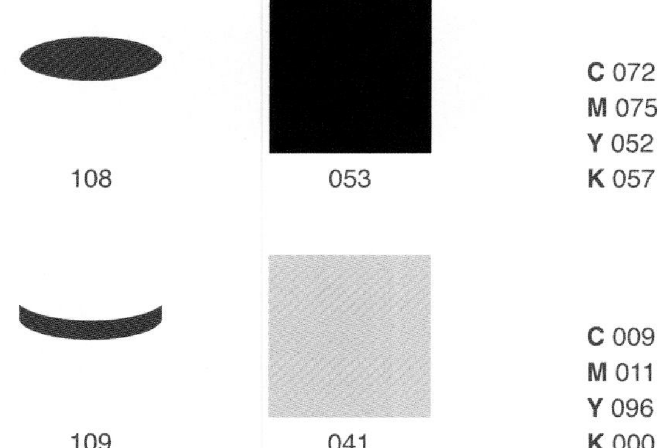

108 053

C 072
M 075
Y 052
K 057

109 041

C 009
M 011
Y 096
K 000

slumdog millionaire

what does it take to find a lost love?

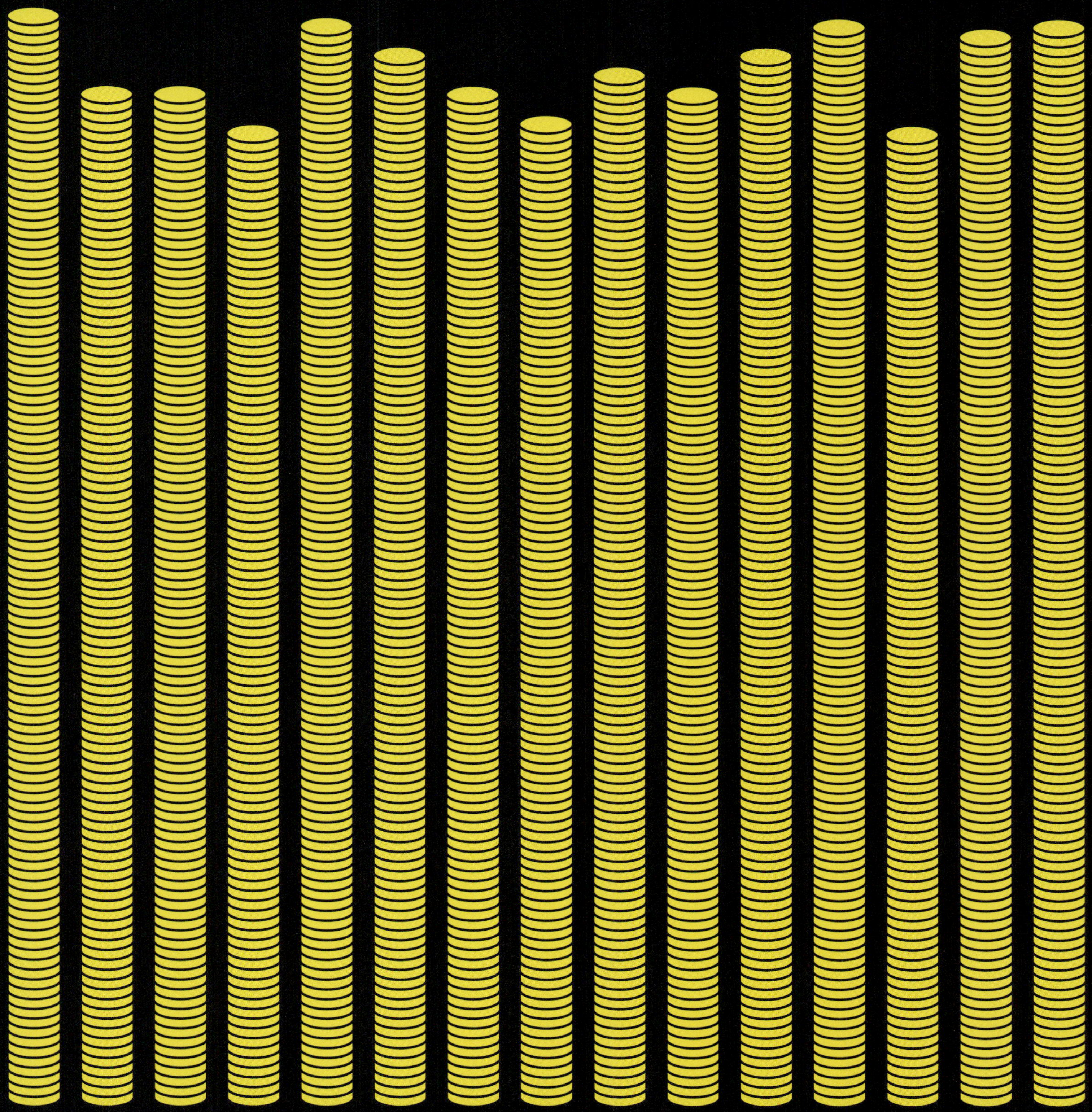

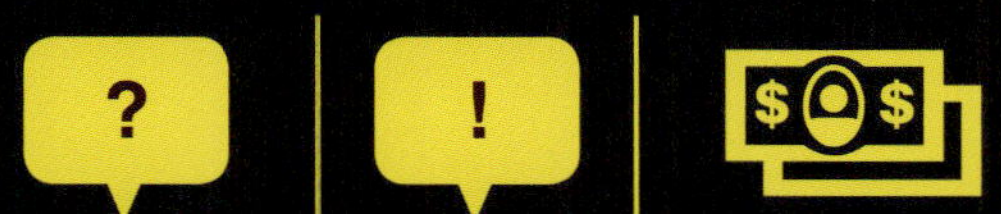

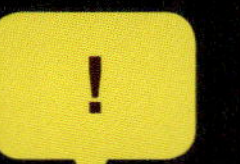
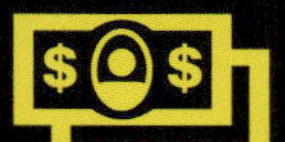

005

013

C 003
M 000
Y 013
K 000

045

C 031
M 030
Y 005
K 000

vanilla sky

lovehatedreamslifeworkplayfriendshipsex.

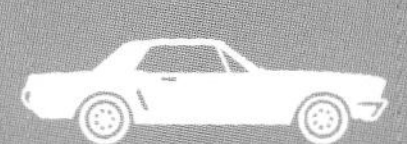 |  | 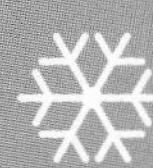

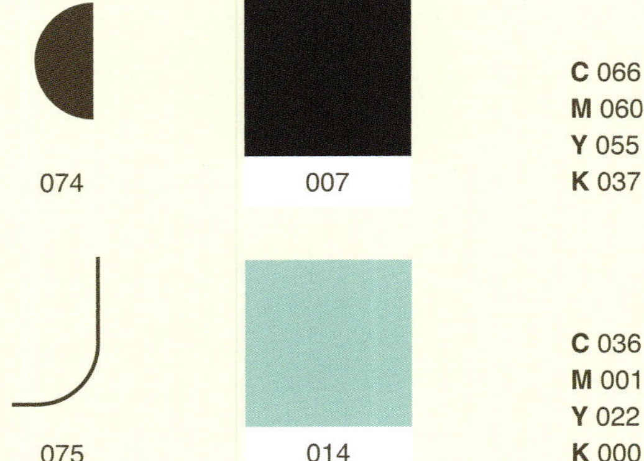

074

007

C 066
M 060
Y 055
K 037

075

014

C 036
M 001
Y 022
K 000

the lives of others / / /
nothing is private. nothing is sacred.

das leben der anderen

in einem system der macht ist nichts privat.

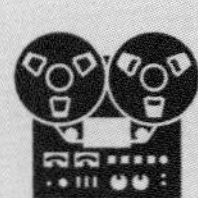  

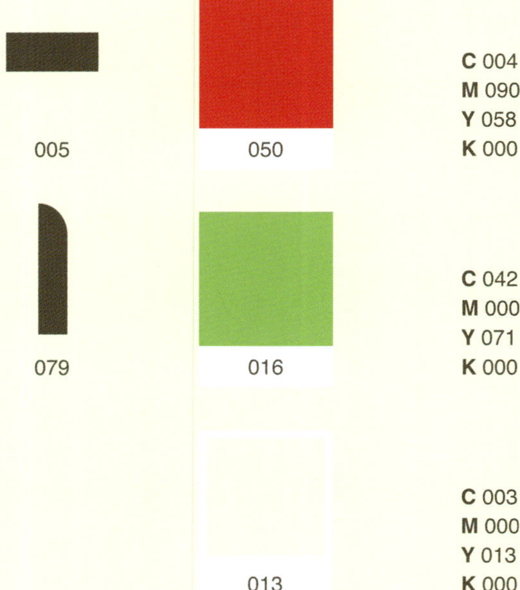

005

079

050

016

013

C 004
M 090
Y 058
K 000

C 042
M 000
Y 071
K 000

C 003
M 000
Y 013
K 000

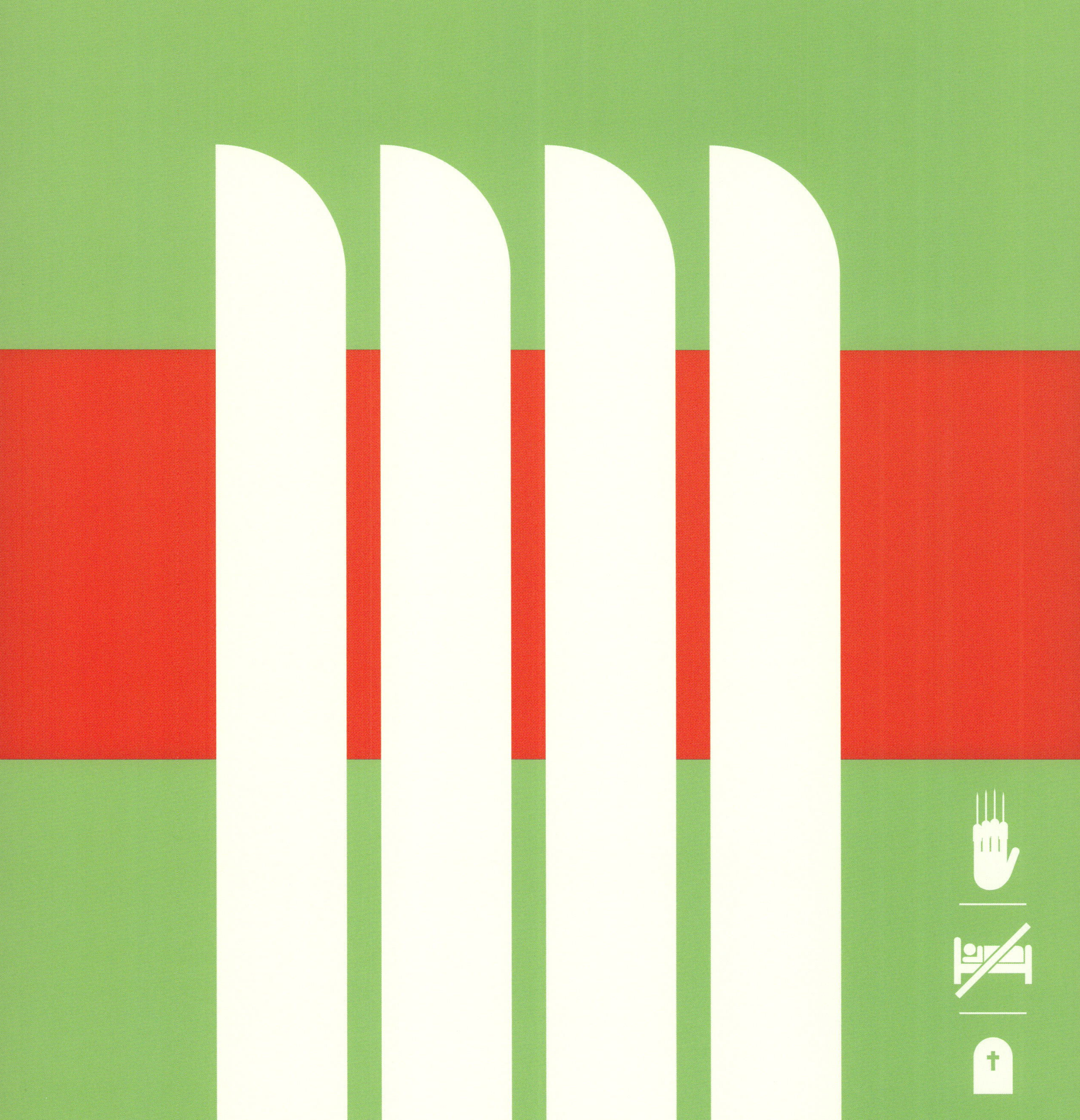

05
33
a nightmare on elm street
if nancy doesn't wake up screaming, she won't wake up at all.
195

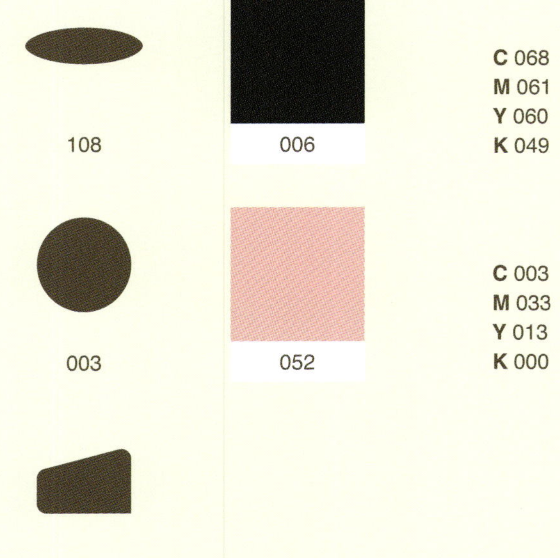

108

003

055

006

C 068
M 061
Y 060
K 049

052

C 003
M 033
Y 013
K 000

jurassic park

an adventure 65 million years in the making.

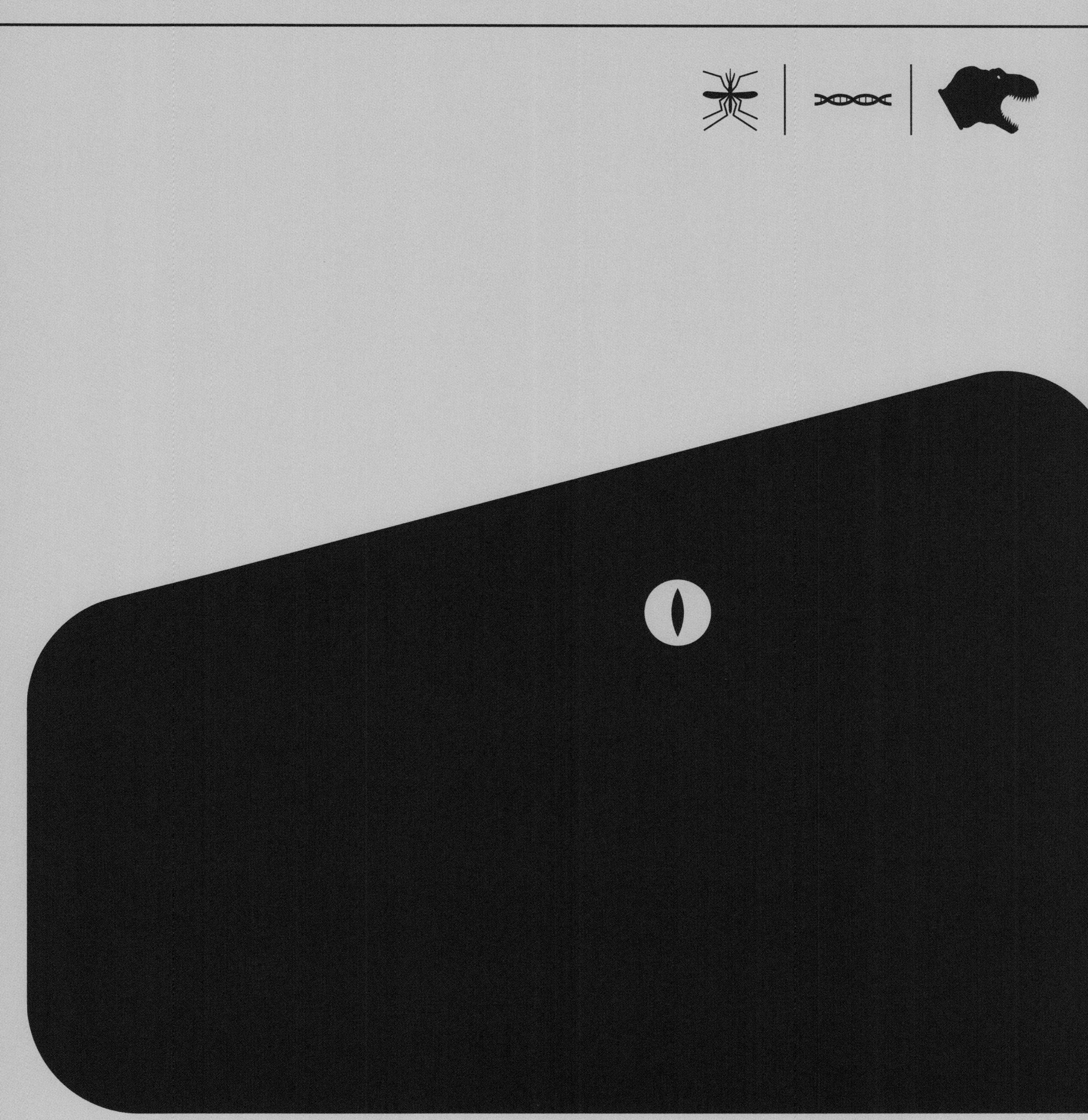

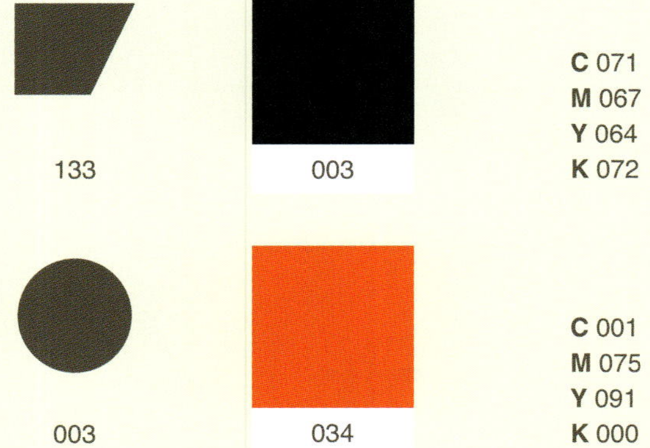

133
003
003
034
C 071
M 067
Y 064
K 072
C 001
M 075
Y 091
K 000

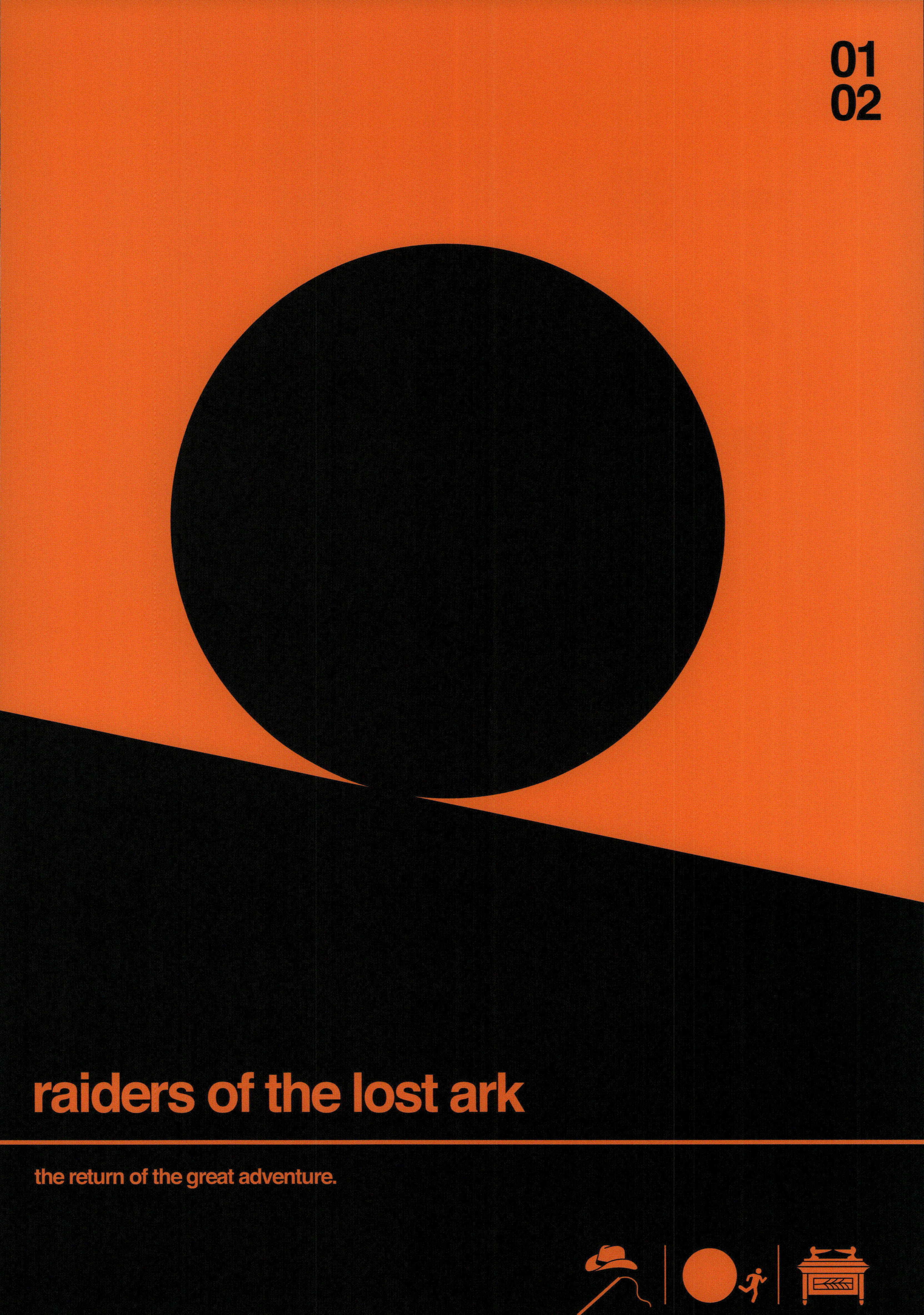

raiders of the lost ark

the return of the great adventure.

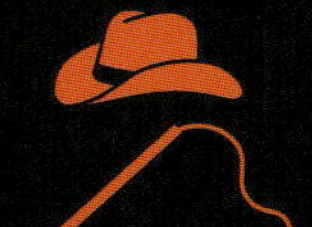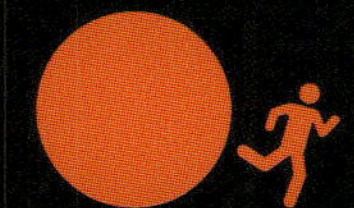

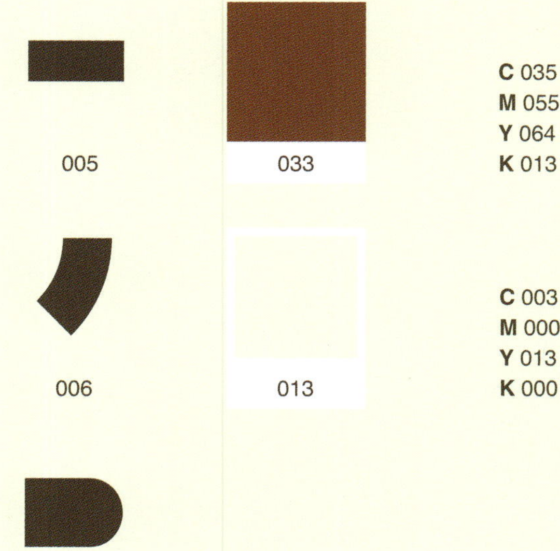

005

006

009

033

013

C 035
M 055
Y 064
K 013

C 003
M 000
Y 013
K 000

dances with wolves

inside everyone is a frontier waiting to be discovered.

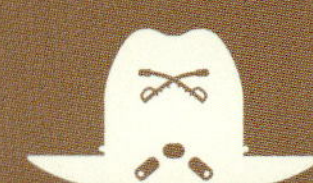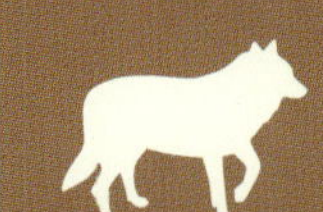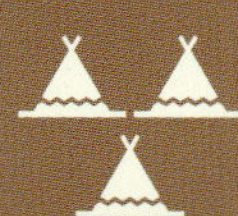

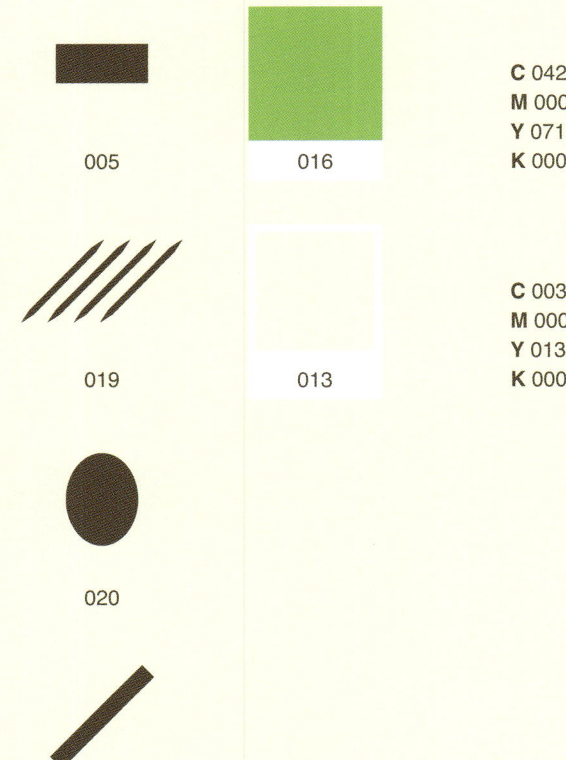

005

016

C 042
M 000
Y 071
K 000

019

013

C 003
M 000
Y 013
K 000

020

023

narcos

there's no business like blow business.

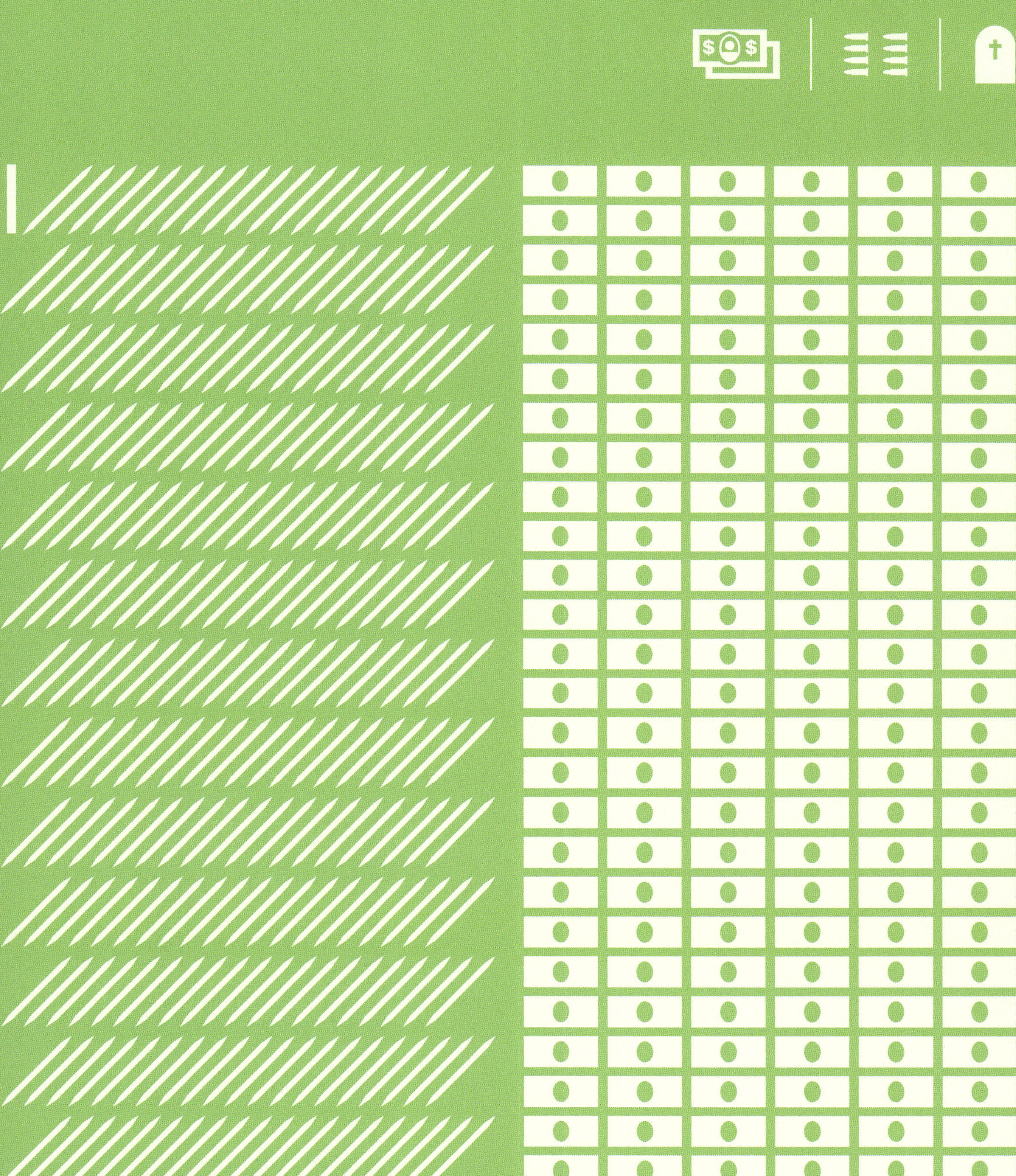

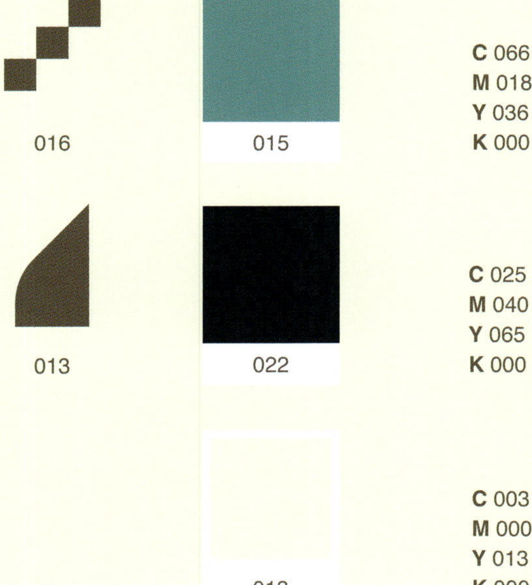

016

015

C 066
M 018
Y 036
K 000

013

022

C 025
M 040
Y 065
K 000

013

C 003
M 000
Y 013
K 000

the legend of 1900

an epic story of a man who could do anything... except be ordinary.

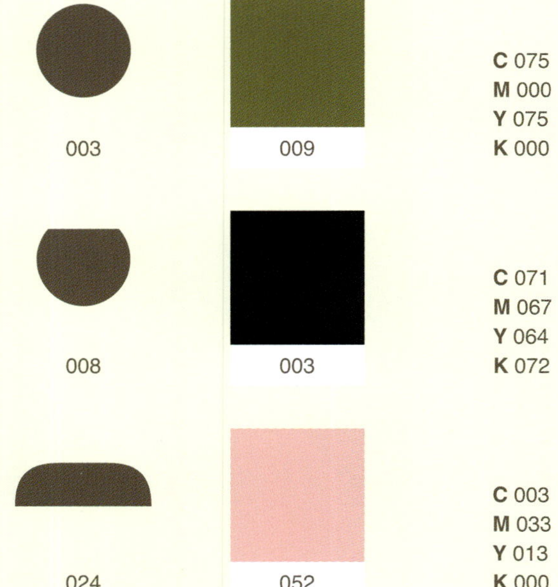

003

009

C 075
M 000
Y 075
K 000

008

003

C 071
M 067
Y 064
K 072

024

052

C 003
M 033
Y 013
K 000

hannibal

break the silence.

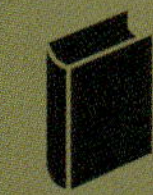

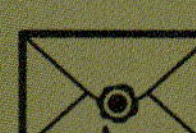

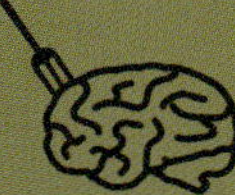

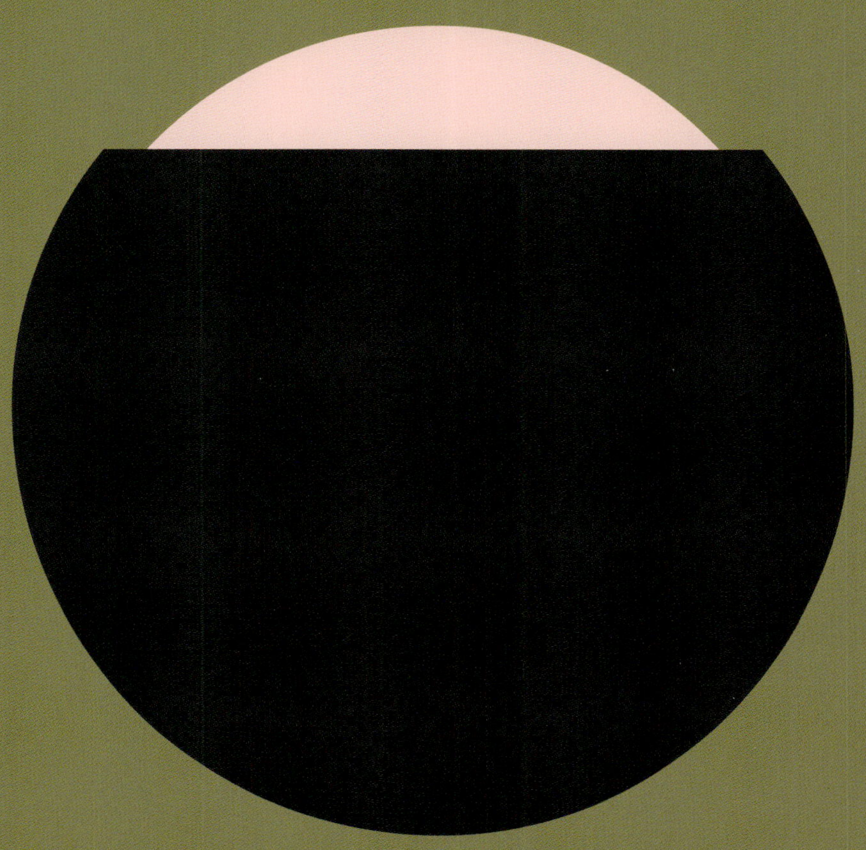

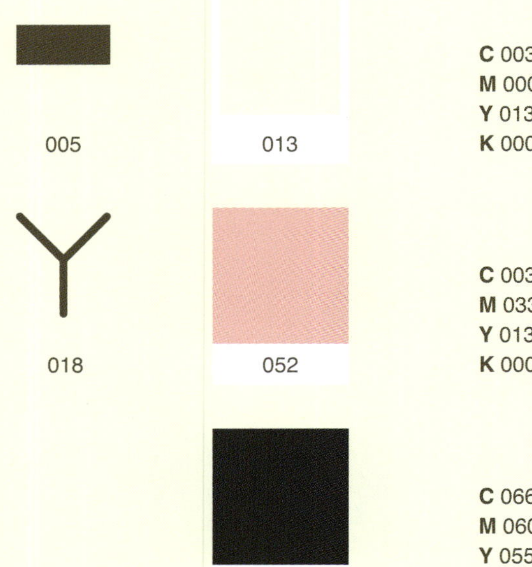

005

018

013

C 003
M 000
Y 013
K 000

052

C 003
M 033
Y 013
K 000

007

C 066
M 060
Y 055
K 037

basic instinct

a brutal murder, a brilliant killer, a cop who can't resist the danger.

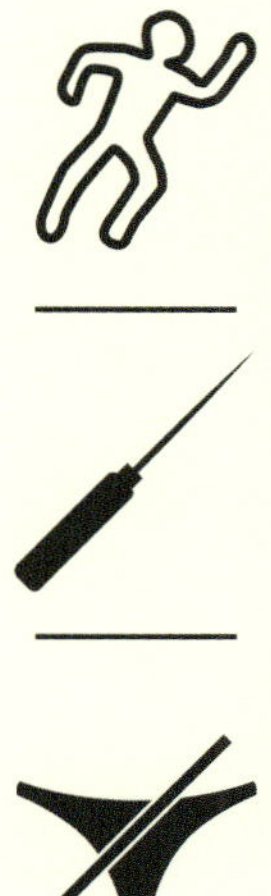

005

055

C 050
M 050
Y 065
K 000

013

C 003
M 000
Y 013
K 000

the curious case of
benjamin button

time is passing, even backwards.

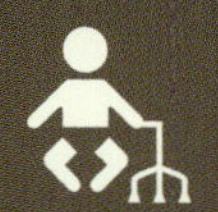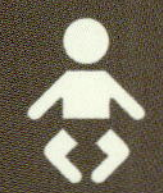

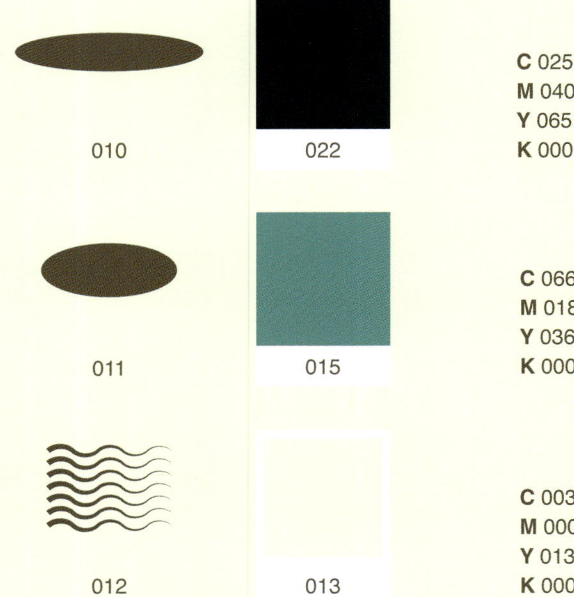

010

011

012

022

015

013

C 025
M 040
Y 065
K 000

C 066
M 018
Y 036
K 000

C 003
M 000
Y 013
K 000

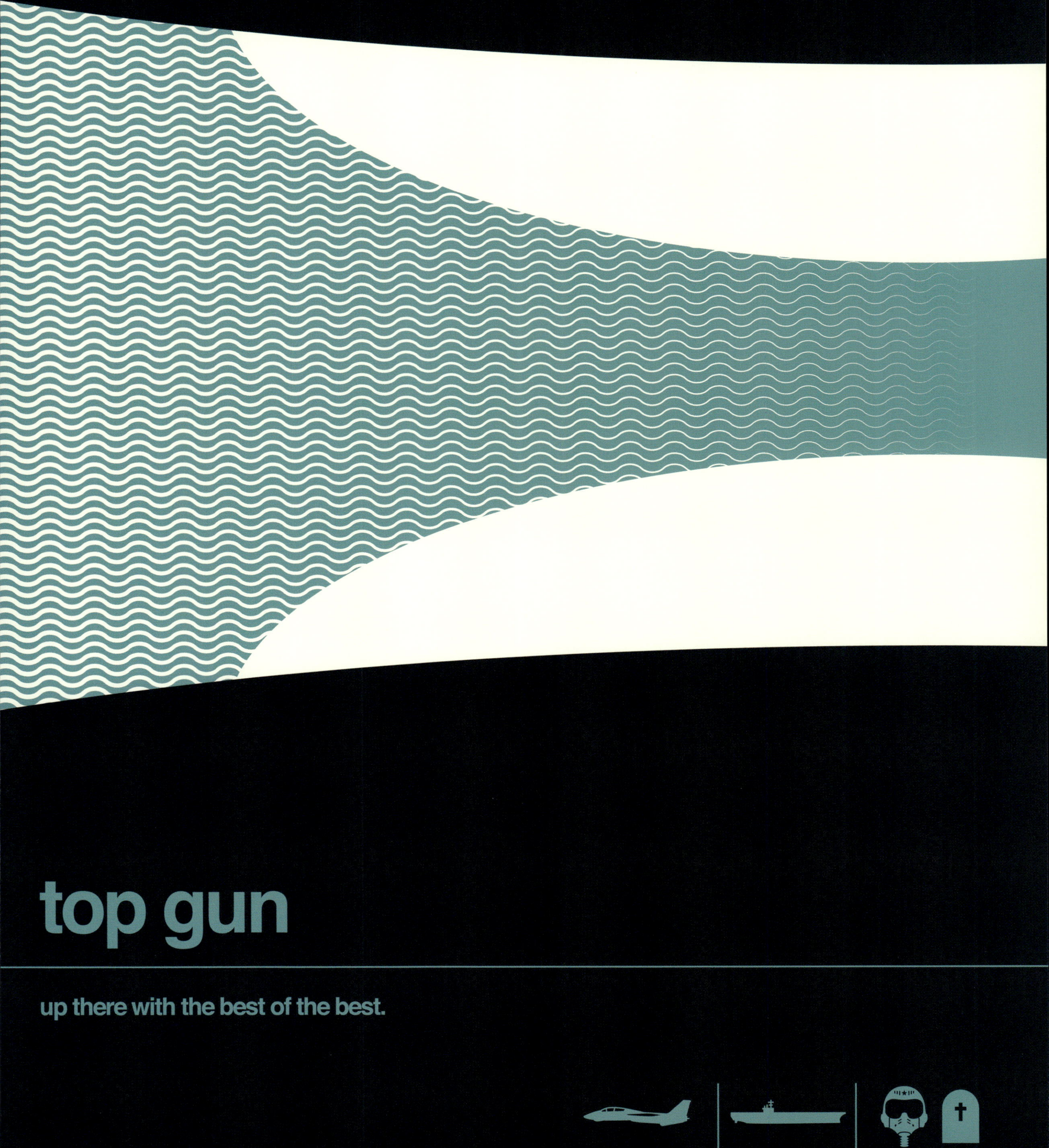

top gun

up there with the best of the best.

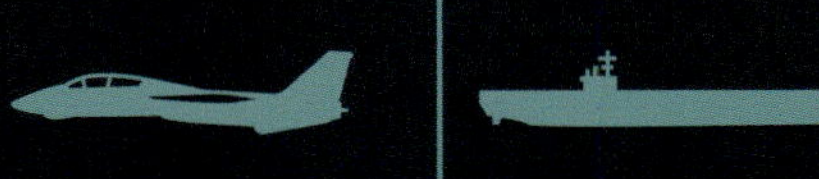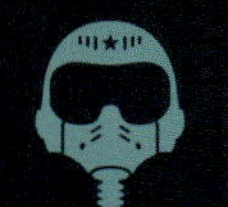

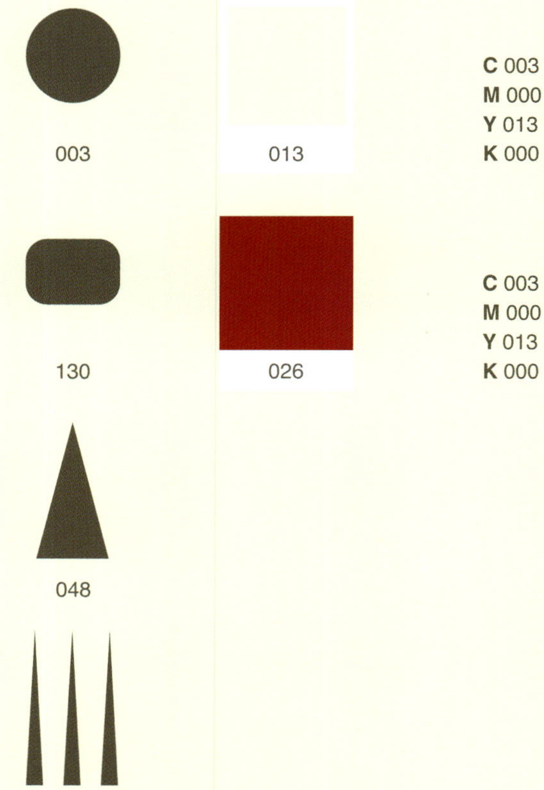

003

130

048

047

013

026

C 003
M 000
Y 013
K 000

C 003
M 000
Y 013
K 000

amores perros / / /

love. betrayal. death.

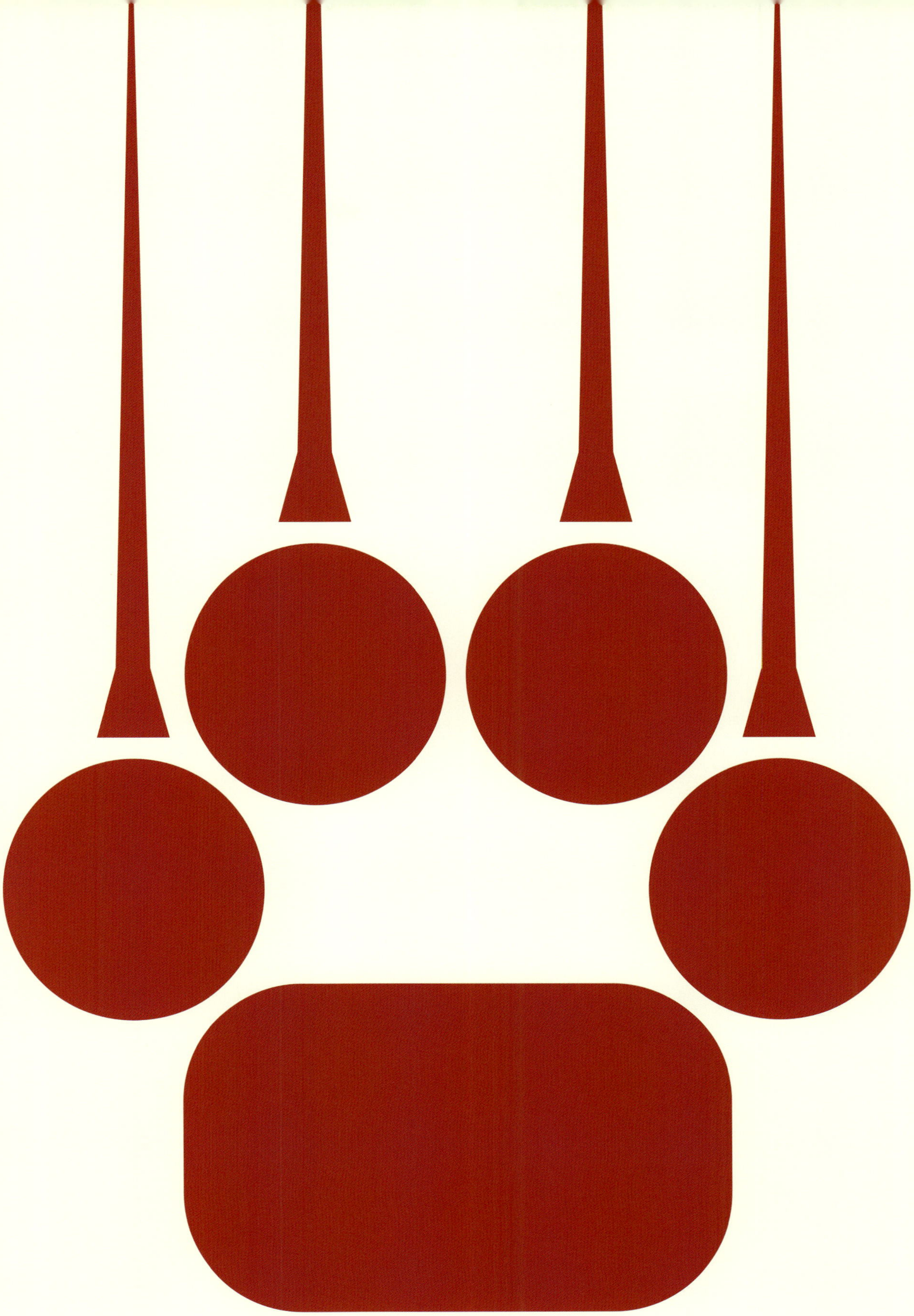

amores perros

traición. angustia. pecado, egoísmo. esperanza. dolor. muerte.
¿qué es el amor?

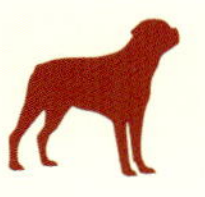 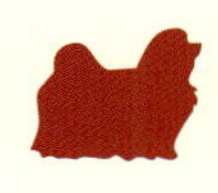 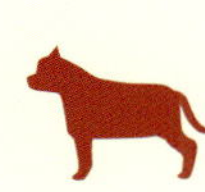

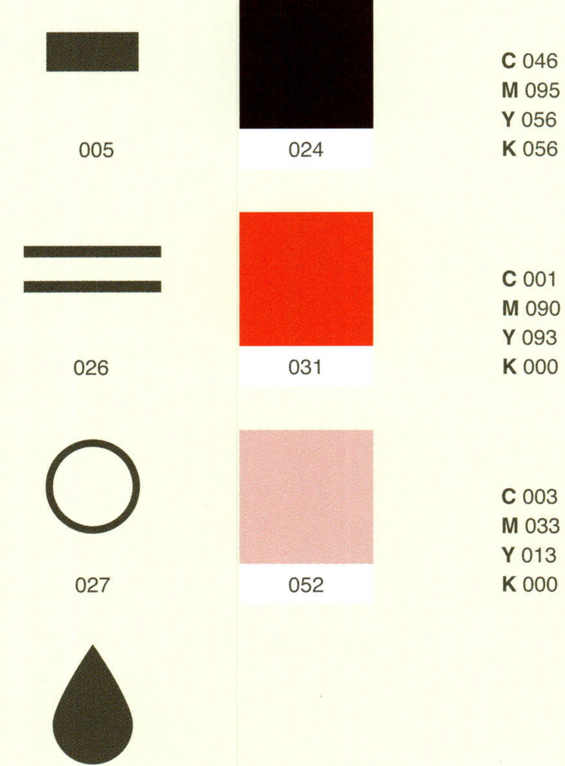

005

024

C 046
M 095
Y 056
K 056

026

031

C 001
M 090
Y 093
K 000

027

052

C 003
M 033
Y 013
K 000

030

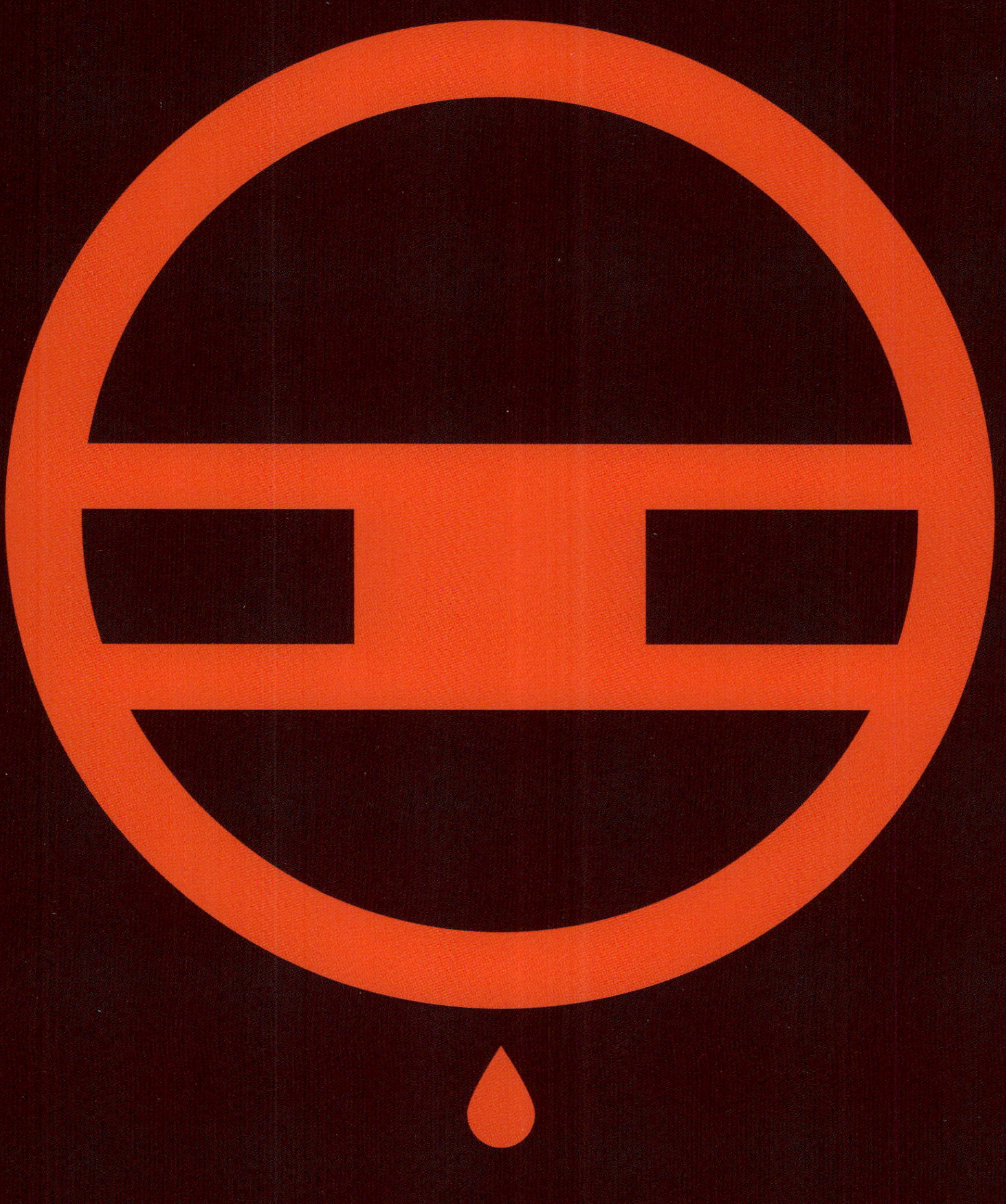

19
73
drive
there are no clean getaways.

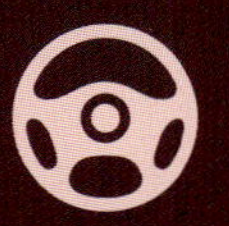
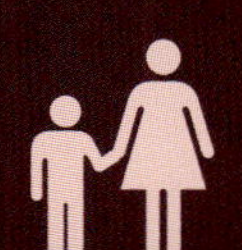
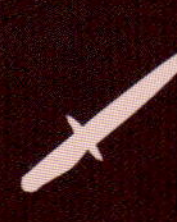

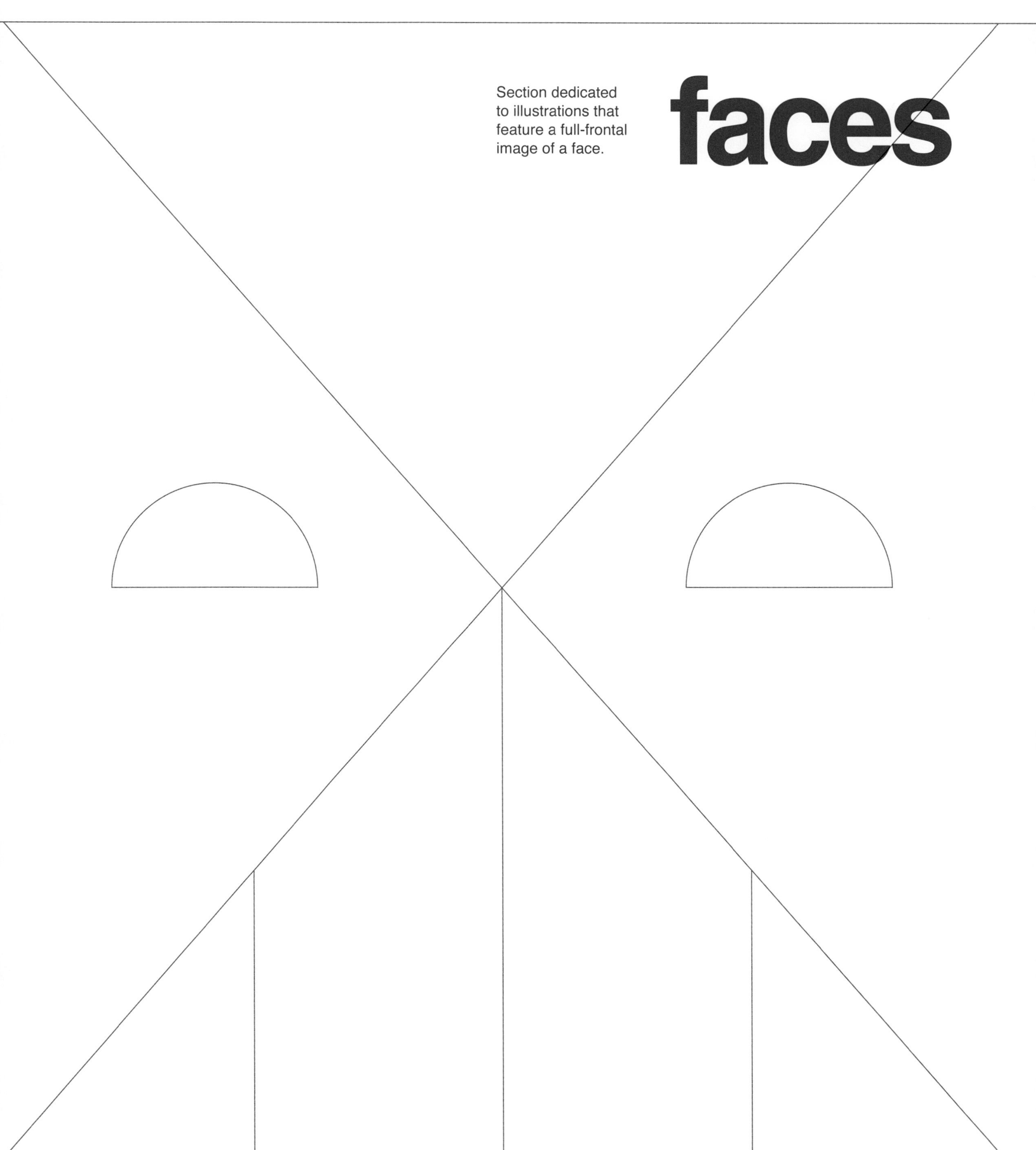

Section dedicated
to illustrations that
feature a full-frontal
image of a face.

faces

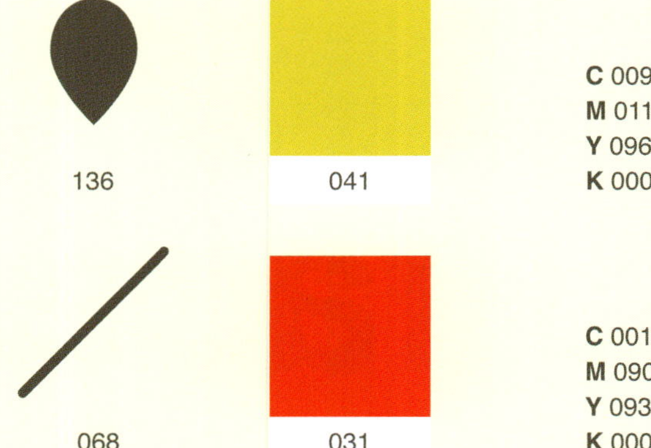

136   041

C 009
M 011
Y 096
K 000

068   031

C 001
M 090
Y 093
K 000

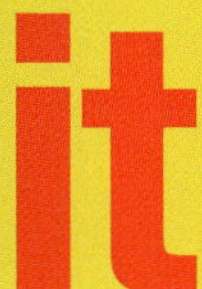

88
27
it
you'll float too.

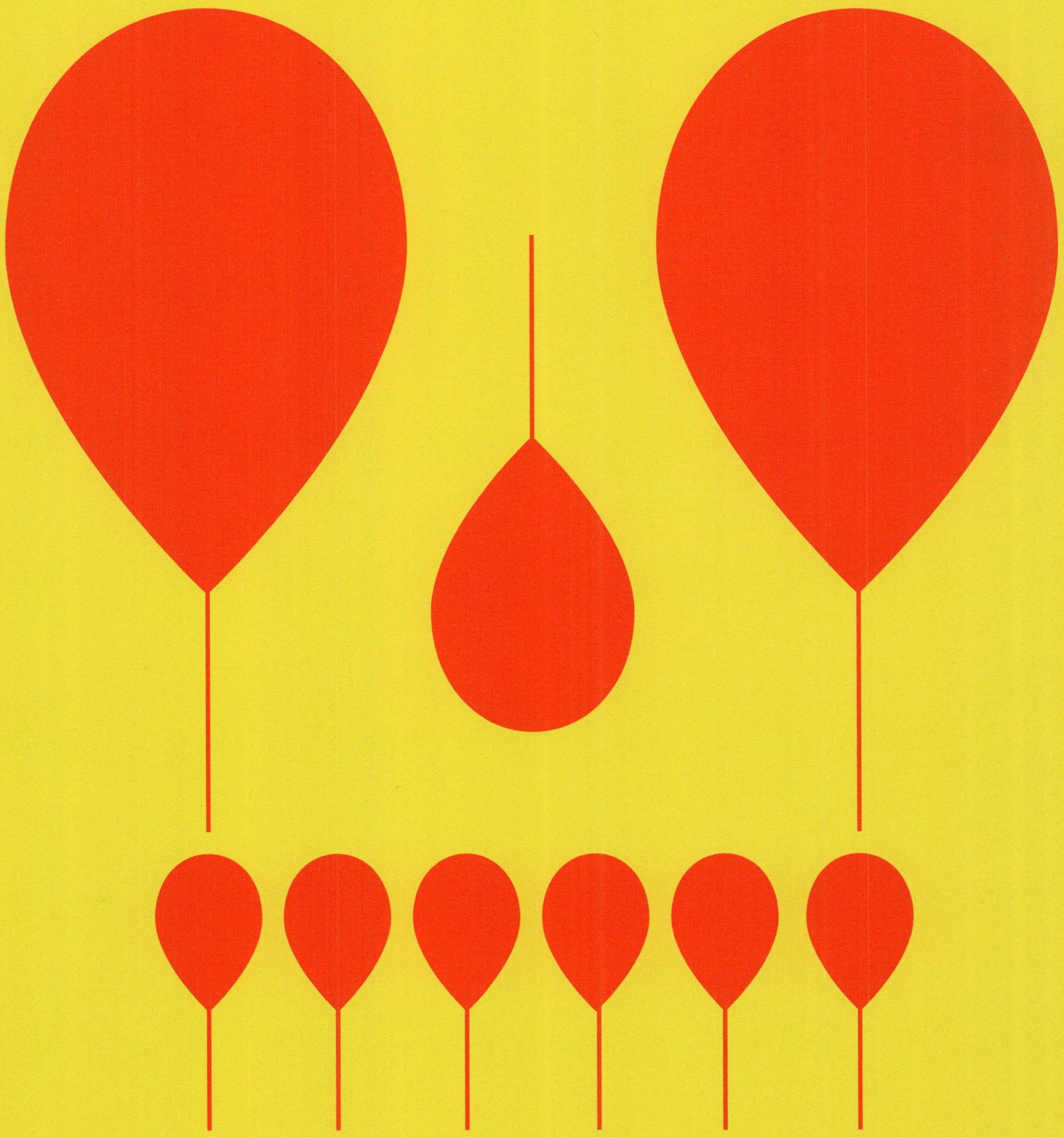

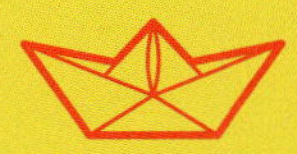

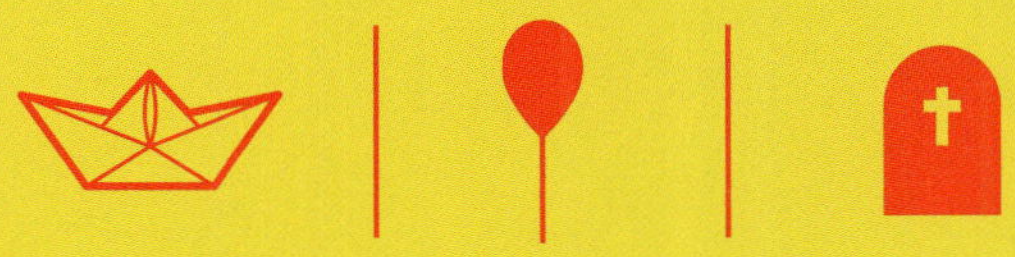

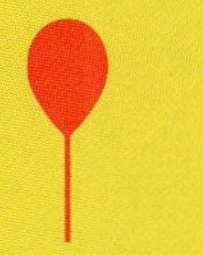

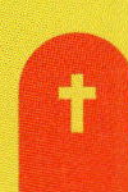

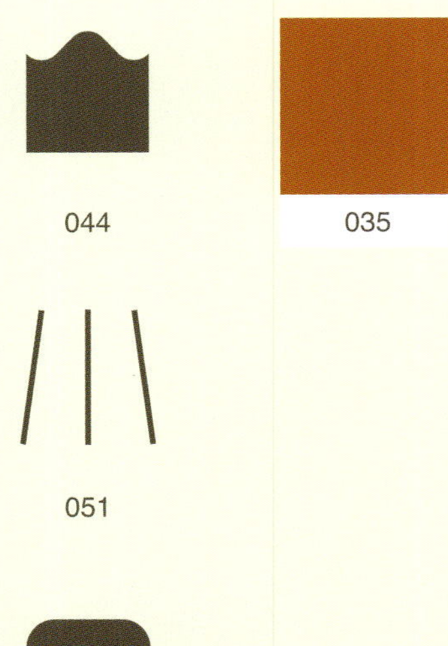

044

035

C 003
M 000
Y 013
K 000

051

130

the silence of the lambs

to enter the mind of a killer she must challenge the mind of a madman.

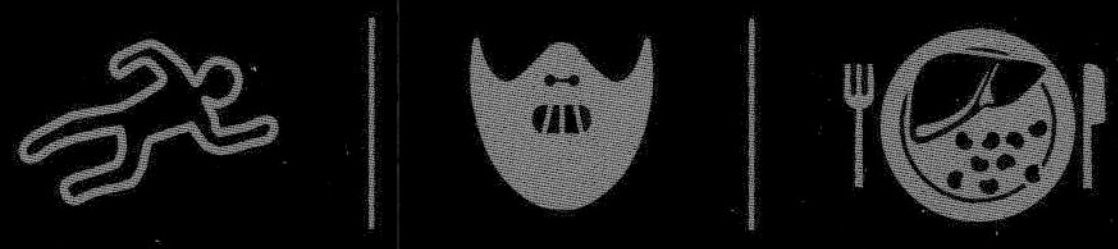

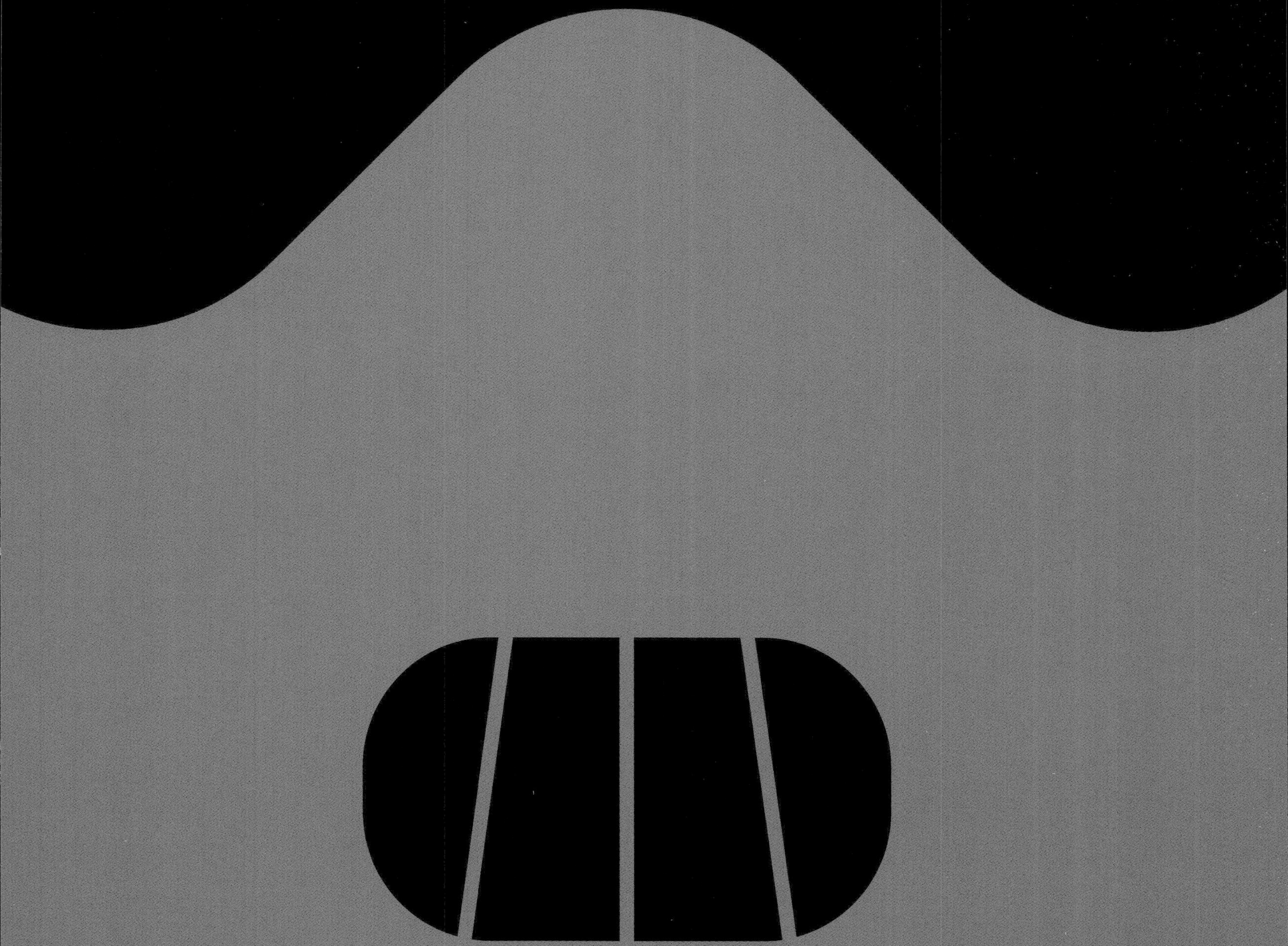

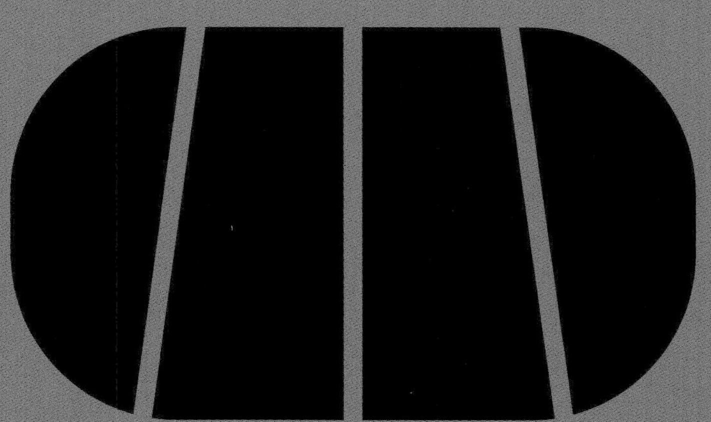

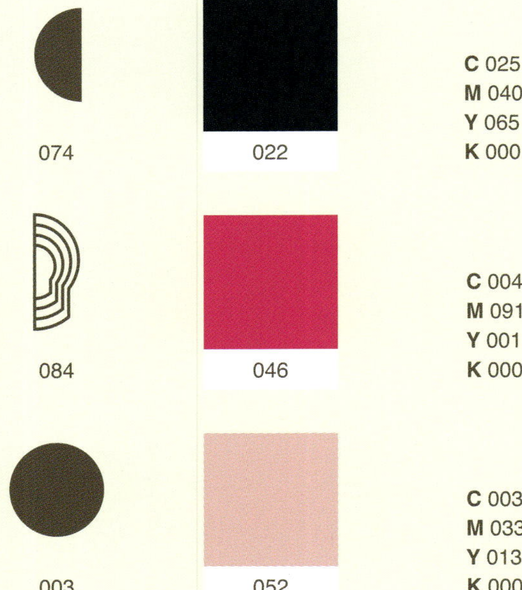

074

022

C 025
M 040
Y 065
K 000

084

046

C 004
M 091
Y 001
K 000

003

052

C 003
M 033
Y 013
K 000

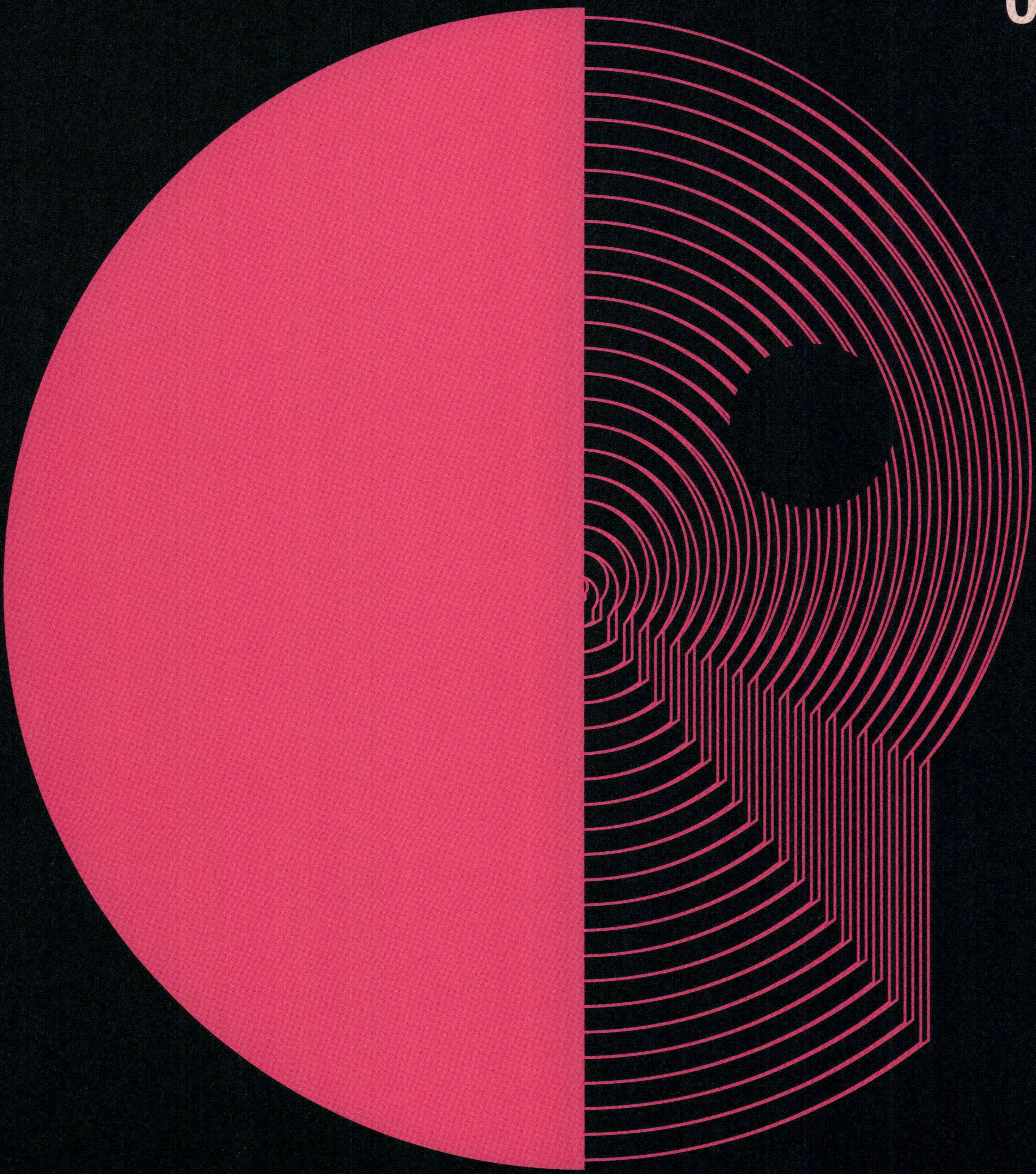

the dark knight

welcome to a world without rules.

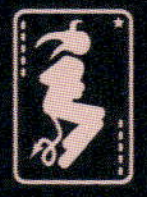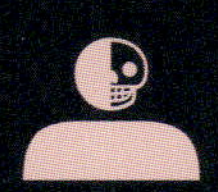

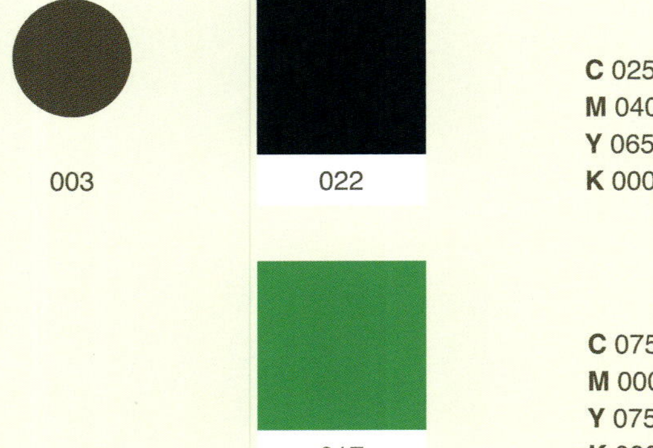

003
022

C 025
M 040
Y 065
K 000

017

C 075
M 000
Y 075
K 000

monsters university

school never looked this scary.

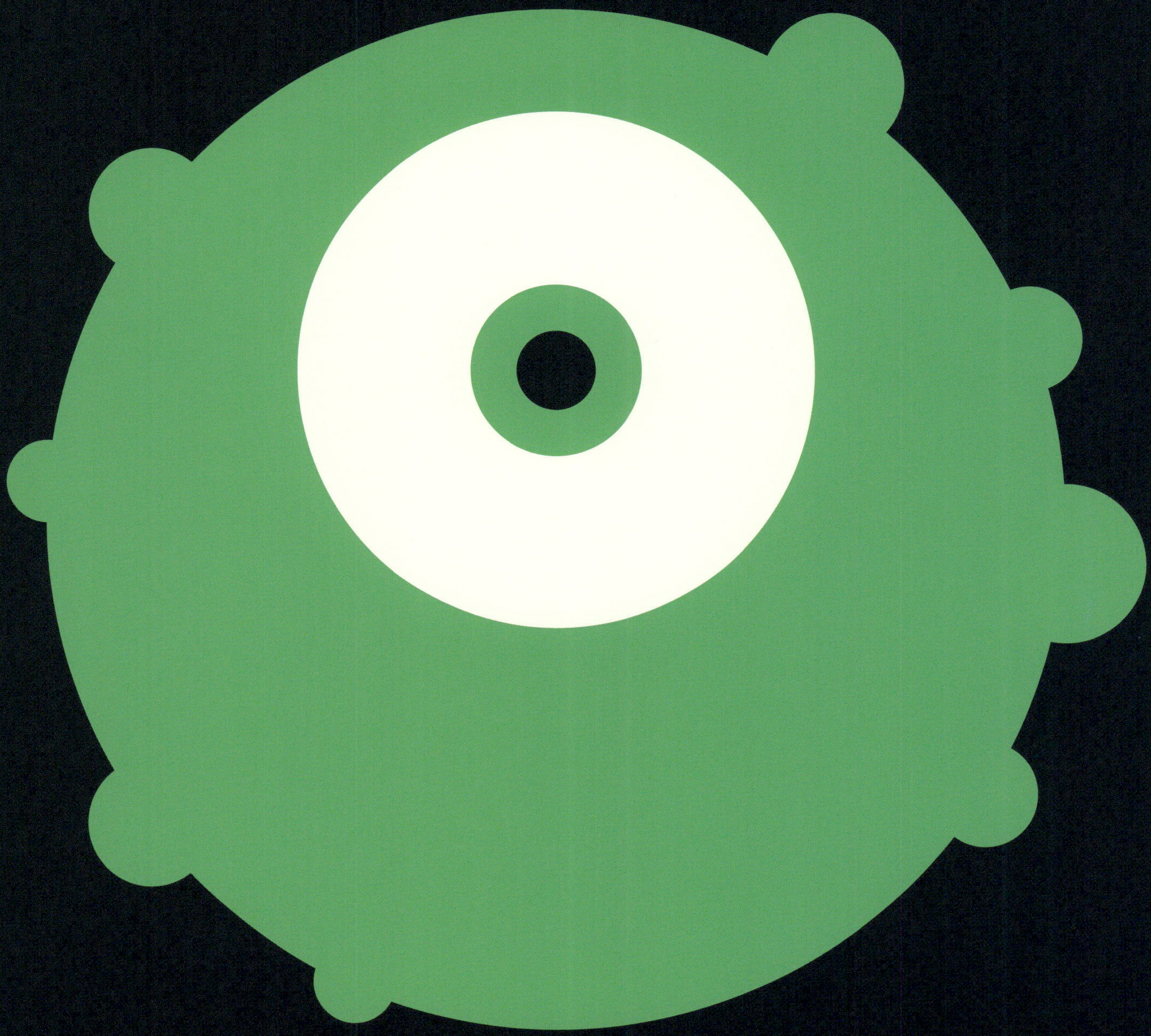

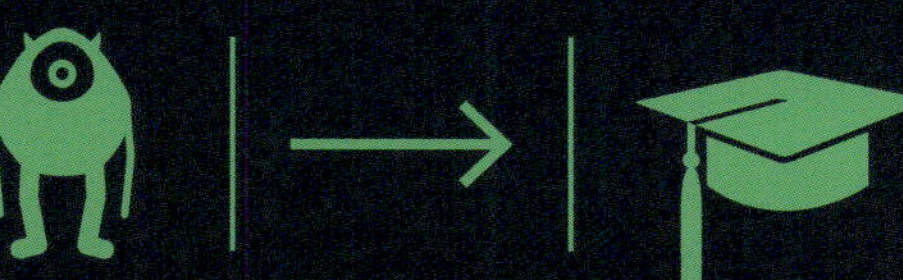

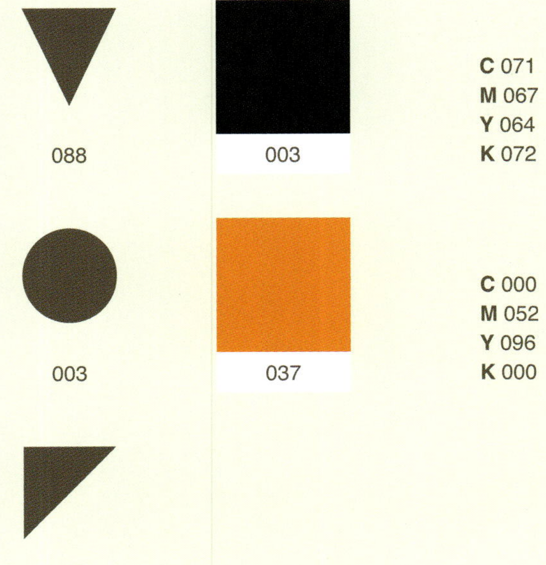

088

003

C 071
M 067
Y 064
K 072

003

037

C 000
M 052
Y 096
K 000

004

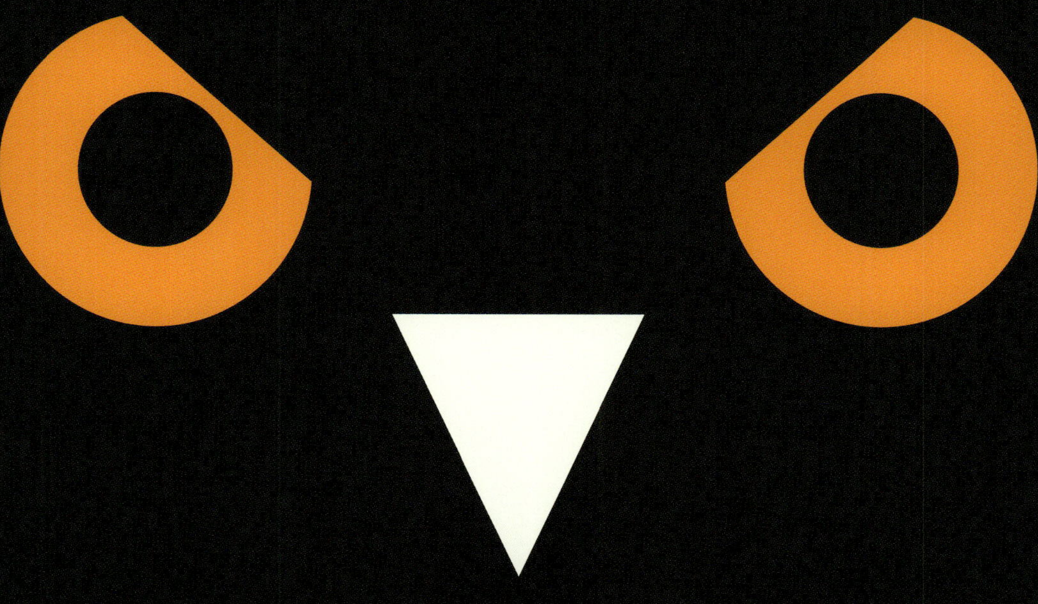

harry potter

something evil has returned to hogwarts.

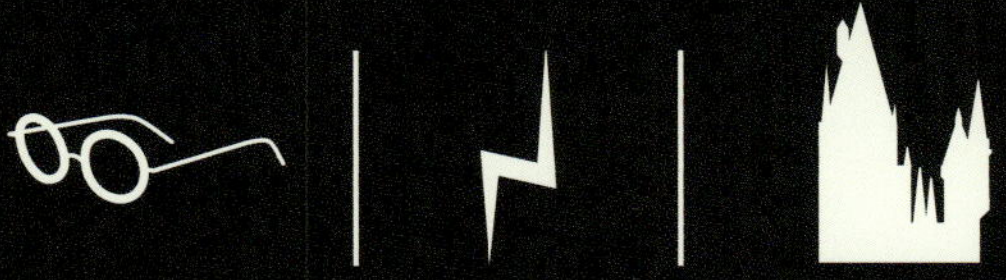

229

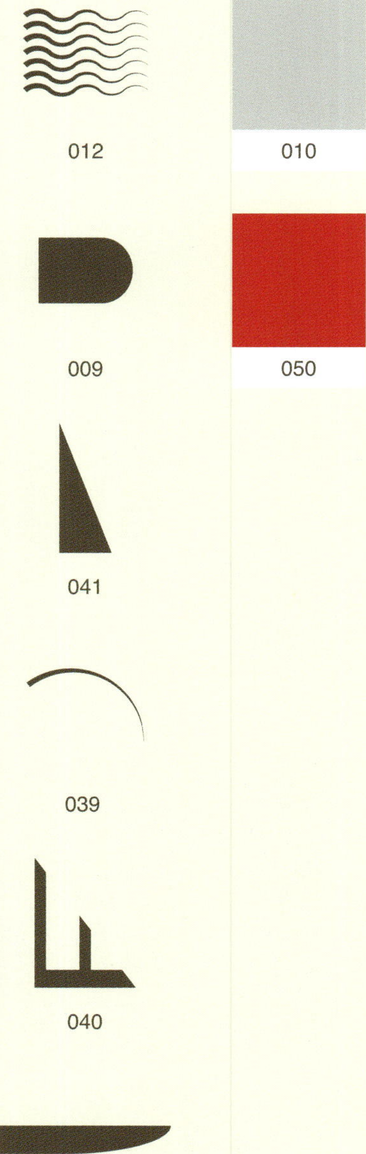

012

009

041

039

040

045

010

050

C 020
M 015
Y 015
K 000

C 004
M 090
Y 058
K 000

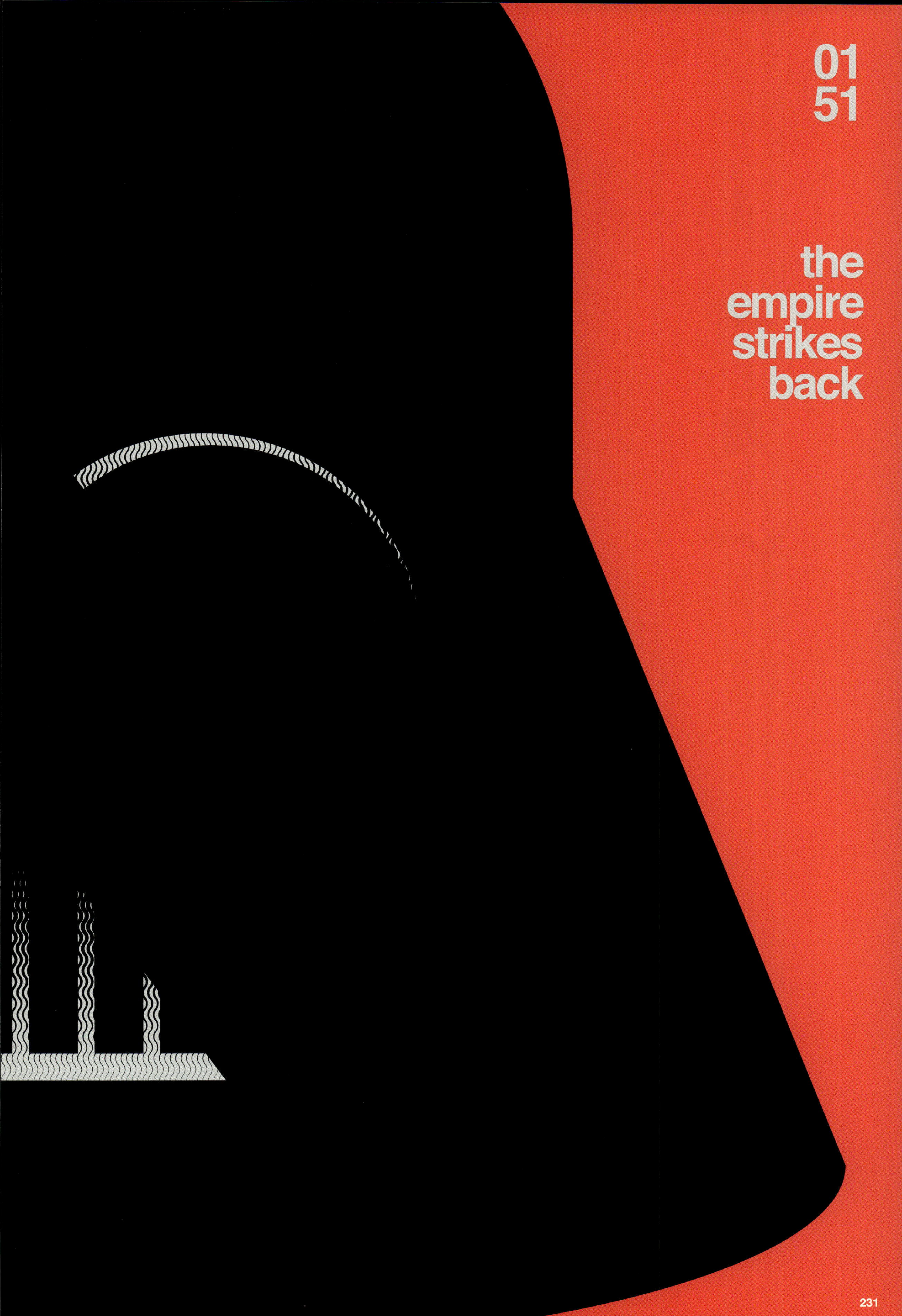

the
empire
strikes
back

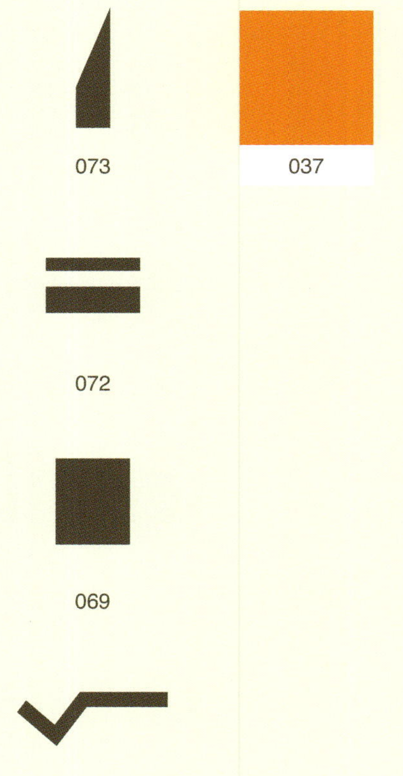

073

072

069

067

037

C 000
M 052
Y 096
K 000

iron man

heroes aren't born.
they're built.

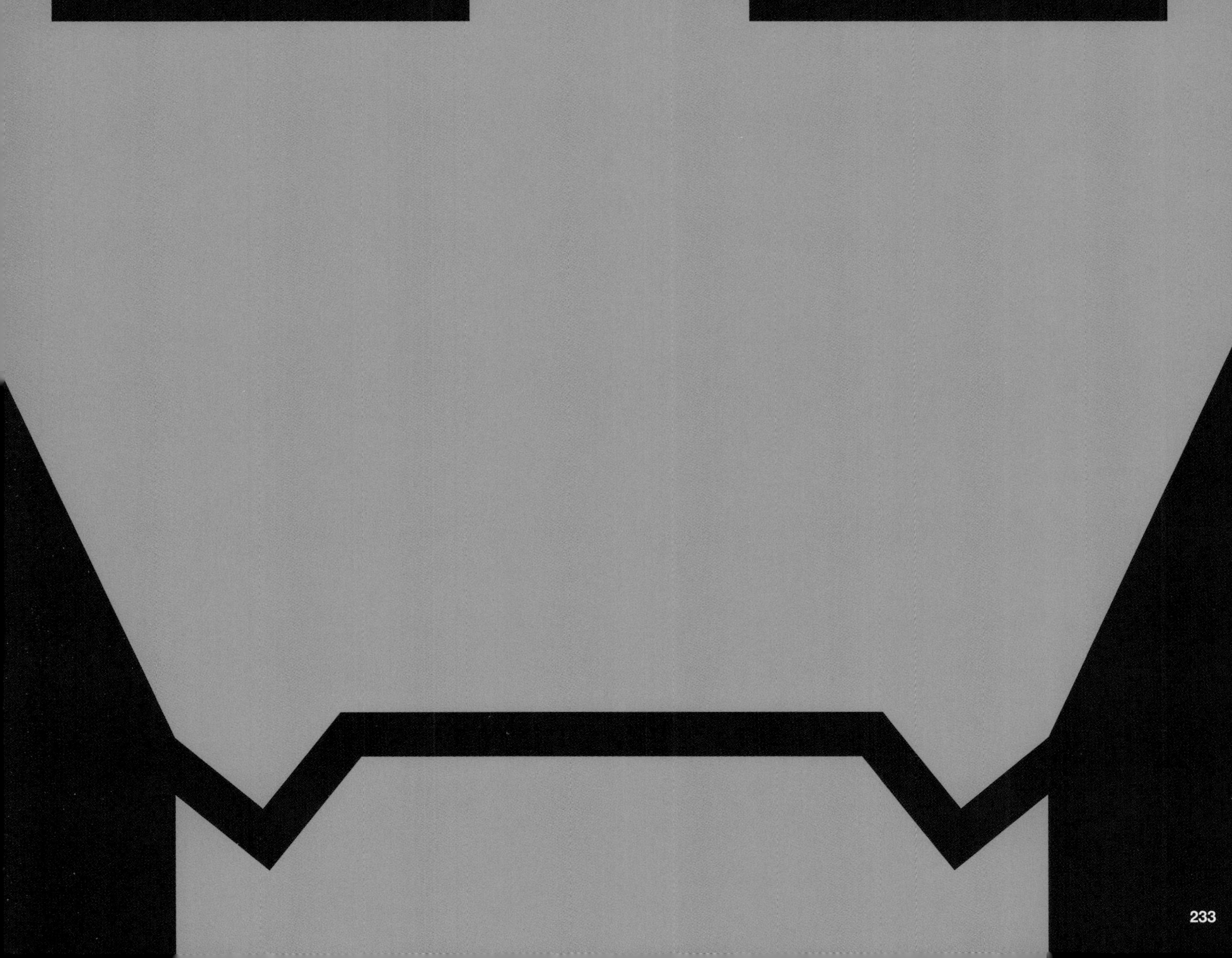

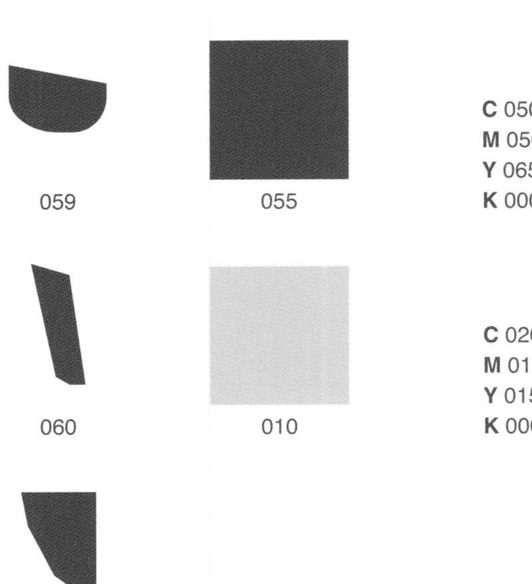

059

055

C 050
M 050
Y 065
K 000

060

010

C 020
M 015
Y 015
K 000

061

069

048

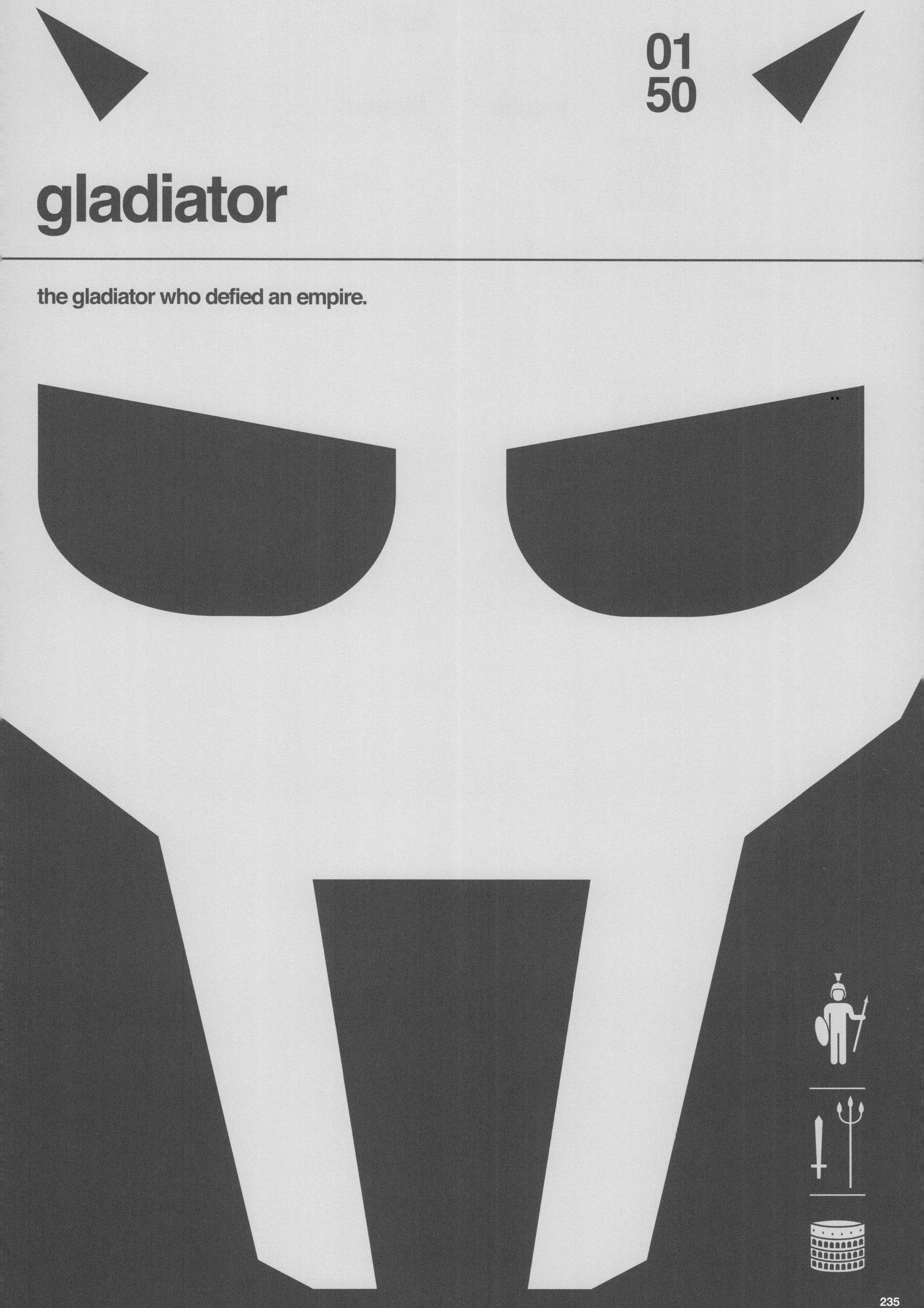

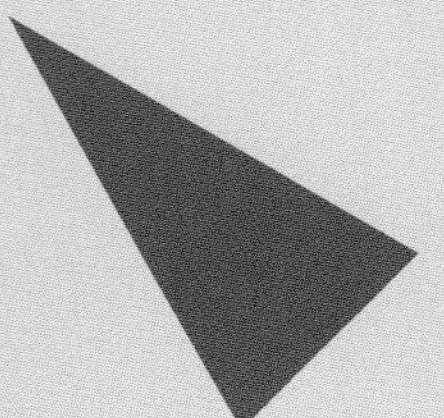

gladiator

the gladiator who defied an empire.

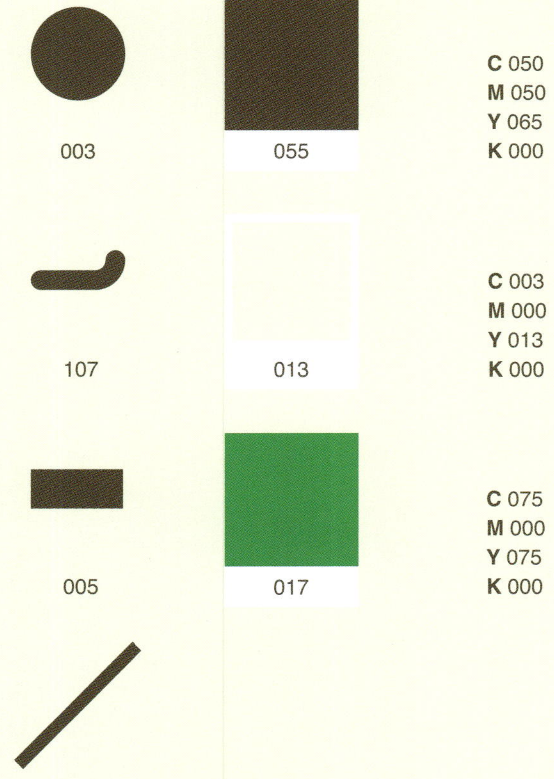

003

055

C 050
M 050
Y 065
K 000

107

013

C 003
M 000
Y 013
K 000

005

017

C 075
M 000
Y 075
K 000

054

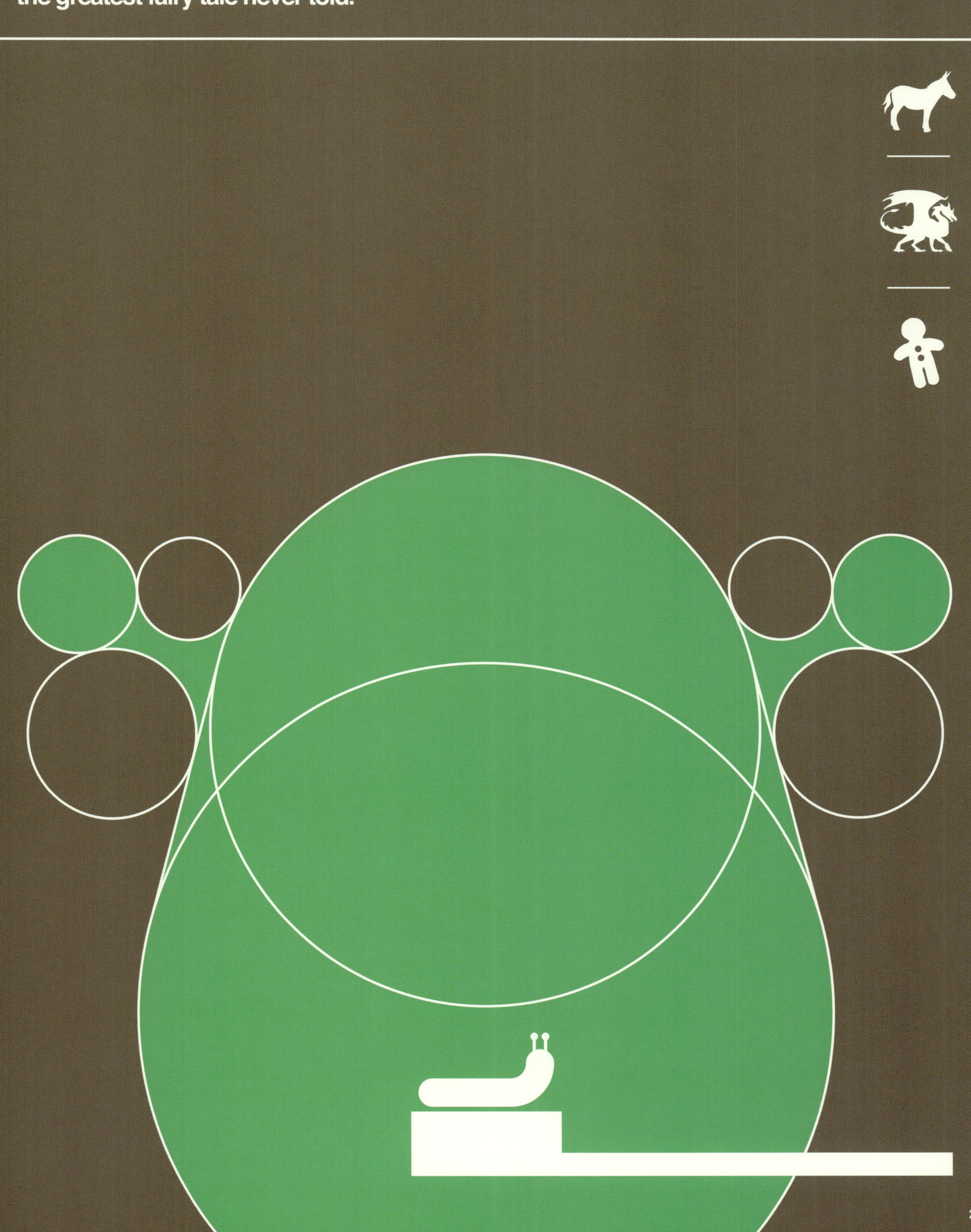

1991
shrek
the greatest fairy tale never told.
237

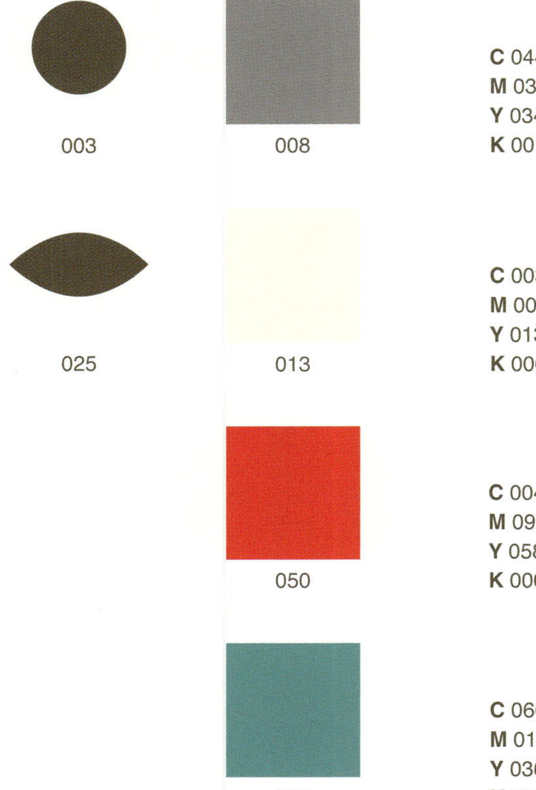

003

008

025

013

050

015

C 044
M 037
Y 034
K 001

C 003
M 000
Y 013
K 000

C 004
M 090
Y 058
K 000

C 066
M 018
Y 036
K 000

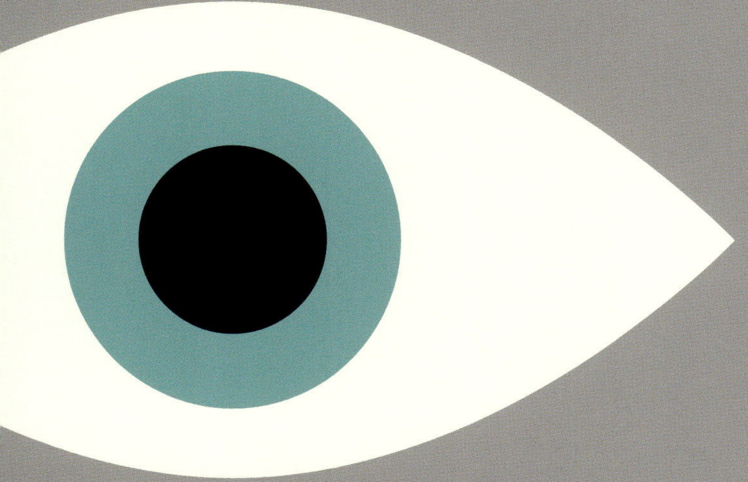
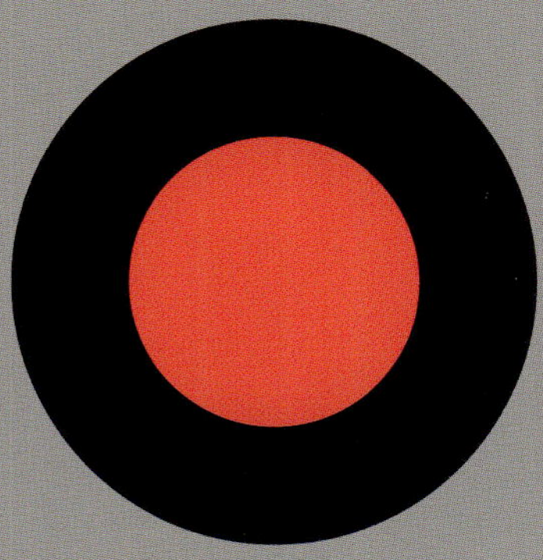

the terminator

your future is in its hands.

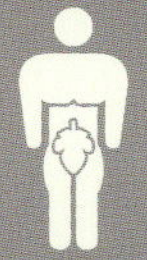

239

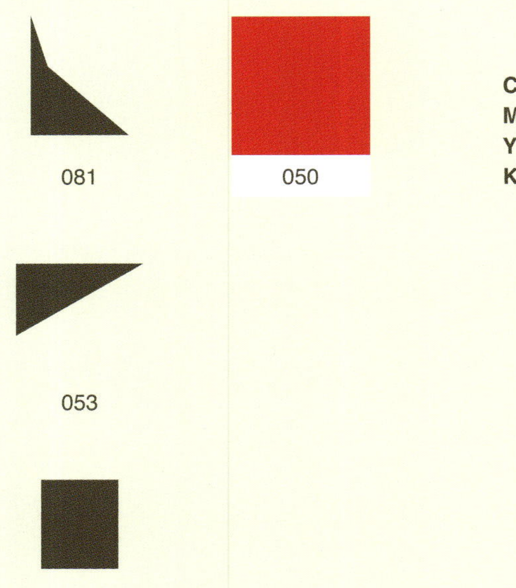

081

053

069

050

C 004
M 090
Y 058
K 000

king kong

the eighth wonder of the world.

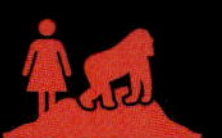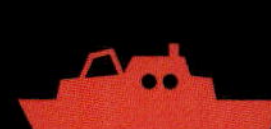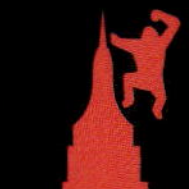

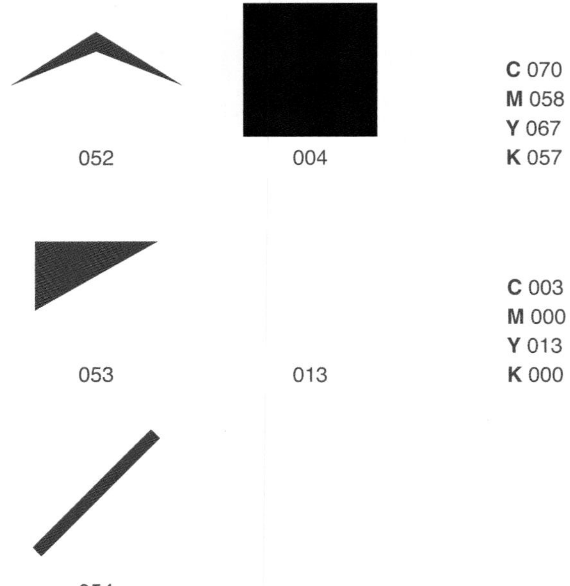

052

004

C 070
M 058
Y 067
K 057

053

013

C 003
M 000
Y 013
K 000

054

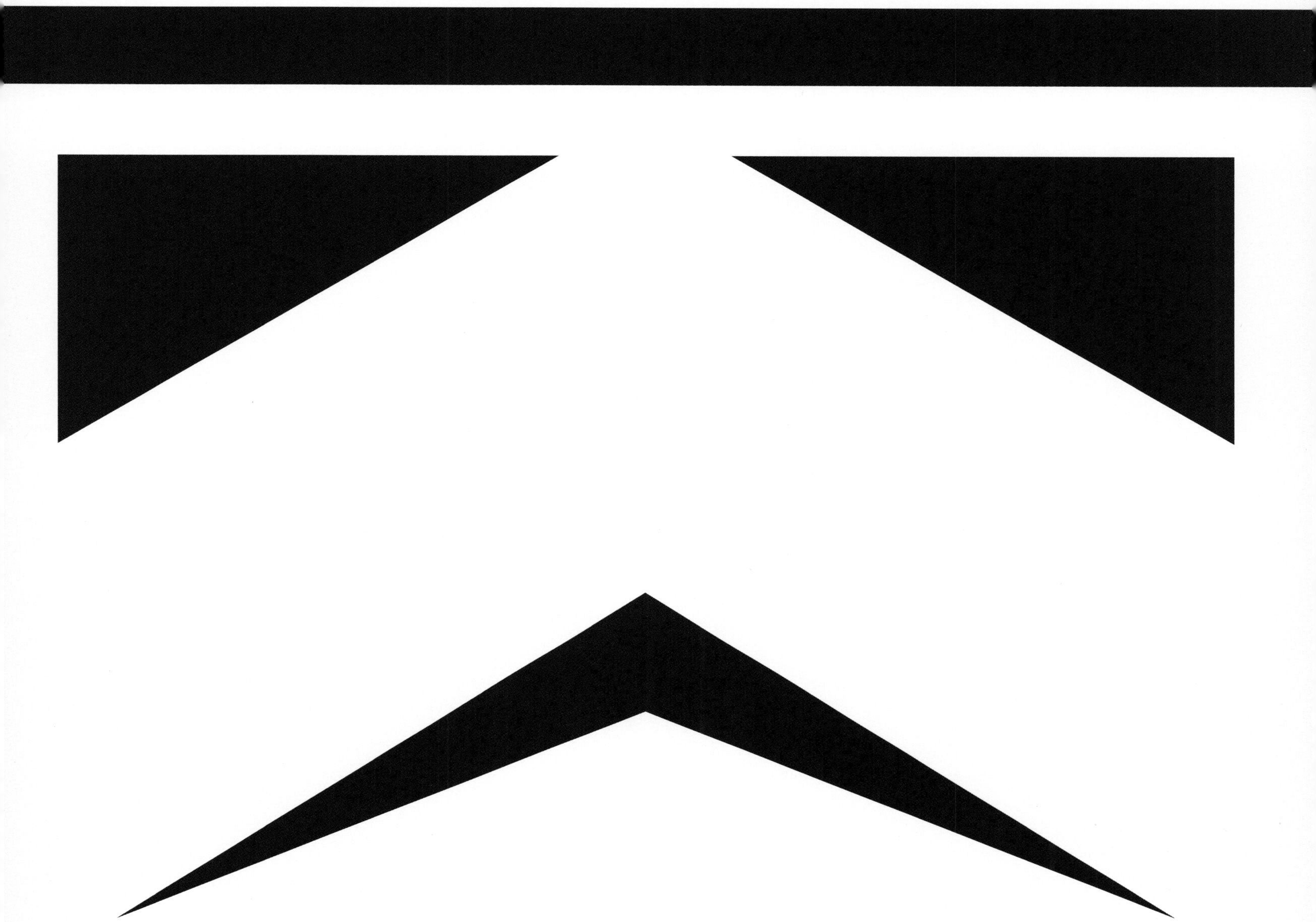

star wars

somewhere, in space, this could all be happening right now.

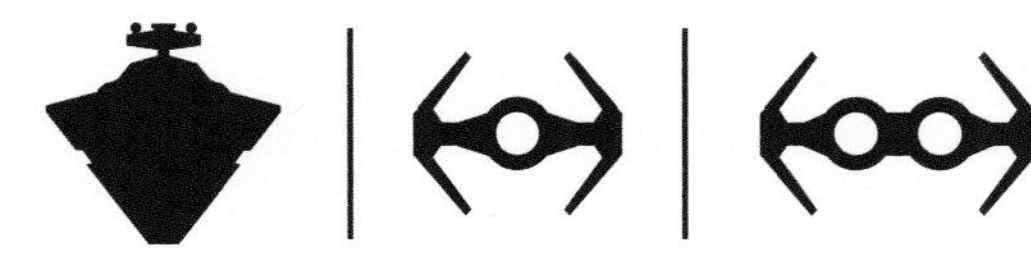

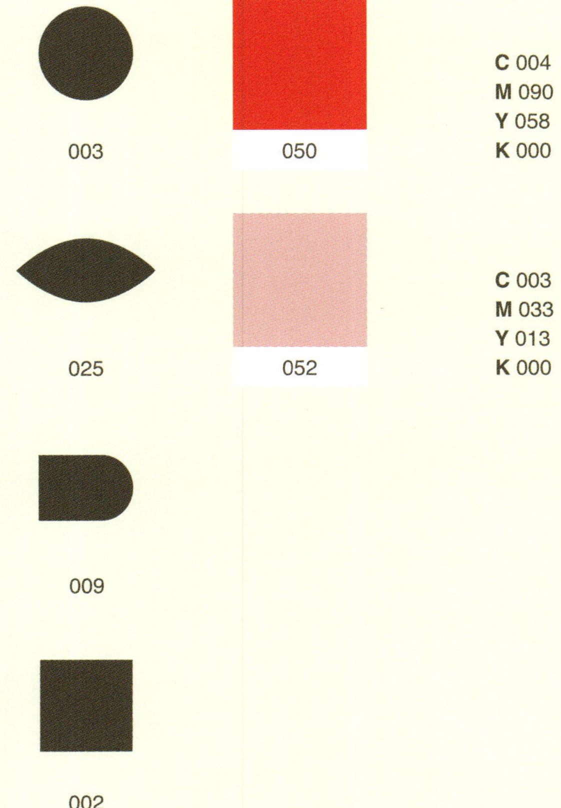

003

050

C 004
M 090
Y 058
K 000

025

052

C 003
M 033
Y 013
K 000

009

002

pan's labyrinth / / /

what happens when make-believe believes it's real?

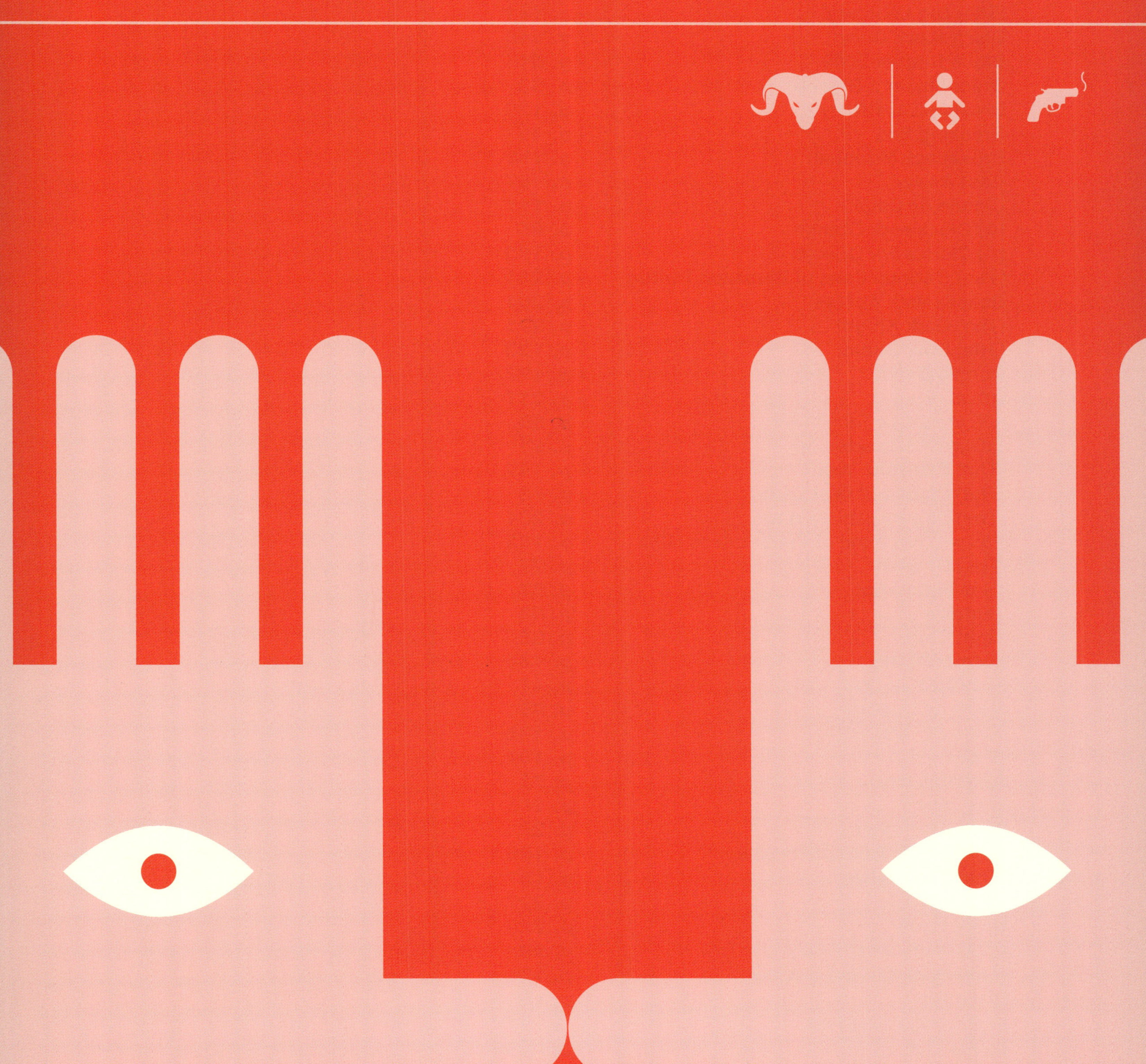

19
44
el laberinto del fauno
la inocencia es más fuerte que el mal.
245

film index in alphabetical order

0002 - *North by Northwest:* 2 minutes into the film, Alfred Hitchcock makes one of his famous cameo appearances.

0003 - *Amores Perros:* The film is divided into 3 parts, which take place in 3 different periods.

0003 - *Minority Report:* 3 precogs predict the future.

0005 - *Inside Out:* The protagonist has 5 main emotions in her head.

0006 - *Relatos salvajes:* The story is made up of 6 episodes.

0007 - *Game of Thrones:* 7 Kingdoms, 7 Gods. A recurring number in the universe created by George R. R. Martin.

0007 - *Predator:* 7 soldiers take part in the mission.

0010 - *Hannibal:* The narrative takes place 10 years after *The Silence of the Lambs.*

0011 - *Star Wars:* The Stormtroopers' standard-issued weapons are called E11 Blasters.

0012 - *Arrival:* 12 is the number of spaceships that landed on earth.

0013 - *Fantasia:* This Disney masterpiece contains 13 musical compositions.

0015 - *Se7en:* All of John Doe's books were actually written for the making of the film, and they cost $15,000.

0020 - *Slumdog Millionaire:* 20 million rupees is the sum won by the film's protagonist.

0020 - *The Big Lebowski:* "White Russian" is the protagonist's favorite drink and has an alcohol content of 20%.

0033 - *Cidade de Deus:* There were 33 kick-ups before the ball was blown up by a bullet.

0039 - *Iron Man:* The first appearance of Tony Stark is in "Tales of Suspense" no. 39.

0047 - *Star Trek:* A number that recurs frequently in the whole saga is 47, no one knows why.

0075 - *Forrest Gump:* Forrest has an IQ of 75, much lower than average.

0076 - *Interstellar:* Calculated from Earth, Cooper traveled for 76 years.

0082 - *Moulin Rouge:* 82 is the street number of the Moulin Rouge in Paris.

0088 - *The Legend of 1990:* A piano has 88 keys.

0101 - *Kill Bill:* 101 is the number of the apartment where Bill lives with Beatrix's daughter.

0102 - *Ghost:* 102 Prince Street, New York, NY is the address of the loft where it was filmed.

0102 - *Raiders of the Lost Ark:* "And there went out fire from Yahweh, and devoured them, and they died before Yahweh." Leviticus 10:2.

0120 - *Jurassic Park:* The island where the story plays out is 120 miles north-west of Costa Rica.

0125 - *A Clockwork Orange:* The piece sung by the woman at the Korova Milk Bar is Beethoven's Symphony No. 9, Op. 125.

0130 - *The Silence of the Lambs:* The moth symbol of the film, African death's head hawkmoth (Acherontia atropos), has a wingspan that can reach 130 mm.

0134 - *Fight Club:* 0134 (without an area code) is Marla Singer's phone number.

0134 - *Memento:* Teddy's telephone number is the same as Marla Singer's in Fight Club.

0150 - *Game of Thrones:* So far, there have been more than 150,000 deaths in the series. Animals included.

0150 - *Gladiator:* The games organized by Commodus at the Colosseum take 150 days.

0151 - *The Empire Strikes Back:* Darth Vader reveals to Luke that he is his father 1 hour and 51 minutes into the film.

0160 - *Star Wars:* The Death Star is 160 kilometers in diameter.

0174 - *The Grand Budapest Hotel:* The film had a budget of only 23 million, but made 174 million.

0193 - *Monsters, Inc.:* Sully uses locker nr. 193 to hide Boo's belongings.

0210 - *Eternal Sunshine of the Spotless Mind:* Lacuna, Inc. is located at 210 E Grand St., New York, NY 10019.

0220 - *The Truman Show:* 220 countries were tuned in during his first steps.

0246 - *Rain Man:* 246 is the number of toothpicks Dustin Hoffman correctly counts on the restaurant floor.

0250 - *Vanilla Sky:* The protagonist dreams about being in a deserted Manhattan, driving a Ferrari 250 GTO.

0288 - *Donnie Darko:* The real Donnie Darko died on October 2, 1988.

0311 - *The Prestige:* A magic act consists of 3 parts, there are 11 letters in the word abracadabra.

0350 - *Inception:* A dream can be explored in 3 levels; the protagonists have spent 50 years in one of these.

0381 - *King Kong:* At the end of the film, King Kong scales all 381 meters of the Empire State Building.

0393 - *Black Hawk Down:* The mission starts on October 3, 1993.

0407 - *Jaws:* On July 4, the authorities decided not to close the beaches, despite the shark alert.

0426 - *Alien:* LV426 is the name of a moon in the imaginary universe of Alien.

0440 - *The Exorcist:* The movie grossed 440 million dollars, a record for a horror film.

0533 - *Nightmare on Elm Street:* Freddy was born in May 1933, following a violent rape.

0604 - *Mad Max: Fury Road:* There are 5 runaway wives, one of them pregnant who, unfortunately, will die on the journey.

0608 - *Rogue One:* 0608 is the identification code of the shuttle used by the rebels to steal the Death Star plans.

0635 - *Thelma & Louise:* FRS 635 is the number plate of the car they drive during the movie.

0666 - *Pulp Fiction:* The code to open Marsellus Wallace's briefcase is 666.

0727 - *Breakfast at Tiffany's:* The street address of Tiffany's flagship store in NYC.

0796 - *Eyes Wide Shut:* 7, 9, 6 are the numbers from the taxi license that is often seen during the movie.

0800 - *The Terminator:* The famous T-800 is one of the cyborgs interpreted by Arnold Schwarzenegger.

0813 - *Inglourious Basterds:* There are 8 "basterds," 13 is the number of German officers killed by Sergeant Hugo Stiglitz.

0924 - *Magnolia:* 9 characters' stories intertwine within a 24-hour period.

1010 - *The Shape of Water:* October 10 is the date that the protagonist wants to free the creature, as marked on the calendar.

1015 - *Breaking Bad:* the numbers in the formula of methamphetamine, $C_{10}H_{15}N$.

1017 - *The Hunt for Red October:* Red October 1917 is the month related to a series of events of the Russian Revolution.

1020 - *28 Days Later:* The zombie-making virus has an incubation period of between 10 and 20 seconds.

1021 - *Blade Runner:* The last digits of the date engraved on the famous wooden horse is 1021.

1117 - *Schindler's List:* There were 1117 names on his list.

1138 - *Star Wars:* 1138 is a recurring number throughout the saga and can be found almost everywhere.

1200 - *Apocalypse Now:* Napalm reaches a temperature of 1200° during combustion.

1212 - *Murder on the Orient Express:* There are 12 suspects after a body with 12 stab wounds is found.

1313 - *Monsters University:* The number linked to the protagonists' fraternity is 1313.

1500 - *Cast Away:* The protagonist was on the island for 1,500 days before escaping on a raft.

1803 - *The Curious Case of Benjamin Button:* 1918–2003, the birth and death of Ben.

1863 - *Dances with Wolves:* The story takes place in 1863, during the Civil War.

1875 - *American Beauty:* 1875 is the year in which the American Beauty, a special variety of rose, was created.

1905 - *Battleship Potemkin:* The events of the film are set in 1905.

1912 - *Titanic:* Titanic set sail for the first, and last, time in 1912.

1933 - *The Untouchables:* 1919–1933, the years of Prohibition.

1942 - *The Thin Red Line:* The film is set in 1942.

1944 - *El laberinto del fauno:* The movie, released in 2006, is set in 1944.

1955 - *The Godfather:* Don Vito died in 1955.

1970 - *Ratatouille:* The story plays out in 1970.

1973 - *Drive:* The protagonist drives a 1973 Chevrolet "Chevelle".

1973 - *Mad Max:* Max's car was inspired by the 1973 Ford Falcon XB GT Coupé.

1984 - *Das Leben der Anderen:* The film starts in Berlin, in 1984.

1991 - *Shrek:* the year in which Spielberg acquired the rights to the film, even before the existence of DreamWorks.

2032 - *Top Gun:* 20.32N 64.24E, the coordinates of the MiGs' interception over the Indian Ocean.

2505 - *Edward Scissorhands:* The bank branch number where Edward asks for a loan to open his beauty salon is 2505.

2517 - *Pulp Fiction:* Ezekiel 25:17 is the famous biblical passage quoted by Samuel L. Jackson.

2736 - *Basic Instinct:* The cult classic scene where Sharon Stone crosses her legs happens at 27 minutes and 36 seconds into the movie.

3092 - *Full Metal Jacket:* 3092 is the platoon identification number that appears on the flags during training.

3107 - *Harry Potter:* The birthday of Harry, and J. K. Rowling, is July 31.

3500 - *The Empire Strikes Back:* Han Solo, at the end of the film, is trapped in carbonite, which has a fusion point of 3,500.

3503 - *The Green Mile:* The story is set in 1935, 3 years later than in the book.

3791 - *The Lord of the Rings:* Sauron distributed rings to each of the kings of the various races of Middle-earth – 3 elves, 7 dwarves, 9 men, and 1 ring of power for himself.

4544 - *The Hudsucker Proxy:* Barnes falls from the 45th floor, or 44th if you don't count the mezzanine.

4721 - *The Shining:* 07/04/1921, the date of the gala event immortalized in the photograph.

4757 - *Psycho:* The killer was inspired by Ed Gein, who confessed to killing two people between 1947 and 1957.

4782 - *Narcos:* The atomic number for silver is 47, 82 is the number for lead. "Plata o Plomo?"

5057 - *The Shawshank Redemption:* The zip code of the place in Mexico where the characters meet at the end of the film is 5057.

5376 - *The Artist:* The major awards won by the film were 5 Oscars, 3 Golden Globes, 7 BAFTAs and 6 César awards.

5575 - *The Deer Hunter:* The years of the Vietnam War, 1955–1975.

5671 - *A Clockwork Orange:* 5671 is the identification number for LSD at the American National Center for Biotechnology Information.

secret numbers

6000 - *Ghostbusters:* The evil entity that threatens the Earth during the film dates back to 6000 BC.

6290 - *The Elephant Man:* Joseph Merrick, 1862–1890.

6297 - *Dracula:* 1462 is the year in which he became a vampire, though the film is set in 1897.

6383 - *Brokeback Mountain:* The year in which the protagonists meet is 1963. However, one of them dies in 1983.

7197 - *Léon:* The address of the building on 97th Street in Manhattan where Léon lives, and of the shop where he buys his two liters of milk.

7810 - *Match Point:* The music is taken almost entirely from a 78-rpm vinyl, there is a 10-minute gap between the murder of Mrs. Eastby and that of Nola.

7908 - *The Dark Knight:* Heath Ledger, 1979–2008.

8110 - *The Matrix:* The protagonists in the film use Nokia 8110 phones.

8169 - *E.T. the Extra-Terrestrial:* The first take was on September 8, 1981 in Los Angeles, and filming wrapped after 69 days.

8555 - *Back to the Future:* Marty started in 1985 and arrived in 1955.

8827 - *It:* 1988, the year in which the boat scene is set, 27 are the years that It goes into "hibernation".

9000 - *2001: A Space Odyssey:* Al 9000, the name of the famous computer in the film.

9472 - *Rear Window:* The movie starts at 94°F and ends at 72°F.

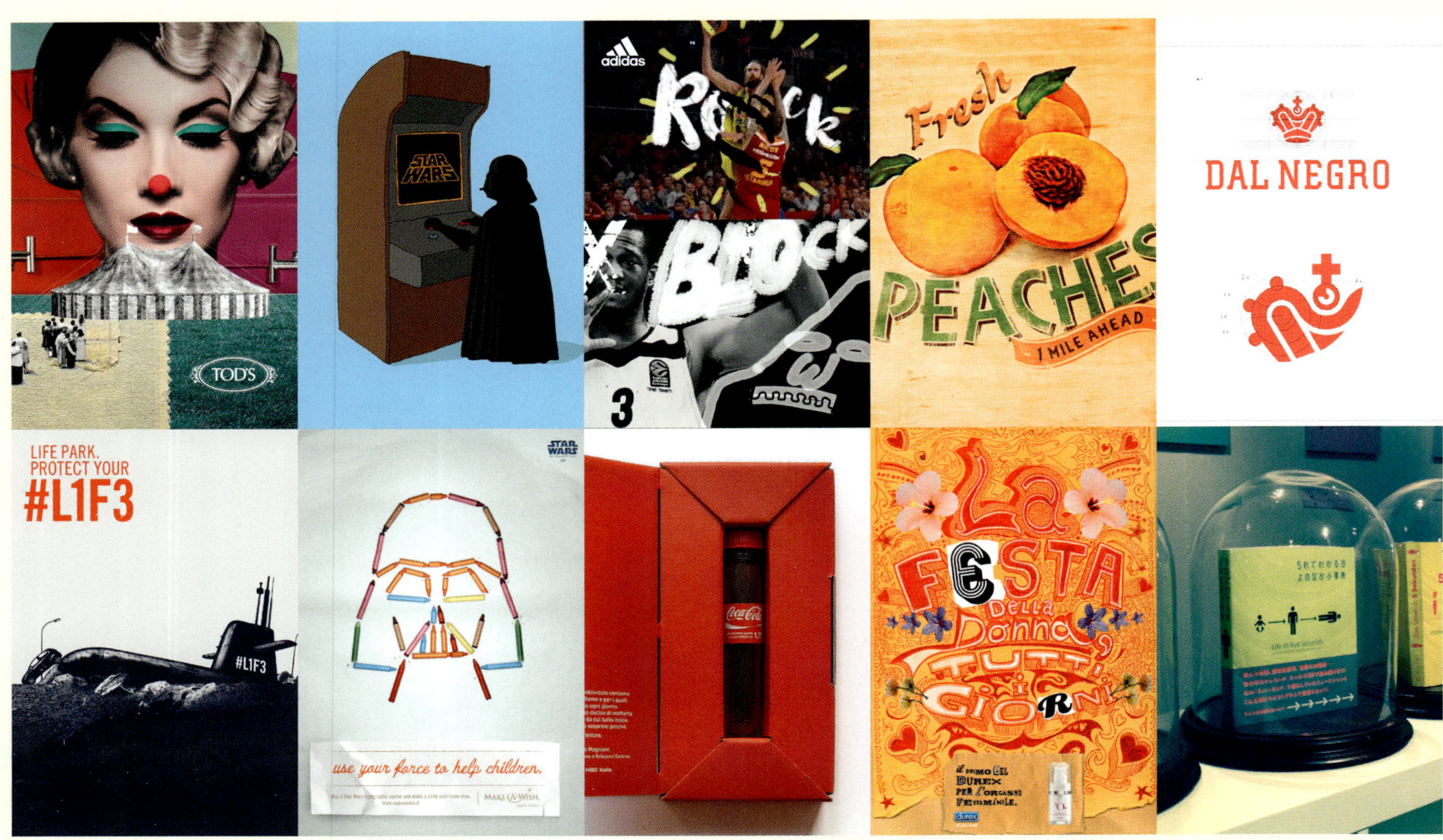

matteo
civaschi

In the summer of 1985, struck by the cover of the first Van Halen album, he decided that his life would be dedicated to graphic "creation." This was followed by fantastic years, drawing absolutely everything while attending art school. Despite this, his father wanted him to become a doctor, but he refused to give up on his dreams. His tenacity paid off when he was awarded a scholarship by Fondo Sociale Europeo (the European Social Fund), and he then attended Nuova Accademia di Belle Arti (the New Academy of Fine Arts) with great satisfaction. At the end of his 3rd year at the academy, while diving in the mud as a goalkeeper for a local amateur soccer team, he noticed his mother on the sidelines, screaming something unintelligible: McCann (a well-known advertising agency) needed him for an emergency:

one of his brother's friends, who worked there as art director, needed an assistant to complete an important presentation. Thanks to that ''emergency,'' his professional career was launched: McCann for 10 years, DLV-BBDO for 1 year, followed by another 6 years at McCann, working as creative director for Gazzetta dello Sport. But something was still missing. He founded H-57 in 2004, first as a clothing line, and then as a Motion Graphics and Design Studio. In 2011, he created Shortology, with 20 books published around the world. His book, *Life in Five Seconds*, won a Lion at the Cannes Festival in the "Design" category. In addition to his work as a creative and an author, he has been a speaker at Ted, Wired, Malofiej (Infographic World Summit) and various other conferences in the world of design and story-telling.

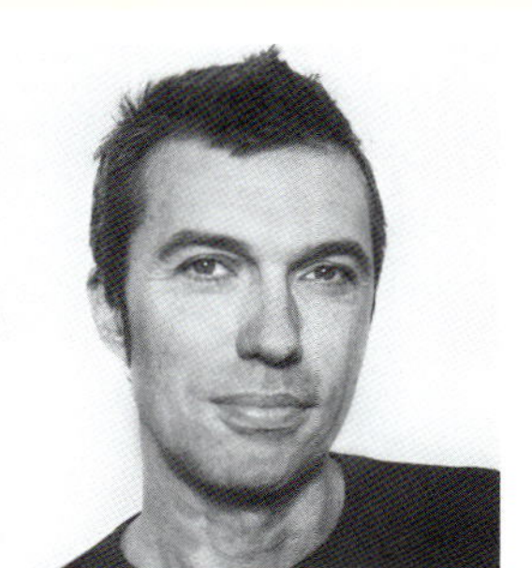

LE2015

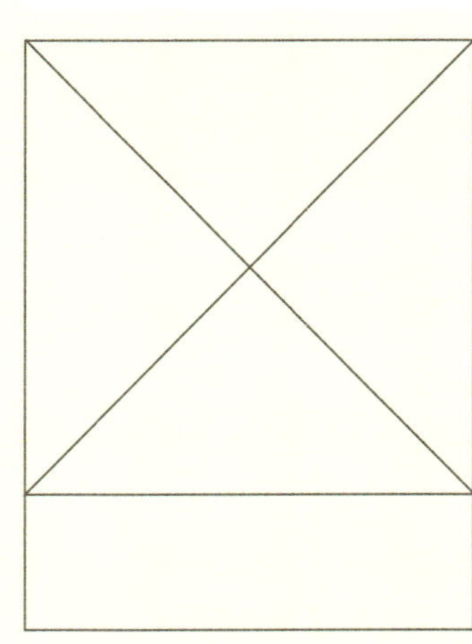

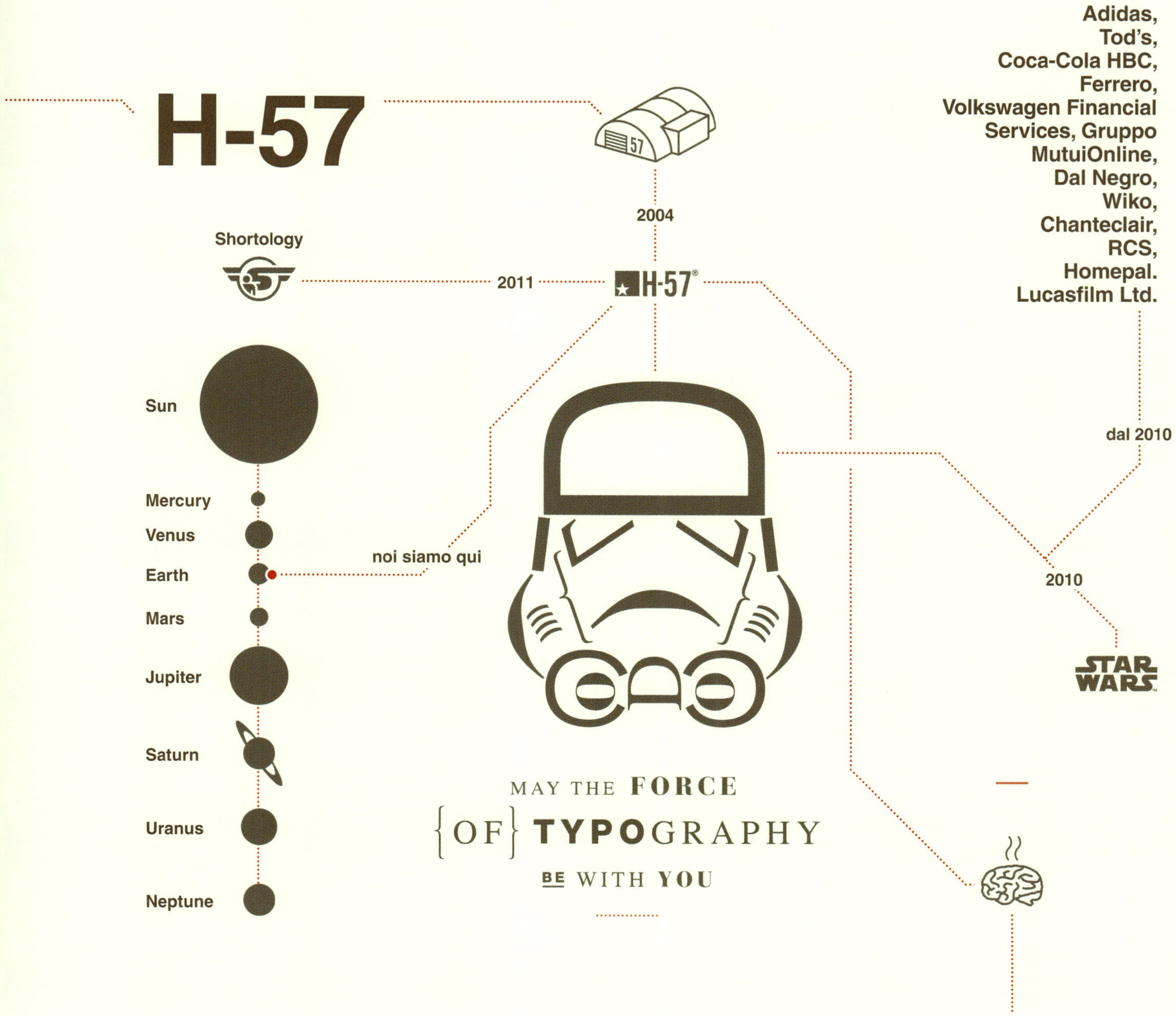

H-57 is a design and advertising studio, officially born in Milan on January 12, 2004. The name derives from the infamous Hangar 57, located in an almost legendary Soviet military base built on an island in the Aral Sea during the years of the Cold War. The base, and in particular Hangar 57, is said to have contained every sort of atrocity: from the most unusual weapons of mass destruction to laboratories for crazy biological experiments that no sane mind would ever even remotely consider. At the beginning, remaining faithful to its ominous name, H-57 was dedicated to the design and creation of a provocative and menacing line of t-shirts. Then, fully grown and with a good head on its shoulders (albeit slightly off-kilter), it discovered its true nature as a studio for design, typography, illustration, animation and advertising. H-57 was reborn in its final form. Soon after, they started collaborating with major advertising agencies and international clients, including Adidas, Tod's, Coca-Cola HBC, Ferrero, Volkswagen Financial Services, Gruppo MutuiOnline, Dal Negro, Wiko, Chanteclair, RCS, Homepal and Lucasfilm Ltd. – for whom they created three typographical posters dedicated to the *Star Wars* saga, which were sold for charity and the proceeds donated to Make-a-Wish Italy – and many others.

The H-57 troop consists of Matteo Civaschi, Marco Dalbesio and Sabrina Di Gregorio, assisted by a group of young and talented creatives, graphic designers, animators and art directors.

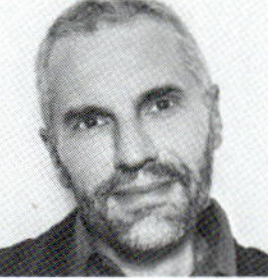

Marco
Dalbesio

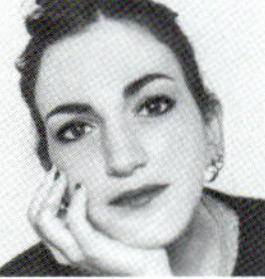

Livia
Albanese

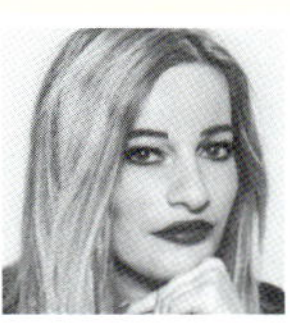

Sabrina
Di Gregorio

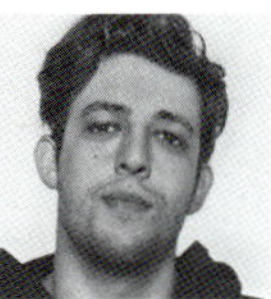

Marco
Bottini

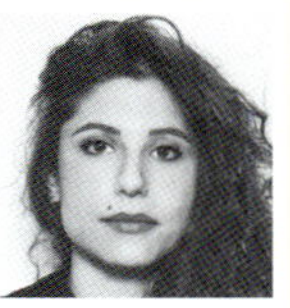

Alessia
Chiaravalloti

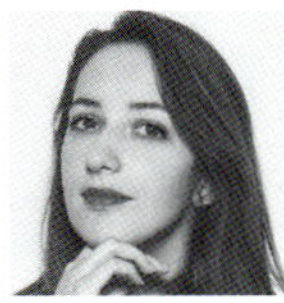

Katia
Monguzzi

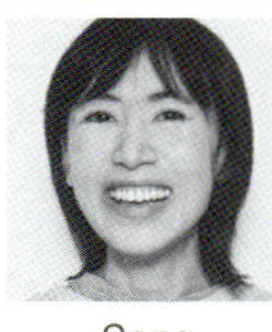

Sang
Shang

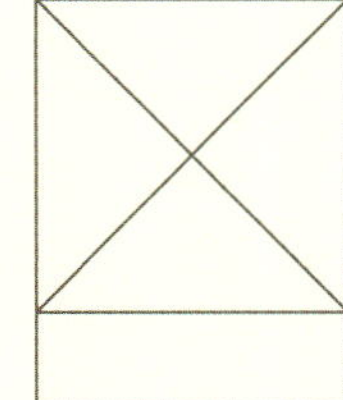

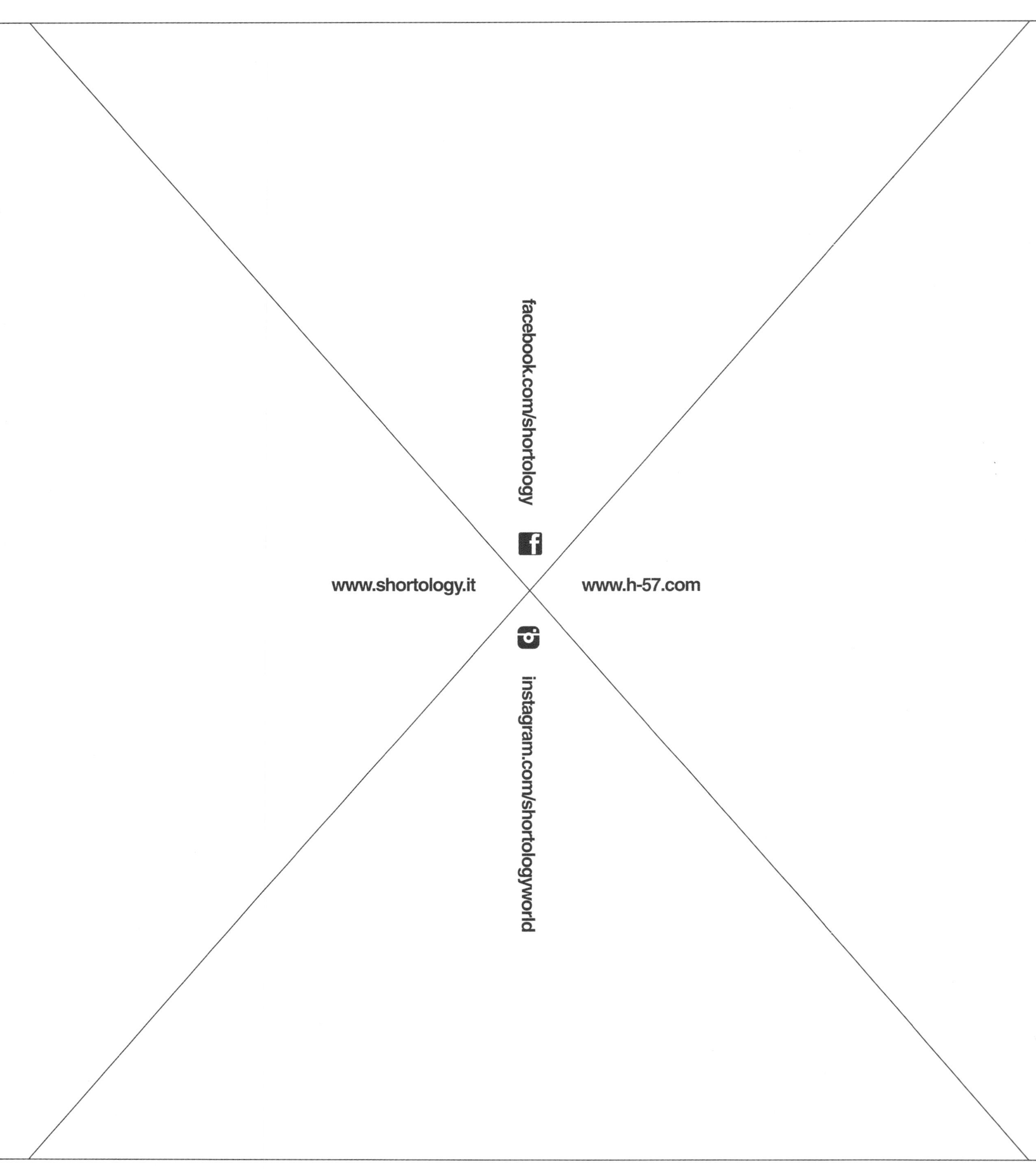

facebook.com/shortology
instagram.com/shortologyworld
www.shortology.it
www.h-57.com

acknowledgments

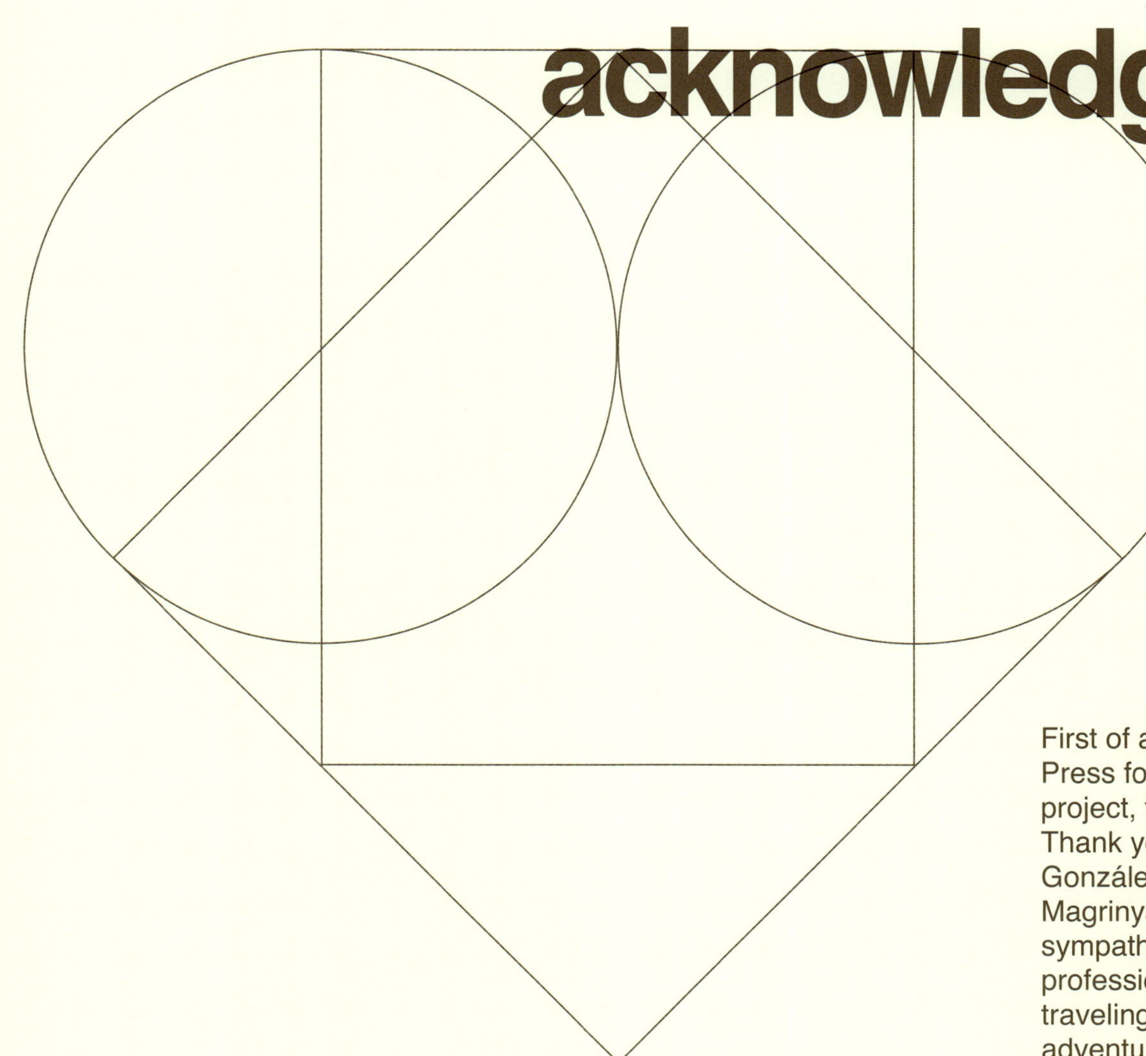

First published in Italy in 2018 by
Skira editore S.p.A.
Palazzo Casati Stampa
via Torino 61
20123 Milano
Italy
www.skira.net

© 2018 Shortology / H-57
© 2018 Skira editore, Milan

Printed and bound in EU. First edition
ISBN: 978-88-572-3967-5

Distributed in USA, Canada,
Central & South America by ARTBOOK |
D.A.P. 75 Broad Street Suite 630,
New York, NY 10004, USA.
Distributed elsewhere in the world
by Thames and Hudson Ltd.,
181A High Holborn, London WC1V 7QX,
United Kingdom.

First of all, I'd like to thank Flow Press for believing in this bizarre project, thank you very much! Thank you to Diego Rosembuj González-Capitel and Oriol Magrinyà Domingo for their passion, sympathy and, above all, great professionalism. I thank my loyal traveling companions in this latest adventure in the design world: Marco Dalbesio, Livia Albanese, Sabrina Di Gregorio, Alessia Chiaravalloti, Katia Monguzzi, Marco Bottini, Sang Shang and Beatrice Porri. I thank Sabrina Messineo and my son Lucas Civaschi. I thank Matteo Pavesi and Fondazione Cineteca Italiana (Italian Film Library Foundation).

I thank all the Shortology fans who have supported us during these years, you are wonderful. I thank Ridley Scott, Christopher Nolan, James Cameron, George Lucas, David Fincher, Quentin Tarantino, Denis Villeneuve, Danny Boyle, Neill Blomkamp, Stanley Kubrick, Alfred Hitchcock, Steven Spielberg, Guillermo del Toro, George R. R. Martin, Vince Gilligan, Bryan Cranston, Hans Zimmer, Wolfgang Amadeus Mozart, Neville Brody, Chuck Palahniuk, Niccolò Ammaniti, Diego Armando Maradona, Cristiano Ronaldo, Edward Van Halen, Roger Federer, Maurizio Cattelan, Stephen Hawking, Nikola Tesla and Matt Groening for inspiring me all these wonderful years.

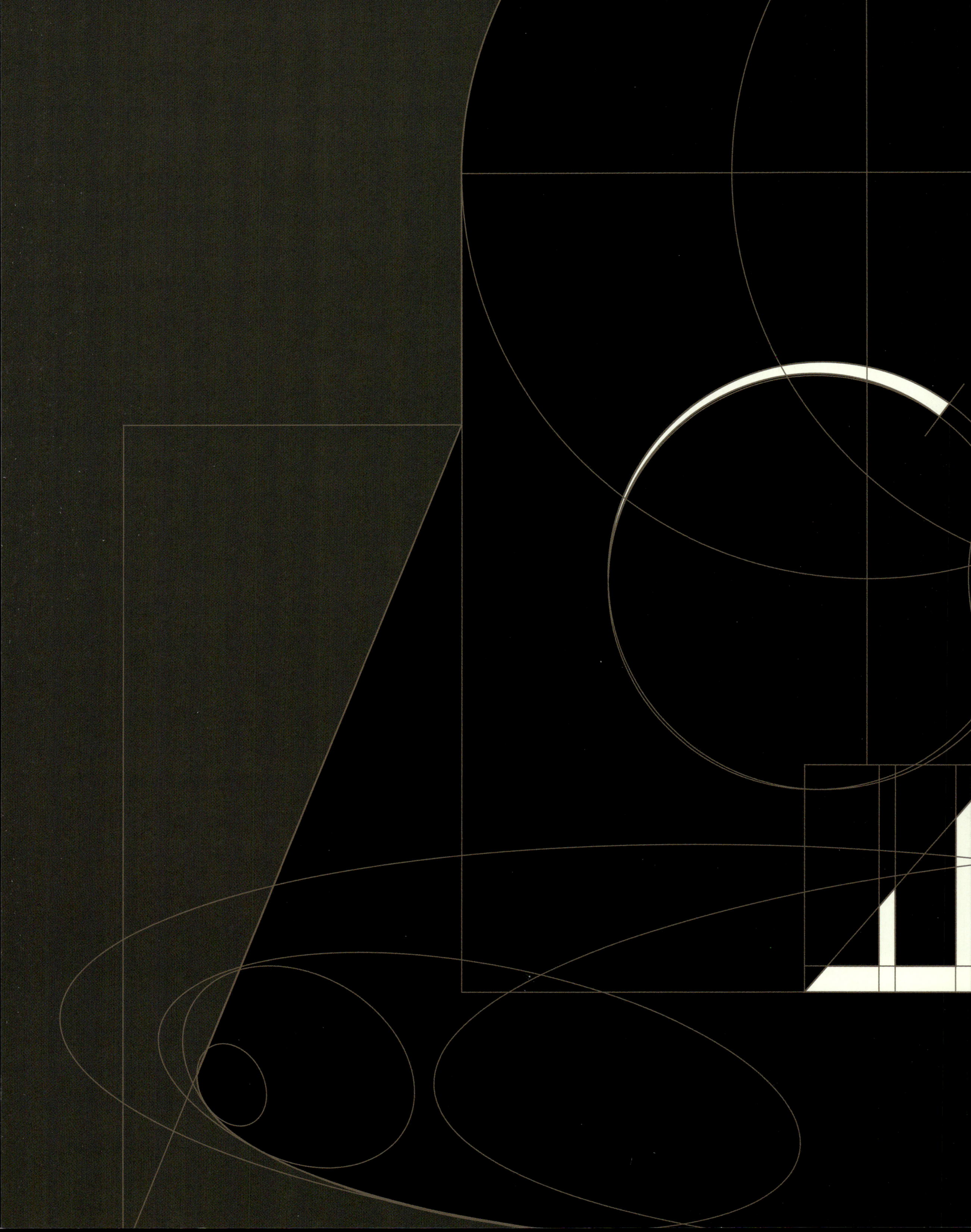

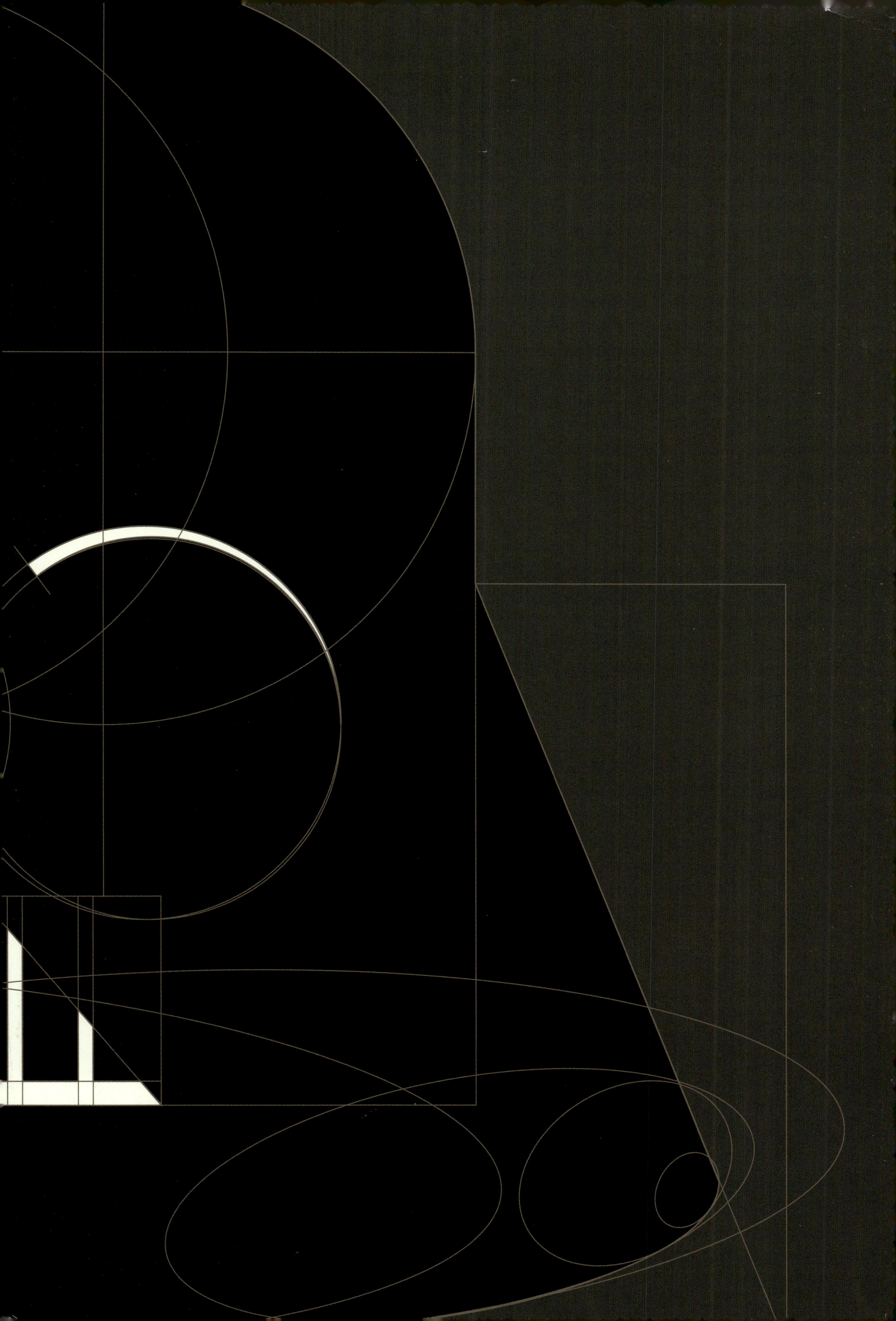

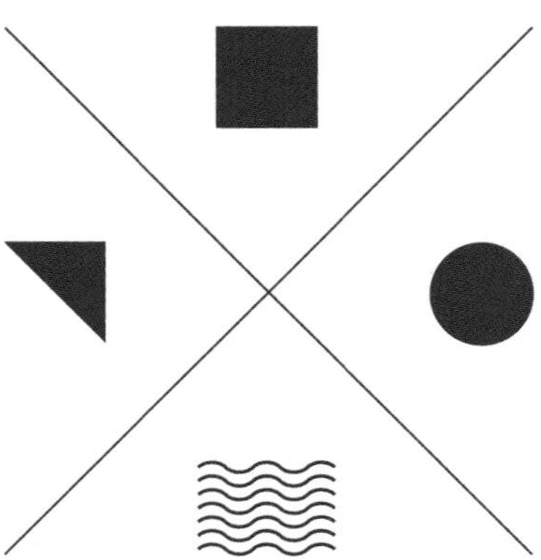